Henry W.J Thiersch

On Christian Commonwealth

Henry W.J Thiersch

On Christian Commonwealth

ISBN/EAN: 9783744652674

Printed in Europe, USA, Canada, Australia, Japan

Cover: Foto ©ninafisch / pixelio.de

More available books at **www.hansebooks.com**

CHRISTIAN COMMONWEALTH.

PRINTED BY MURRAY AND GIBB,

FOR

T. & T. CLARK, EDINBURGH.

LONDON, ... HAMILTON, ADAMS, AND CO.
DUBLIN, ... ROBERTSON AND CO.
NEW YORK, ... SCRIBNER, WELFORD, AND ARMSTRONG.

ON
CHRISTIAN COMMONWEALTH.

Translated and Adapted,

UNDER THE DIRECTION OF THE AUTHOR,

FROM THE GERMAN OF

DR. HENRY W. J. THIERSCH,

AUTHOR OF "THE CHURCH IN THE APOSTLES' TIME," "CHRISTIAN FAMILY LIFE,"
"THE PARABLES OF CHRIST," ETC.

EDINBURGH:
T. & T. CLARK, 38 GEORGE STREET.
1877.

PREFACE.

THE other works written by the same author are too well known to require any apology from me for bringing this, one of his latest works, under public notice. I could only wish that he had found some one more capable than myself of rendering his clear, terse, and classic style of writing. However, I hope that my language will convey with accuracy the meaning of the author.

I have termed this an adaptation, for the sole reason that the greater portion of the notes with which the original is furnished have been omitted. Consisting, as they do, mainly of references to German writers, they are of more interest to German than English readers. Such portions of the notes as I have deemed indispensable to the meaning, I have incorporated into the main text.

The subject of the work is one which, in some shape or another, is at the present time occupying the minds of all those who take an interest in our national prosperity; and my desire is that, by giving easier access to the ideas of so deep a thinker, I may be the means of enabling some one, who has the power as well as the will, to apply those ideas to England.

The object of the work is of a strictly pacificatory nature. It treats of the proper moral appreciation due to the various political and social parties. No attempt has been made to show that any are entitled to unalloyed praise on the one hand, or to unmitigated censure on the other. An endeavour has been made to bring to light such features in each of the various systems as appear to be capable of justification.

Special attention is called to those chapters which show how all Christian principles are opposed to oppression and misuse of power; how those principles promote and favour liberty of conscience, civic freedom, and the material as well as the spiritual prosperity of the people. True liberty and political advancement can only exist where there is mutual confidence; and such confidence can only be established upon a durable basis when the various component parts of the commonwealth and of society are convinced that all other parts may be justified upon and deduced from Christian principles.

The nature of our subject itself shows us that, in considering it, we must recognise two primary divisions. In the one division we have those universally admitted truths,—such as, the derivation of all authority from on high; the duty of the government to care for the well-being of the people; the duty of subjects to be faithful, respectful, and obedient; the difference between temporal and spiritual power; the duty of making all legislation to accord with the divine commands. All who honestly hold to the Holy Scriptures and ancient Church tradition, will probably be of one mind on these points, and be prepared to admit and uphold them.

In the other division, we must place all attempts to apply the above axioms to the course of history. For a due consideration of these points, we require an exact knowledge of facts, practical intelligence, and, so to say, a discerning of spirits. Here individual opinion comes into play. Take, for example, the ideas expressed in this work about absolute monarchy, about what is right and what is wrong in the latest ecclesiastical strifes, about social reforms, and about the right of punishment. All these are mixed and intricate questions, regarding which every one may hold his own opinions. It may be that, in the variety of aspect from which the subject can be regarded, some of the historical facts, or even cognate axioms of other affinitive sciences, may seem to require correction; but no intelligent critic will assert that the need of such adjustment impugns the principles which we are discussing. Any thesis derived from Christian verity continues to be true, although the hypotheses taken from history may contain an element of error.

In the present day, every citizen has a recognised right to express his opinion and to make use of the freedom of the press, if he believes that he can thereby advance the good of the commonwealth. This work does not pretend to treat its subject in an exhaustive manner, but the rapidity with which events are passing around him has warned the author not to delay its publication any longer, for fear of being overtaken by the current; and the applicability of many of the arguments it contains to our island home has appeared to me a sufficient reason for desiring that its contents may be more widely known amongst us.

The Established Church of England is being attacked on all sides; her foes without are ever looking for a weak point against which to direct their assault; whilst the garrison to whom her defence is entrusted are either quarrelling amongst themselves as to some minor point of ritual, or lulled to sleep by the whisperings of the arch enemy, who proclaims peace when there is no peace: they rely upon the strength of her outworks and fortifications, forgetting that the strongest of those natural defences are of but little avail against an active and unscrupulous enemy, unless manned by a vigilant and determined army of defenders. But of what use are vigilance and determination unless the construction of the fortress and its resources are well known? The aforesaid good qualities are prone to lead to over-confidence; some weak point is left unguarded until too late, and the enemy effects an entrance where least expected, turning the weapons which were designed for his repulse and annihilation against those whom they should have protected.

The times are perilous; the working man is combining daily more and more with his fellow against the capitalist, whom he looks upon as his enemy, quite overlooking the fact that it is owing to the careful and well-considered application of that capital, under God's providence, that England has assumed her present proud position among the nations. Still we are all of us more quick in detecting the shortcomings of others than in recognising our own, and if the capitalists of England would leave their antagonists without excuse, they must be careful to see that they have not provoked the unnatural strife by past omissions and neglect. But what if neither party will consent to give way, and by mutual concessions to return to a more healthy relation between employers and employed? Do our legislators intend to stand by doing nothing until the two hostile forces have thrown aside all pretence of friendship, have cut away all the links and cords by which they are at present, at least to a certain extent, united, and are drawn up in battle array. It will then, perhaps, be too late; the would-be mediator may find all the animosity with which the two combatants regard each other combined against and poured out upon himself.

Not a session of Parliament has of late years passed without the position, action, and bearing of the throne being made the subjects of virulent attack, — such attack as would, a few short years ago, have been deemed impossible.

In the everyday life of society, religion is looked upon either as infatuation, or as designed to curtail our pleasures, and therefore as a bore, or, finally, as a purely Sunday affair. It has become a common saying that business and religion are incompatible.

These are all points which show whither the current of events is hurrying us. The foundation of all ancient rights is not only undermined, as was the case in 1848, but it is about to sink away from under our feet, and will be carried away by the waves of the sea. He who feels himself impelled to do anything towards defending the remaining fragments of Christian State policy, must make no long tarrying.

J. W. WATKINS,
Captain H. P. Royal Artillery.

LEIPSIC, 1st *December* 1876.

TABLE OF CONTENTS.

CHAP.		PAGE
I.	DEFINITION OF A CHRISTIAN COMMONWEALTH,	1
II.	CHRISTIANITY IN ITS RELATION TO EXISTING AUTHORITY AND THE VARIOUS FORMS OF GOVERNMENT,	6
III.	CHRISTIANITY AND ABSOLUTE MONARCHY,	15
IV.	CHRISTIANITY AND MODERN LIBERAL TENDENCIES,	30
V.	THE TEMPORAL AND SPIRITUAL POWER,	44
VI.	COMMON GROUND: EDUCATION AND MATRIMONY,	58
VII.	THE STATE CHURCH—FREEDOM OF CONSCIENCE—CHRISTIAN AND NON-CHRISTIAN TOLERATION,	63
VIII.	THE EMANCIPATION OF THE JEWS,	82
IX.	SEPARATION OF CHURCH AND STATE,	96
X.	THE LAWFULNESS OF TAKING AN OATH IN A CHRISTIAN COMMONWEALTH,	111
XI.	THE POSITION OF A CHRISTIAN STATE TOWARDS SCHISM IN THE CHURCH AND THE VARIOUS SECTS,	117
XII.	THE POSITION OF A CHRISTIAN STATE TOWARDS THE PRETENSIONS OF THE PAPACY,	129
XIII.	THE DUTY OF A CHRISTIAN COMMONWEALTH WITH REGARD TO THE WORKING CLASSES,	149
XIV.	ON CRIMINAL LAW,	187
XV.	WAR AND INTERNATIONAL LAW,	222
XVI.	THE DUTIES OF SUBJECTS,	235
XVII.	THE DUTIES OF RULERS,	248

CHRISTIAN COMMONWEALTH.

CHAPTER I.

DEFINITION OF A CHRISTIAN COMMONWEALTH.

THE legislature and the entire condition of society in our country is convulsed, and we live in a period of transition, of which the future and final results are still shrouded in darkness. There was a time when the best men of the age endeavoured to work out a Christian state of society. Now it is not so; that task is set aside and other results aimed at, not only on account of weariness, but of set purpose, and with full prescience of the result. As, at the end of the last century, the public mind of France was betrayed into the demented assertion, "The State is atheist, and ought to be so!" so we find now in German papers the foolhardy expression, "A Christian State is Utopian," whereby they would accuse of folly all those who endeavour to realize that ideal. Still, if we grant that, with such materials and means as we have at command, it may be impossible perfectly to solve so lofty a problem, since when has the principle been recognised, that because the ideal is unattainable, all endeavour to attain at least to as near an approach to it as possible should be given up? If it were allowable to arrange the affairs of the State without regard to Christian principles, it would be equally justifiable in each individual to abstain from endeavouring to become really virtuous, because this also, taken in its fullest sense, is an ideal which is far beyond the reach of average men.

The employment of the abstract term "State" or "Commonwealth" renders the solution of the question the more difficult. We approach the reality and the understanding of it better, if we think of the people, or the nation, and its rulers; that is to say, those who are invested with the authority without which no community can exist. The nation, with its leaders,—and all such as have any civic authority are to be numbered amongst the latter,—forms one corporation. Just as a family, consisting of children, servants, and other inmates of the house, with father and mother at the head, forms one moral entity, one responsible personality, so also the nation, gathered under its rulers, forms an abstraction, which we express by the word "State" or "Commonwealth."

Who will be bold enough to deny that a family ought to be guided and ordered according to Christian principles? Every individual member, and, therefore, also the family as a whole, is called upon, and is bound, to order itself, as to conduct, entirely according to Christian principles. The same calling, the same duty, attaches to a nation when it as such—*i.e.* the majority of its component members under the guidance of its rulers—accepts the Christian religion and professes allegiance to it. This has occurred. It is no supposition or fanciful proposition, but a grand, irrefutable, historical fact. Every one of the European nations which exist at the present day, with the exception of the Jews, who dwell amongst us as strangers, and the Osmanlis, who came amongst us as intruders, have taken this very step. Every European nation has set aside its old heathen religion, and adopted as its own the Christian faith and worship. In that individuals have been baptized, the body, which is composed of such individuals, has received Christian baptism. But, together with the benefits of Christianity, we must accept its duties. The confession of Christ of necessity includes also a vow to obey His commands. Christian faith without Christian works is open to that sentence of condemnation which Christ expressed in the saying, "Why call ye me Lord, Lord, and do not the things which I say?" But if the matter be seriously gone about, to bring the laws of the land, the public institutions, the mode of action of the authorities, and the life of the nation into accordance with the laws of Christ, what is this but an endeavour to realize and to render corporate a Christian State or Commonwealth?

Thanks to this endeavour, we have no slavery, with its absence of legal status, no immoral worship amongst us; the claims of the poor are recognised, the sick are cared for, the young are educated, and the dignity of human existence, as established and ennobled by Christianity, is acknowledged.

Such virtues as flourished in the ancient heathen States, for instance, in the best days of the Roman Republic, as faithfulness to an oath, uprightness of the judges, incorruptibility of officials, and self-devotion to the country, have acquired, through Christianity, a new status and a higher sanction than before. Amongst the greatest benefits which have accrued to the nations in consequence of their acceptance of Christianity may be reckoned the principle that God is no respecter of persons. Whereas the whole of the ancient heathen nations inclined to the deification of their kings, and thereby fostered the worst depravities, all who profess Christianity admit the divine principle that the highest amongst the people, as well as the lowest, are equally responsible for their deeds to a heavenly Judge, and that one moral code is binding upon all.

It would be unintelligible how any one could deny the principle that the State should be formed on a Christian plan, if, in the days when this principle was universally and publicly acknowledged, abuses and degeneracy had not crept in. But thus it was, and the fact is undeniable. Even during the whole of the Middle Ages we find antagonism existing between the Christian profession and antichristian mode of life. We have the most explicit confession of Christ, in public announcements, ceremonials, and laws, co-existing with injustice and tyranny, impure living, cruelty, and persecution. This ancient evil assumed even a worse form in despotically governed States after the Reformation under the old *régime*. Since schism entered the Church, the various parties have sought, each in their own way, by insisting upon their own especial orthodoxy, and by the want of forbearance connected with it, to arrive as it were at the highest pitch of Christianity. But as at the same time the national life was neglected, and corruption gained the ascendancy in the upper ranks, untruth, and those internal anomalies from which the Christian States of the Middle Ages suffered, also became intensified. That we are all bound to strive to render the State Christian, is an eternal moral truism; but that a Christian Commonwealth ever was realized under Henry VIII., Ivan the Terrible, Philip II., Ferdinand II., or Louis XIV., —to assert that would be a monstrous untruth.

The better a thing originally is, the worse it becomes when it degenerates.[1] The falsity of the nature of the so-called Christian States has not only caused delay and injury, but has also brought about disintegration. The fact of boasting of enjoying a Christian Commonwealth, and at the same time not obeying the highest commandments of God, is hypocrisy; but hypocrisy is

[1] "Corruptio optimi pessima."

repulsive to the best elements in the breast of man. This antagonism is directed not only against the perversion, but against the principle itself. The worst elements of human society take advantage of the opportunity. Under the screen of righteous indignation a resistance is organized, which, whilst far from endeavouring to make virtue a reality, wishes to do away with the effects of Christian principles on the national and individual life. Thus the want of virtue in the clergy, and the causes of offence furnished by them, have not only weakened the faith of the people, but have also opened the door to heterodoxy and scandal; the immorality and tyranny of rulers, who took the name of Christ upon their lips, has lighted up the fires of hatred, revolutions, and mania for destruction amongst the people. He who now takes upon himself after all this to plead for the setting up of a Christian State, has to combat with prejudice, as though he desired to reintroduce the abuses and depravities which existed under the old state of things. We hope to be able to show that a Christian State, properly understood, contains in itself all the conditions necessary for the public weal. However much it may have degenerated in the hands of men, still the problem has to be solved; and it is plainly the duty of each and all to aim at a better solution than has ever yet been attained.

CHAPTER II.

CHRISTIANITY IN ITS RELATION TO EXISTING AUTHORITY AND THE VARIOUS FORMS OF GOVERNMENT.

WHEN the Christian religion became operative in the Roman Empire — when it was announced to our Teutonic forefathers, it found itself in both cases face to face with an established form of government. The preachers of the gospel did not require to construct anything of the sort; and even if we suppose that opportunity for so doing had been afforded them, they had no commission, no authority, no warrant for any such undertaking. This is clearly evident from the behaviour of Christ and His apostles. Whilst they recognised the existing authority, they claimed no temporal power for themselves, and deduced from their high calling no right to participation in the framing of laws, dispensation of justice, or administration of the State. The narrative of the life of Christ upon earth commences with a statement of the fact that a census was being taken under the authority of the Emperor Augustus. Whilst the orthodox Jews held it to be unseemly to pay taxes to a heathen ruler, Christ said, "Render unto Cæsar the things that are Cæsar's." Christ drew the clearest possible distinction between His own servants and the temporal rulers. When Peter drew his sword against the myrmidons who laid hands upon the Just One, Christ rebuked him with the words, "Put up thy sword again into his place, for all they who take to the sword shall perish with the sword." When Christ stood before the judgment-seat of Pilate, He solemnly recognised his office as judge, and the delegated power of life and death which he wielded. Thus He removed the sword from the hand of His own servant Peter, but allowed the servant of Tiberius to retain it. Here we have the foundation laid for those teachings which we find in the epistles of the apostles upon the subject of the authorities ordained of God.

It is very remarkable to observe how foreign it was to the intention of the apostles to cast any doubt upon the legitimacy of the ordinances which existed in the Roman Empire. The origin of these was in many respects allied with guilt; the system upon which the provinces were governed was oppressive. In the very commencement the abuse of authority was seen in the persecution of Christians. But with all this we hear of no reproach being heaped upon the existing imperial organs. The Christians took no part either in the Jewish war or in any insurrections, and during the cruel persecutions it never occurred that the Christians joined any revolutionary movement in order to put a stop to their own sufferings.

When the gospel found acceptance amongst the Germanic nations, it entered a sphere where more noble relations existed. It entered a Teutonic kingdom. Here no despotism founded upon usurpation and conquest reigned. Each of the German tribes had a king of its own; and although in war his power was almost absolute, still, in the normal condition of peace, it was limited. Christianity also recognised the German kingdom and German legislature. Although ancient church history furnishes us with no example in which Christianity entered into a republic, such as the Grecian republics in olden times were, still we may with certainty conclude from its general behaviour, that any existing form of government, even though republican, would have met with recognition from the servants of Christ.

The question as to which of the different forms of government agreed best with Christian principles was never raised in the Middle Ages. Only in the movements of later times, which commenced with the revolution in England, did this question come prominently forward. Since then conflicting political parties have appealed to Christian doctrine, and each of these would assert that the form of government which they strove to inaugurate was the one commended by the word of truth revealed by God. English history affords the most instructive illustration of this. There both extremes have presented themselves, each with this bold assertion of the divine sanction.

After the royal prerogative had been brought to its highest pitch by Charles I. and Lord Strafford, Filmer asserted, in the interest of the house of the Stuarts, the theory of the absolute authority of kings, as opposed to which no privileges of Parliament, no rights of the people, might be set up. That such did exist he admitted, but he asserted that they were not original, and had no independent existence, being mere gracious gifts from the king, which he had granted in the absolutism of his power, but which he could also, when he considered expedient, circumscribe or revoke. This inalienable power was given him from above. And he asserted that such kingship, restrained by no other power, was the one ordained of God,—the form of government which corresponded to Christian principles.

The contrary proposition was set up by Oliver Cromwell and his adherents. A republic was the only form of Christian government. The kingship, misused by the Tudors and Stuarts, had become an object of mistrust and disgust to all earnest men. From that quarter nothing was to be hoped for for the people, or for the setting up of a Christian national life. The people must take the matter in hand themselves, and a righteous, God-fearing, and morally pure government could only be established in the form of a Christian democracy. Under Charles II. some unfortunate people were executed because they would hear of no king but Jesus.

When the waves of the first and second revolutions had passed away in England, the views of both parties became more temperate. The political systems of the Whigs and Tories were developed. The form of words in which they expressed their views ran thus: One said, "Authority is from God;" the others, "Authority exists for the sake of the people." These watchwords serve, even in the present day, as excellent descriptions of the fundamental ideas of both parties.

They are clearly not contradictory. If one of these statements be well founded, that by no means excludes the possibility of the other being also true; and, in fact, each contains a moral truism, neither can be rebutted from a Christian point of view, and the synthesis of the two might serve as an exact expression of the Christian view. Authority is ordained of God, and the divine intention is to promote and secure the welfare of the people. The entire object of authority is to serve for the good of the people, and thus the divine intention, upon which the ordinance rests, is fulfilled. The assertion of the Whigs is Christian, and the reply of the Tories is Christian, so long as both are merely asserted in the positive form. But it would be untrue, and in its consequences contradictory to Christian principles, if either one or the other assertion were set up in a negative or exclusive form. To say that authority does not exist for the people, or that authority is not ordained of God, would in either case be distinctly false.

The battle which was practically fought out in England was philosophically worked out by sharp-witted thinkers on the Continent, in connection with speculations on the root of social evil and the origin of authoritative power. At the present day they still exist as two scientific theories, which have never been exhaustively examined, and which still await decision.

One doctrine starts with the assumption of an original equality inherent in all mankind; it assumes the existence of a natural condition of this kind at first, but which could not continue because it had no organization. For the purpose of living together in safety, a certain order, a protecting power, became necessary. Then the majority voluntarily transferred a portion of their rights to a few, who should assume the task of protecting the life and property of all, and carry on the general business. It is supposed that authority was founded in this manner. Everything was conducted naturally and humanly, as when, in the present day, a party of emigrants and gold-diggers in California constitute themselves into a community of some sort. The Commonwealth, thus built up according to the ideas of men, is, agreeably to this conception, only a mutual assurance office for the life and property of those who take part therein. Grotius and Puffendorf have set forth this doctrine of the *status naturalis.* Rousseau, in his *Contrat Social,* has deduced the final sequences from it, and his doctrine became the programme of the revolutionary party in all Europe and America.

As opposed to the one-sidedness and vacuity of this theory, the defenders of authority and the ancient order of things rely the more emphatically upon the contrary principle. The family, so they say, is the oldest form of authority, and in the family paternal authority is the basis of all. A father, who is bound to nourish, protect, and defend his own,—who is bound to preserve unity, justice, and decency in his family circle,—is the origin of all authority. From the paternal authority the civic authority is derived. In ancient times the family grew by the accession of servants, slaves, and wards, by the increase of territorial possessions and general prosperity, to a primitive State. Job and Abraham were kings, just as in Homer the great landed proprietor appears as a king, leaning upon his sceptre, contemplating the labours of the ploughmen, and handing them the refreshing cup. The original State was the patriarchal.

Now, as the paternal authority in the family certainly is not based upon human invention, nor upon any articles of association signed by the children, in which they abdicated their rights, but upon a divine appointment and law, which preceded the existence of the individual and is out of the pale of man's will, so also civic authority. Later forms of government are derived from the patriarchal State; it is necessary to retain the connection with the latter, and the entire arrangement and form of the national life must conform to that model.

Has the natural condition of affairs, as presupposed by Locke and his successors, ever existed? Experience and common sense both inform us that this state of perfect equality, and enjoyment of similar privileges by each individual, never has existed and never could exist. It is a phantom, as is also the supposititious transition from that condition into a full-blown State by a regular form of agreement, and affords no reliable basis for further consideration. Louis von Haller has once for all disposed of this idea in the first volume of his *Restoration of Political Science*. Moreover, it by no means coincides with the facts recorded in history to suppose that all civic ordinances have been derived from the patriarchal State. Even admitting that the ancient despotic monarchies of Nineveh and Babylon, Egypt and China, were raised upon such a basis, still in the constitution of European States, such as the Grecian, Roman, and above all those of the Teutonic Middle Ages, we find totally different sources of origin. The paternal power of an individual is not the basis, no single authority suppresses all other; but, concomitant with the dignity of the head of the State, we find a second element, that is to say, a body of free and independent men, who have entered into a compact for mutual aid and protection. The ancient history of Iceland, as related by Conrad Maurer, is about the most remarkable instance of a State having arisen from the voluntary association of independent and co-equal heads of families. In such historical facts we are able to arrive at the truth which is at the bottom of the theory of a condition of nature, and the constitution of States therefrom.

The most noble and most active forms of constitution are just those in which we find the two features of headship and fellowship most distinctly retained. Both these principles existed even in pre-historic times, and it is the endeavour to maintain these principles in action, and to bring them into accord, which underlies the history of the most favoured nations. Whenever we find one principle absorbed by the other,—if such a case were possible, for it probably never will be completely effected,—we find distorted and miserable forms of government, whether it be apathetic and unyielding despotism, or a restless, wild, and self-destructive democracy. If the theory be true that the movement of the heavenly bodies depends upon the action of two forces which control each other, called the centrifugal and the centripetal forces, we seem to have in nature a constitution analogous to the two forces, which are the postulates of civic order, namely, liberty and authority. When both are developed, when both are brought into harmony and consolidated by the experience and labours of centuries, then we have the most perfect constitution of the State conceivable, and the one which satisfies the human wants most completely. The English constitution is the one which most closely approximates to this ideal; and it is the one held up as an example to be followed, alternately by sticklers for authority and by the enthusiastic worshippers of liberty. It is this very admiration accorded by both parties which may be accepted as proof of the fact that in this instance the two legitimate elements of constitutional existence have been able to assert themselves more thoroughly than elsewhere.

These principles, the effects of which may be traced in the existence of nations from the very commencement, are embodied in the two great parties whose strife is the topic of the present day, of which one has inscribed Conservatism, the other Reform, upon its banners. Thus also we are bound to admit that both of these parties has grounds for existence. It is primarily inaccurate to say that one is Christian, the other antichristian, in principle. Egotism is an element in all political strife, and no party is free from error. But this renders it all the more dangerous for Christianity to identify itself with either of these parties, otherwise it too would be thereby held responsible for their excesses.

If we desire to arrive at a just and moral appreciation of the political contrasts of our times, we shall never be able to do so as long as we only distinguish two parties. For besides the moderate and reasonable partisans, whether of Conservatism or Reform, we have the extremes, who either affectionately cling to ancient and oppressive abuses, or else are guilty of an irreverent love of demolition. We must not only consider two, but four parties. Only thus can we attain to a just appreciation of them and their relations to Christianity, and only thus will it be possible to bring about an approximate understanding between the opponents.

The ministers of the gospel should, in this combat between Conservatism and Reform, avoid placing themselves in the ranks of either party; otherwise they will embitter the strife by shortsightedly declaring one principle to be Christian, the other to be antichristian, instead of, as their calling requires of them, using their influence to bring about a reconciliation between both parties.

Christianity does not set up governments, and it does not pull any down. But wherever it finds acceptation, and is allowed to influence public opinion, it assists in softening down asperities and egotism, and in spontaneously opening up a way to the most perfect form of organic development. Christian doctrine has a humanizing effect upon the feelings and manners. It reminds the powerful ones of their dependence upon God, and of the account which they will have to render to Him; it endeavours to attune their hearts to good will towards and confidence in their subjects; and at the same time it establishes in the subjects feelings of reverence. It ratifies respect for the law; it endows the ministers of the law with a higher sanction—all of which are results from before which the extravagances of despotism and the egotism of democracy must give way.

CHAPTER III.

CHRISTIANITY AND ABSOLUTE MONARCHY.

IF what we have said be correct, and if Christianity does recognise the various forms of government, whether monarchical, aristocratic, or democratic, it may be supposed that under each the realization of a Christian Commonwealth is possible. As one may say in regard to the public weal, every form of administration is good if only well administered; so also a Christian State will everywhere be realized and flourish, where the rulers, the framers and administrators of the law, consider themselves bound by the laws of Christ, and permit themselves to be guided by Christian principles. History has confirmed this assertion. Even although the ideal has never been attained to anywhere, still a Christian form of government and national life has flourished both in monarchies and in republics—*e.g.* in Geneva, Holland, and the States of New England. These statements, which are calculated to allay and to still all passionate feeling, appear to be admitted on all hands, and to be self-evident; nevertheless we cannot pass over one argument needful for their confirmation. The elder ones of our contemporaries can relate much from sad experience about the mighty activity of one party, which had inscribed the motto of a "Christian State" upon their banner, and maintained that an absolute monarchy alone was suited to its realization; that this was above all the form of government desired of God, and the form which harmonized best with Christian principles. It was admitted that the privileges of corporate bodies, as they existed in the Middle Ages, were admissible under such a monarchy; but that all modern ideas of liberty, such as have come to the surface since 1789, and the constitutions which have emanated from them, were objectionable. Hence the duty of a Christian was to range himself on the side of absolute monarchy, and to oppose the constitutional system. It is the system of anti-revolution, which obtained amongst the greater and lesser powers of the Continent for some fifty years after the fall of Napoleon. The excesses of the democratic party in the French Revolution, and the sufferings with which Europe was threatened by the intrinsically revolutionary empire of the first Napoleon, led to this reaction. The wave of the liberation movement which had passed over Europe retired, and it was believed that in re-erecting the old monarchical system one might boast of being in communion with revived Christian principles, and that therefore the entire retrograde movement could be justified. It was Count Joseph de Maistre, the Roman Catholic diplomatist, who applied a religious hue to the systems represented by Metternich and Gentz. In Prussia the matter was clothed in the garb of evangelical piety. It was customary to extol the Prussian kingdom by means of quotations from the Messianic Psalms. It seemed as though a thirteenth article had there been added to the other twelve of the Apostles' Creed, and that this new article was the assertion of the absolute power of kings. Vilmar required that every Christian, and especially every German Christian, should repeat and subscribe to a political creed recognising the absolute power of princes, and denying the constitutional principle. A well-known newspaper, called the *New Prussian Journal*, proposed the following as a charter for the constitution:—

Sec. I. The king commands.

Sec. II. The people obey.

We have here only to do with the assertion that this system is an eminently Christian one. We regret the necessity which arises for differing from such as evidently are striving after a Christian State. We would much rather not do so, and would prefer not to oppose a tendency whose star is, whether or no, on the wane, were not the spiritual injury which has arisen from the mixing up of the sacred subject of Christianity with the desecrated absolute monarchy so great. By this intermixture the Christian faith was compromised. Prejudice assumed enormous proportions, as though every distinctly Christian profession was in league with despotism, and orthodox doctrine was an invention of tyranny for the oppression of the people. The moral code of Christianity was adulterated with the assertion that princes were above the reach of the law, and could retract their pledged word. Any one who in the present day will plead for a Christian State has to fear being called upon to appear at the bar of public opinion as a participator in those dreadful errors, and as a conspirator with such powers as are inimical to the people. Hence it becomes a duty to defend the Christian State from its friends and worshippers; and every one does a good work who assists in rebutting so dangerous an error, and disentangles the cause of Christ from that of the despots.

Is absolute monarchy based, more than any other form of government, upon biblical and Christian doctrines, or even recommended by them?

In the Bible such an arbitrary and unrestrained power is mentioned; but how is it spoken of?

It is Nebuchadnezzar, the ruler of the Babylonian Empire, of whom it is said, "Whom he would he slew, and whom he would he kept alive; and whom he would he set up, and whom he would he put down." Such was the form which royal power had assumed upon Eastern soil. But it is certainly not held up before us as an example of that which is right and desirable. On the contrary, a totally different object was set before the kings of the people of Israel. For it is said in the Mosaic law: "It shall be when he—the king, chosen by the Lord thy God; the anointed one, whom no one dare lay hands upon—when he sitteth upon the throne of his kingdom, that he shall write him a copy of this law in a book out of that which is before the priests, the Levites. And it shall be with him, and he shall read therein all the days of his life, that he may learn to fear the Lord his God, to keep all the words of this law, and these statutes, to do them; that his heart be not lifted up above his brethren (his subjects—his brethren!), and that he turn not aside from the commandment to the right hand or to the left: to the end that he may prolong his days in his kingdom, he and his children in the midst of Israel" (Deut. xvii. 18-20).

This distinction between the heathen and Israelitish rights of kings comes even more prominently to light in the history of King Ahab. The king wished to purchase the vineyard of Naboth, which lies near the palace, and to make for himself a garden of herbs. Naboth declined to part with it, basing his refusal upon the privilege and duty of every head of a family in Israel to hand down the inheritance of his father to his children. So Ahab came into his house heavy and displeased, and he laid him down upon his bed and would eat no bread. Then came to him Jezebel his wife, the daughter of the heathen king of Tyre, the zealous worshipper of Baal; and when she heard the cause of his humour, she said, "Dost thou now govern the kingdom of Israel? Arise and eat bread, and let thine heart be merry; I will give thee the vineyard of Naboth the Jezreelite" (1 Kings xxi.). That was the heathenish, Oriental idea of royal power which the Phœnicians had brought with them from the court at Tyre, and which they wished to introduce into Israel, that no royalty could exist if laws and the rights of individuals were allowed to present an impassable barrier interfering with the will of the ruler.

In the Psalms and in the writings of the prophets the kingdom of the Messiah is foretold. The ruler of it is to appear furnished with divine power, righteousness, and wisdom. But such passages refer to Christ and His future kingdom. In Him dwelleth the fulness of the Godhead, and His rule will indeed bear out the sayings of the prophets. To refer such prophecies to any mortal ruler, whether David, Solomon, or any Christian king, would be idolatry. Who dares to place the statements contained in the Messianic prophecies upon an equality with the Apotheosis of Augustus by Horace? In the whole volume of Holy Scripture we find nothing repudiated and rebuked so earnestly and with such detestation as the idolizing of men.

It is very true that in a Christian kingdom there ought to be a reflex of the royal action of Christ; the Christian king should be an image of Christ in his dignity and his working. Granted; but it must not be forgotten that this image is of clay. With reference to the 82d Psalm, Bacon says in his *Essays*: "A king is a mortal god upon earth, unto whom the living God hath let His own name as a great honour; but withal told him that he should die like a man, lest he should be proud, and flatter himself that God hath with His name imparted unto him His nature also."

It is true that Scripture teaches us to recognise in the royal office a divine commission, and to respect the same; but, at the same time, in no other book in the world is the weakness, infirmity, unworthiness, and nothingness of man so prominently insisted upon as in the Bible. It would be a monstrous fallacy to wish to deduce from the divine commission that any superhuman wisdom and insight had been imparted. It is as certain that the king is not omniscient, as that he is not immortal and not omnipotent. On the contrary, he is born with the same spiritual and corporeal weaknesses as all other mortals. One difference certainly does exist, and that is, a prince ought to be more deeply impressed with his need of aid, because his duties are so vast and the temptations which surround him so many.

It is not enough that he consider himself amenable to the eternal laws of righteousness, truth, and charity, and bound to conform to the limitations imposed thereby—an axiom which only a godless person can question; but also within those limitations he is restrained in the exercise of his power by his human imperfections. His Christian principles will be the very thing which will impress upon him the consciousness of such restriction.

There are two considerations which lead to the same conclusion from different causes. The king requires wisdom, and he will seek it from God; similarly to Solomon, who, on ascending the throne, did not pray for riches, honour, and victory over his enemies, but for an obedient and wise heart, that he might be capable of ruling the people of God. But still he will not only look upwards to attain this wisdom, he will also look about for it upon earth; for if he has the power of deciding in all weighty occasions, insight does not pertain to him alone. As Bacon says: "The wisest princes need not think it any diminution to their greatness, or derogation to their sufficing, to rely upon counsel." The most pregnant action of a king is the promulgation of a law. In this, comprehensive knowledge of the circumstances, and the experience of centuries, is above all things needful; hence an appreciation of his duties will lead a Christian prince to seek the advice of his subjects. He will seek for the best advice which is to be found amongst his people, the most varied, impartial, and unselfish that is to be had. It is a justifiable desire on the part of the people to see their ruler surrounded with the most trustworthy councillors, that the sufferings and the wishes of his people may not be hid from him, and that neither justice nor mercy may be deficient in his rule. Suppose that in any State there were no law binding the king by the consent of his councillors in the promulgation of a new law, or forbidding him to decide contrary to them, still there is a moral obligation, and in a Christian-minded ruler this would have exactly as much effect as a constitutional limitation of his power.

The other consideration is this: individual rights are under divine protection. Not only the rulers of the country, but also the head of the family, the landowner, and every proprietor, has within his own border certain rights due to the grace of God. In the history of the people of Israel, it is palpable that these rights existed even prior to the rights of kings. The former are, therefore, equally of divine sanction with the latter. But the very nature of a community and of a State requires that each individual shall be prepared to sacrifice a portion of his own rights for the welfare of all. A form of government necessitates, for the execution of its functions, the payment of taxes and personal service from the people. With new imposts and new laws, fresh demands are made upon the tributary people. But as the life and property of each individual are sacred, a Christian ruler will only make such demands upon the liberality of his people as are actually necessary for the well-being of the whole. To be able to form a correct judgment on this point, again, is a matter requiring the wisest consideration. A Christian prince will not here decide for himself. His conscience will move him to seek counsel of his people, and in the impost of fresh burdens to obtain the consent of those concerned. How far the people are to be allowed to participate in the framing of the laws, and the mode in which the opinion of the nation respecting fresh taxes is to be gathered, are matters which must be ruled by laws which have passed into the domain of history. The principle itself follows, as a matter of course, from the fundamental ideas of prince, people, authority, State, and rights.

If absolute monarchy be the form of government most consonant with Christianity, there ought to be observable a similarity of constitution and nature between it and the Christian Church; but, as a matter of fact, the contrary is the case. In the Christian Church quite different fundamental ideas are prominent.

The rule of Christ is of a very different kind from that of the despots of heathenish antiquity. It is true, He is King and Lord in the fullest sense of the terms; but He it is who offered Himself up for the good of His people, and who holds dear each individual soul, even that of the least and poorest. In His dealings as Head of the Church, He regards the sufferings of His subjects; He listens to the voice of His Spirit in the prayers of those seeking help; He judges the transgressors of His laws; but the homage which He expects is voluntary, and even in His chastisements He does not override the free-will of man.

By the appearance of Christ upon earth, rule has become something very different to what the world ever saw before. Every participation in government is now destined for the well-being of the subjects.

Government has become, as Franz von Baader says, in reality a service, and being governed has become an act of being served.

In the Christian Church both principles, that of liberty and that of authority, are intertwined. In the apostles, and in the bishops and elders ordained by them, a higher commission, a reverence-requiring authority, was unmistakeably put forth. The Christian ministry did not come into existence as a thing begotten by the community; it existed previous to the latter. On the other hand, in every member the dignity of Christ is recognised and respected to the utmost. The welfare of all the members constitutes the aim of a religious community, and authority exists in it for the purpose of realizing this aim. It is true that in the course of time the harmony between these two principles has been disturbed; and on the one hand the authority of the office-bearer, and on the other the liberty and the rights of the community, have been pushed beyond bounds. But at the same time the Church has, owing to the fact of these two elements being combined in her and appreciated, contributed to a peaceful development of the national life. In her original, pure, divinely-granted constitution, she is the most perfect of all organizations. With her before them, such as extol a one-sided form of constitution, as being especially Christian, should hide their heads for shame.

If we look at the visible form which the separate communities took, we find that the original arrangement, which should never have been departed from, is the following:—A bishop at the head, who has to guide the whole; under him a body of elders or priests, who assist him with counsel and action; under these the body of deacons, chosen by the community, from whom the bishop and the elders learn the wishes of the congregation. Who can refuse to see in this the organic order of the State, where the king, in the position of temporal bishop and pastor of his people, really governs; the body of elders is represented by the Senate or House of Lords; and the diaconate is shown forth in the representatives of the people or House of Commons? Looked at in every aspect, the organization of the Christian Church, as divinely ordered, is suggestive of a limited, not an absolute monarchy.

Can it be gravely asserted that absolute monarchy is Teutonic? that it coincides with the German spirit and traditions? Such an assertion requires no refutation; still it may be useful, as throwing a light upon the whole subject, to call to mind here certain historical facts.

Tacitus has laid down the fundamental principles of the ancient Teutonic kingdoms. The kings were taken from the most distinguished families; the retainers displayed the utmost faithfulness to their prince, and resolved to die for or with him. To defend and protect him, to enhance his glory by acts of heroism, was the duty of his men. If the king fell in battle, for any to return alive was a lifelong disgrace. This is one aspect. On the other hand, Tacitus asserts that, in important matters, not the princes alone, but the whole assembly of the people, were called upon to decide; and when, in this assembly, the king himself spoke, he endeavoured rather to determine them by persuasive argument than by direct command. Tacitus, in his *Germania*, desired to hold up a looking-glass before the Romans of his time, by extolling the noble qualities of our German forefathers. And thus, too, he cast a side glance of reproach at the omnipotence of Roman emperors, when he penned the words: "Neither have kings infinite or free power."[1] In the better times, it is true that the law was the ruler of the Romans as well as of the Spartans;

---

[1] "Nec regibus infinita aut libera potestas."

but in the evil days of imperial power, matters went so far that the Roman jurists set up the doctrine: "The emperor is not bound by the laws."

During the Middle Ages the Teutonic kingdom preserved, in all material points, its original form. The Frankish kings retained in peace a very limited, but in war—as is necessitated by the position of affairs—an absolute power. Both principles are most beautifully expressed in the old English traditions. No other person shall be superior to the king. The king confirms the law, and without his sanction no law can take effect. But he alone cannot make the law; he is obliged, before publishing any statute, to listen to the advice of the Parliament and to obtain their consent. The proclamation of any new law is announced with the old Norman form, "Le roi le veut." But when once proclaimed, the king himself is subject to it. He above all others is bound to obey it; he must uphold the ancient principle, "Nolumus leges Angliæ mutari." In the Teutonic portion of the Roman Empire, since Charlemagne, the emperor, according to the form of the installation ceremony and his coronation oath, was the supreme protector of rights and guardian of the laws.

In all Christian States of the Middle Ages, Roman as well as Teutonic, it again and again appears that the nation had a voice in the legislature, although in various forms,—sometimes by two estates, as in France; or by three, as in England; or by four, as in Sweden.

It is only after the division of the Church that we come upon those evil times, when, by the growing despotism of the Spanish and French kings, and by the usurped power of the German princes, the ancient rights were ignored and the bounds of princely power removed. The rulers assumed the entire power of lawgiving to themselves. From 1614, the "Etats généraux" of France were never called together until the outbreak of the great Revolution; and yet the better traditions were so far imperishable, that they were still spoken of in the documents of prominent writers. Under Philip III. of Spain, Mariana, and under Louis XIV., Duguet, maintained the principle that the king was morally bound to obey the laws of the land which he at his coronation found existing, and no less also those which he himself gave to the people.

The proposition which we combat is not native on German soil; it has been developed and taken root in other countries. The ancient Oriental despotism assumed a Christian form in the Byzantine Empire; and when Christianity passed over from thence to the Sclavonic nations, it found amongst them a frame of mind closely related to the despotic notions of the East. The Russian autocracy was thus developed, and appeared surrounded with the halo of a supposedly divine and exclusive sanction.

Ivan the Terrible caused 70,000 inhabitants of Novgorod to be put to the sword for no reason whatever, and experienced no resistance; for, as the Russian historian of those days says, "Nothing equalled the cruelty of the czar excepting the patience of his subjects." The Russian priests taught that any one dying in accordance with the will of the czar attains to heaven at once, similarly to the ancient martyrs.

If ever a murmur arose that the magnates of the land should be allowed to participate in the government, the clergy at once declared such ideas to be Manichæan heresy. Manes it was who taught that there were two eternal principles; and any one who spoke of any other power in the State, besides that of the czar, was considered partaker in his errors. So too royalty, which, it is true, has received a portion of the honour and majesty belonging to the eternal King, is confounded with divinity as being a visible God upon monarch. His precursors have ages ago been visible upon the stage of the world's history. They were the ancient tyrants of Babylon and Assyria, and the lawless emperors of heathen Rome.

It is a dangerous matter to tell princes that they may set themselves above the laws, and to accustom the people to a blind and unreasoning obedience, as though that were a virtue becoming to Christians, without regarding the distinctions between right and wrong. Supposing that the present possessor of absolute monarchy is imbued with Christian ideas, what guarantee have we that his successor will be so? What a misfortune it would be that Christian politicians, without intending it, should assist in the setting up of an antichristian throne!

CHAPTER IV.

CHRISTIANITY AND MODERN LIBERAL TENDENCIES.

There is still one word of explanation necessary for those who do not claim an absolute power for rulers, and yet reject all modern liberal tendencies as unchristian. They say monarchy shall be limited, the form of government shall be organic; but the limits of the monarchy shall be determined, as they were in the Middle Ages, by the powerful body of the nobility, the clergy, and the boroughs. They say that the truly organic State is the patrimonial of past centuries, as Louis von Haller has described it in a most masterly manner, and that such a form alone corresponds with the Christian ideal; that, on the other hand, the attempts which have been made since 1789 to divide the power between the crown and a representation selected from the body of the people is antichristian; that it is reprehensible to talk of any contract between princes and people, or to set up a written constitution, and to require an oath of observance to be taken. Such is the doctrine which Gentz, Jarcke, Vollgraff, and the political weekly paper in Berlin have taken up.

Let us put one question here, to begin with. Where does the patrimonial State exist? It has fallen to pieces, and only unimportant fragments thereof remain; upon the ruins of it, absolute monarchy, like that of Louis XIV. and the first Napoleon, was reared. Those precautions against arbitrary rule and misuse of power, which existed in the form of government of the Middle Ages, are no longer to be found. The waves of time have carried them away. If it were possible to resuscitate them, it would have been achieved by the noble endeavours of Frederick William IV. But his attempts to rebuild monarchy upon the basis of the ancient "estates" or "curiæ" resulted in failure, and will not be lightly resumed. Hence the practical question with which we have to deal in Germany, as well as in France and elsewhere, is not whether in a Christian State the power of the king shall be regulated by ancient corporations or by modern inventions, but whether it shall be limited by new arrangements or not limited at all. This is the choice which the well-wishers of their country have found themselves face to face with in Germany, ever since, at the constitution of the German Confederation, a representative constitution was promised; but that promise remained unfulfilled in the two principal German States.

What we demand for the supporters of the modern Parliamentary system, is not the acceptation of each and every one of their principles and measures. What we ask for the entire movement is nothing more than freedom of conscience, an exemption from wholesale anathema on the plea of unchristian sentiments, and a recognition of the fact that a Christian State can co-exist with a constitutional system, and that a Christian conscience is not necessarily antagonistic to constitutional ideas.

How was it that the ancient state of things first fell to pieces in France, and then by a slower process in Germany? Not accidentally, and also not exclusively owing to the self-will, folly, and crime of seditious men; the change in the course of events had a deeper origin. In France, at any rate, there were fearful abuses, social evils, and restrictions of the public well-being, which came to light under the old system, and, in combination with the sins and provocations of those in authority, called forth the divine judgment. But this last, amongst other instruments, makes use of wicked men to carry out its decrees; and yet such decrees in themselves are lawful and needful. It is not true, as Schiller has said, that the history of the world is *the* divine judgment of the world; but it is true that it is *a* divine judgment upon her.

But supposing it possible anyhow to restore the former condition of affairs, as it existed on the eve of the Revolution, we should have the old evils, which attached to the ancient institution, again coming to light, and the old common load of sin would be again heaped upon the supporters of those institutions. The Legitimists of France may in many respects be worthy of sympathy; but if they were to come into power, where would be the advantage, unless they had passed through a fire of purification, and had thereby been brought to a recognition of, and contrition for, their evil ways which produced the Revolution? Wolfgang Menzel, in his chapter on the "Corruption of Courts" (in the eighteenth century) of his modern history, has collated from facts such a description as must deeply move every reader, and ought to open the eyes of every unconditional worshipper of the age previous to the Revolution.

Guizot, in his work on the English Revolution, has argued the question, "Why did it succeed?" and we may also add, "Why did not the French Revolution succeed?" It would be a very wide-reaching inquiry to attempt to solve this question thoroughly—the reflections of Edmund Burke on the French Revolution point out the way to the solution; but here it must suffice for us to give prominence to one mighty difference. The twofold English Revolution was carried out at a time when the fear of God was still a power which ruled nations, and by men whose sole object was to realize a Christian life amongst the people and in the government. The French Revolution broke out at a time, and in a nation, when the Church, having undergone much desecration, had lost its beneficial influence; when the fear of God had disappeared, and atheism had become a power. The movement was conducted by the hands of men who were inimical to Christianity, and had fallen into the delusion that they could, without Christ and without Christian virtues, by means of ideas of liberty and the dignity of mankind, create a new world full of justice, happiness, and peace. The English Revolution, although not free from serious errors, could serve to bring about better times; the French Revolution reduced Titanic assailants of heaven to leaders of a merely impious undertaking, and necessarily collapsed. And yet the requirements and desires which the party in France set forth were in themselves to a great extent well founded and justifiable. Ought it then to have been so difficult to use the same discretion in this historical problem as must be employed in every legal controversy,—that is to say, the power of distinguishing between the justifiable demand and the spirit, perhaps perfectly reprehensible, in which such demand is made?

Thus we find two elements mixed up in the great French overthrow of government, and in all the consequences and imitations which have followed that fearful drama. The entire development of the ideas of liberty since 1789 resembles a turbid, impetuous stream, which hurries along on its troubled surface the most varied matters. But it would be neither just nor politic not to examine it critically. We can hardly suppose that any one will unconditionally uphold the principles of 1789 in common with Napoleon III., nor uncompromisingly repudiate them with Julius Stahl.

Laurentius Stein, in his interesting history of the social movement in France, has shown that the Revolution of 1789 was a social, quite as much as a political transformation. It got rid of great social embarrassments, and procured great benefits for the people, which they had a right to have long looked for from a good form of government. The ideas of humanity with which men were then imbued, and which Fichte has most eloquently advocated on German soil, were, notwithstanding the perverted conception of them, really deduced from Christianity. Those ideas contained the truism, that the dignity of humanity confirmed by the gospel of Christianity ought to be respected in the poorest and least of the members of society.

A series of liberties which have been demanded and acquired since that time may, according to the Christian standard, be said to be indifferent, being neither decidedly Christian nor antichristian in themselves. The freedom of the press, freedom of assembly, free trade, freedom of business, free emigration, may be deemed useful or otherwise; but with the various opinions on these subjects Christianity has no concern. If any party which supported such views were to be termed antichristian on that account, and indiscriminately anathematized, it is to be feared that such party would be only thereby thoroughly prejudiced against Christianity. Such a course would make the party unchristian when it really is not so, and that is a responsibility which must not be lightly undertaken.

Whereas the principles of liberty and equality were, during the French Revolution, pushed to extremes with fearfully consequential determination (whence it also comes that those years 1789-95 form the most instructive chapter of modern history), in Germany the same principles were only partially put into practice during the changes of 1830, 1848, 1866.

In the latter case, some limitations have been retained. A first chamber corresponding to the House of Peers, an unconditional right of veto in the crown, a federal council, are so many points of *appui* against transition into the lawless extreme. At present we are in a transition state, and it would therefore be the less permissible to award unmeasured praise or blame to either party.

People may say of a charter or constitutional contract, that it is not a happy idea to reduce all civil rights to a mere string of paragraphs upon vellum. It may be objected that the tendency of our age is bent upon codifying all laws and privileges. Savigny's objection may be urged, "that the present generation is not called upon to make laws." We call the English nation fortunate, because their constitution is like a forest of ancient oak trees; we pity France, because since 1789 there have been no less than ten attempts to improvise a constitution, and we are not surprised that those attempts have only resulted in a crumbling piece of patchwork. Nevertheless we have no right to assert that it is an unchristian act to lay down and ratify the relations between the crown and the nation, between Upper and Lower House, in a charter. It must not be said that reverence is diminished, and the dignity of the crown denied, as soon as any mention is made of a contract between the ruler and his people. Marriage is a sacrament, a union sanctified and rendered indissoluble by God, and in this alliance the man is the head of the woman; but is it, therefore, unchristian to make out a marriage settlement, in which the monetary relations are arranged, and the powers of disposition of the husband over the property of the wife are defined? Both are perfectly compatible, the sacramental consecration and the temporal contract. Now, what the marriage settlement is as regards the family, such is also the charter as regards the State. It can be agreed to without in any way interfering with the sacred dignity of the chief ruler, and without relaxing the bond of union between prince and people.

There are probably no words more indefinite, none more varied in interpretation, than the expressions "Liberty" and "Progress." And the fact is all the more striking, that the German nation above all others should be so much excited by vague ideas and semi-intelligible phrases. It was so in the sixteenth century, and it appears to be so now. Liberty!—of what? Progress!—whither? Those are the questions upon which but very few appear able to furnish a reasonable answer. Freedom from the debasing and illegal condition of slavery; freedom from the condition of serfdom; freedom from all restrictions as to choice of profession and the higher education of children; freedom to enter into matrimony or to acquire property; freedom from all legal disabilities; freedom from the oppression of a compulsory form of worship which is antagonistic to conviction,—these are all, so to say, social freedoms; and who will take upon himself to say that it is unchristian to strive after them or unchristian to grant them? If there be some irreligious men amongst the mass who demand these and similar freedoms, well, let us prevent such men from obtaining a position of rule; but should we not at the same time recognise and carry out their demands, in so far as they are good, thereby morally disarming and weakening a dangerous party in the State?

But freedom from the duty of reverence to paternal and kingly authority; freedom from the stringency of the matrimonial bond; freedom from the laws of temperance and chastity; freedom to tread all holy things under foot; freedom to cast suspicion upon the best intentions of the Government, anonymously; under the same veil to vilify all who differ from us in opinion, to damage the reputation of innocent persons; freedom to pillage and grind down the poor with usury or oppressive tasks; freedom from the restraints imposed by the decalogue,—these are all freedoms of a totally different character. They are also strivings after freedom, but as different from those enumerated in the foregoing paragraph as light from darkness, as day from night.

There is a progress towards the improvement of the moral and material well-being of the people, a progress towards a condition of life based upon charity and justice. To further such progress is the real object of a Christian ruler and of all patriots; and only in a Christian community can the promises held out by such progress be realized. But there is also a progress towards a condition where the main object is that man begin, continue, and end his existence without God; where nothing is sacred, nothing is sublime, nothing is inviolable; where there shall be no Christian family, no Christian school,—a progress towards chaos, where everything ideal is to die out, where the last remnants of the fear of God and subjection to the moral code shall be exterminated. Such progress means the ruin of the nation.

The strivings after progress of our days are a confused turmoil of various and antagonistic elements. What can then be the advantage of a restless, undefined spirit of progress,—a rushing on, merely on, away from the evils we know of to those we know not of,—a pushing off into the wild dark ocean, without rudder, without compass, without guiding star, without definite destination?

We may well look for a psychological explanation of this curious, undetermined, and unconsidered striving after liberty and progress. One considerable element of the solution lies in an error which is plainly asserted by one party, and is by the other made the silent axiom of their efforts; and that is the idea that mankind is radically good. All crime, all offences against society, are supposed to be only the results partially of ignorance, partially of evil concomitant accidents, poverty, and want. If freedom of action be permitted, and ignorance be dispelled by education, every virtue would at once shoot forth, and a condition of happiness and general contentment would very soon result.

Your true despot is led astray by the opposite illusion. He considers that all mankind is bad, servile, and not to be improved. When a philanthropic schoolmaster[1] once laid his plans for educating and benefiting the people before a despotic king,[2] basing them upon the exceeding goodness of human nature, he was told, "I know this breed; it is an evil race." Naturally, then, such an one believes that mankind is only worthy of the knout. The less freedom of action, the more trammels and despotism, the better. As compared with these views of the despot, the views of those who strive for liberty are noble and amiable. Still there is error on both sides; one is the Manichæan, the other takes the Pelagian form. In human nature, as it at present is, all the germs of evil are contained. If no fundamental remedial procedure be adopted, they come to maturity and bear evil fruit. Knowledge alone does not sanctify or ennoble. By the mere tearing down of oppressive restraint, we cannot raise heroes of virtue.

And yet man is capable of, and called upon to show forth, the highest form of virtue; he only requires a moral conversion, a new spirit, the impartation of divine life. Paternal and maternal education of the childish disposition in love and seriousness, sanctifying influences of the Spirit of Christ who dwells in the

---

[1] Salzmann.   [2] Frederick II. of Prussia.

Church, and the entire power of the divinely-revealed truth, added to the action of a ruling power, which in its justice and mercy is an image of the divine rule, and which assists education by means of public schools conducted upon Christian principles,—these are the powers by the co-operation of which a virtuous nation, and one worthy of freedom, can be trained up.

Those justifiable liberties or freedoms, of which we have spoken above, are grand possessions. But much depends also, as in the case of other possessions of human life, such as property, talents, and physical strength, upon what use is made of them. The more freedom that is granted to a nation, the more moral solidity, respect for the law, self-control, and regard for the common weal ought to exist, so that liberty may be properly used. A republic, if it is to succeed, premises the greatest possible amount of virtue. This is a lesson taught us by history, an incontrovertible truth. And yet it should not be misapplied, as some narrow-minded statesmen have done, in order to retain the nation in leading-strings, and in order to embitter such freedom as exists, under the pretence of a Christian, paternal care, again and again withholding such freedom, though promised, under the same pretext. The possible or actual misuse must be provided against; but the misused possession may not, on account of its abuse, be taken away from a nation. Or has it never occurred that authority has been misused? and is it on that account permissible to tear down all authority? Just in the same position stands the reasonable freedom which has once been granted to a nation.

The famous announcement of the rights of man by the French National Assembly, on 26th August 1789, which has become the basis and model of so many expositions of fundamental rights since then, appears, in the light of experience, and if measured by the standard of Christian axioms, as a wonderful conglomerate of truth and error, of beneficial and hurtful elements.

A fatal error is contained in the proposition, that every individual has an original and inalienable right to an equal participation and co-operation in the formation of the laws,—a proposition which necessarily grants universal suffrage in the election of representatives for the legislative assembly. When in Germany, during the years 1848 and 1866, we had the election law introduced, which is the consequence of that erroneous idea, we had plenty of opportunity of learning by experience the full scope of that error.

The roughest and most ignorant citizen would have by his vote just the same influence upon the legislature as the wisest and most experienced; the former no less, the latter no more. For instance, in a university town the scouts of the students would have more to say to the choice of a representative than the professors, for there are more scouts than professors.

There may be occasions in which a Government may feel disposed to consult all its subjects, without distinction of position or education, when a tax is to be imposed which will fall upon all, and will press most heavily upon the poor and lowly ones; for instance, the introduction of a general obligation to carry arms. But to make this in any way a principle of legislation is an error which all the principal lawgivers of antiquity have avoided. Even the *Thetes* and the *Capite censi* in Athens and in Rome had their representatives, but as a class, not according to numbers. At that time it was properly considered that the wisdom required for legislation was the most valuable and rare of endowments. Now it would appear that people hold it the cheapest and most common of all, and that it may be picked up anywhere in the street. If the autocratic system is bad, because it has no conception of an organized State, this is more than ever the case if we concede to the masses an arithmetically equal amount of co-operation in the legislature. It is the thorough denial of all natural organization in civil society. The right of each individual to be free from slavery, to be able to found a family and to acquire property, to be equal before the criminal law, may be deduced from Christian doctrine; but a right to an equal share in the legislation cannot. Burke long ago expressed the really correct idea on this subject in his *Reflections*, when he says: "I am far from denying the real rights of men. All the advantages for which civil society is made become man's rights. But as to the share of power, authority, and direction which each individual ought to have in the management of the State, that I must deny to be among the direct original rights of man in civil society."

The principles of 1789 were those of pure democracy. They led, of consequent necessity, to a disappearance of royalty; but they did not lead to true liberty. It was supposed that a division of power, by which the entire making of the laws should be reserved to the representatives of the people, and the executive power alone should remain to the heads of the State, would be a guarantee for freedom. But it did not prove to be so; it reverses and becomes a new form of tyranny, in that the legislative also assumes the executive power. Pure democracy does not fulfil its promises; for, as we cannot attain to the requisite unity of mind, we are obliged to revert to the expedient of the decision of the majority overruling that of the minority; and this resource is rendered the more unfortunate, because the result of the voting is often based, not upon intelligence, but upon chance.

And yet we ought not to, as often occurs, employ democracy as a bugbear, and decry the democratic principle as antichristian. A Christian State can co-exist with a republic. Given a Christian people, which in its family life observes Christian manners, a democratic constitution will certainly not be a hindrance to a Christian regulation of the national life. On the contrary, a people which chooses its own rulers and determines its own laws,—a people which at the same time is filled with a reverence for God, that has for its object the good of all, and takes the divine moral code for its guide, is a sublime spectacle, and one worthy of all admiration.

In a republic, also, the character of the ruler makes itself felt as a divine institution. The regents and officials chosen by the people must be impressed with the idea that their duties should be carried out as in the sight of God, and that they will have to render an account of them to the Supreme Judge. Who does not believe that the office of judge under a republic is just as sacred a one as under a monarchy?

In a democracy, the sovereignty of the people is recognised. It is a grievous mistake to declare that this is the one original, necessary, and always valid principle. The sovereignty of the people was called into play as a desperate resource against the misuse of royal and aristocratic power; and, as the history of all modern revolutions shows us, it never did any good. It was only another power of evil. In places where the sovereignty of the people exists as an actual fact, and is based on historical data,—as, for instance, in Switzerland and in the United States of America,—it has a title to recognition. We have no right to say, "Away with it;" but rather, "Employ it in a manner which shall be pleasing to God." It is, however, a very different thing when a people declares its own sovereignty in defiance of God and His laws. If the principle be asserted in the latter form, and the will of the people be set up, in opposition to the divine commands, as the supreme and only fountain of law, then no form of words can be too strong for protesting against it. But this may be said not alone of the sovereignty of the people. Every form of idolizing men, and the will of men, is antichristian. As Pharaoh of old exclaimed, when he refused to grant permission to the Israelites to go and worship, saying, "Who is the Lord, that I should obey His voice?" so also it is equally reprehensible when a democratic mob does away with Christian worship. It is not democracy itself that is objectionable, but the repudiation of the moral code. Every form of government is antichristian which raises its head against God, whether it be wielded by the people or by an autocrat.

CHAPTER V.

THE TEMPORAL AND SPIRITUAL POWER.

ROYALTY and priesthood, temporal and spiritual power, are quite distinct,—they may not be confounded; the two offices cannot be combined in one person. That principle is distinctly expressed in the doctrines and ordinances of the Christian Church.

The axiom is peculiar to Christianity. During the pre-Christian era it was never distinctly expressed, and at one time the fusion of both powers was usual. At the time of the patriarchs, Melchizedec appears both as king and priest. In Moses, again, we have a royal and priestly action combined. From that time the two powers separte,—the priesthood is hereditary in the house of Aaron, of the tribe of Levi; the kingdom is made over to the house of David, of the tribe of Judah. When King Uzziah took upon himself to offer incense in the sanctuary, he was smitten with leprosy as a punishment for the encroachment. The recombining of the two offices, which, notwithstanding the previous warnings, took place in the priestly race of the Maccabees for a short time, was something abnormal. Priestly action on the part of kings was a common occurrence in the times of heathen antiquity, and the Roman Imperator was, *ex officio*, chief priest.[1]

The position assumed by Christ forms the most unmistakable contrast to all of these. It is true that, agreeably to His vocation, and of right, He is King; but here below His only crown was one of thorns.

[1] " Pontifex maximus."

He withdrew from the people who desired to set Him upon the throne. In a condition of humility, He fulfilled His prophetic and priestly mission, and He imparted to His disciples a share of this before His departure to the Father. They are to walk in His steps; they continue, as does the Church of Christ generally during this dispensation, in a condition of humility, patience, and servitude. It is only in the coming dispensation that Christ will appear as King, and then, too, will the hidden dignity of royalty, which doubtless dwells in His Church also, be revealed.

The self-negation of our Lord went so far, that He declined the office of arbitrator in a worldly quarrel. A man said to Him, "Master, speak to my brother, that he divide the inheritance with me;" and the Lord replied, "Man, who made me a judge or a divider over you?" (Luke xii. 13, 14.)

As Christ carefully kept Himself at a distance from worldly matters, so also ought His servants to act, whom He has called to a ministerial office, and made it their duty to imitate His example.

As long as the temporal rulers and their subordinate officers were inimical, or strangers to Christianity, the servants of Christ continued in their borders. They not only actually held themselves aloof from any form of participation in political affairs, from any entanglement in State concerns, and from differences respecting *meum* and *tuum*, but they also proclaimed, without hesitation, the principle that spiritual rulers had no power to command in temporal affairs, and temporal rulers none in spiritual matters. That was the time when the Christian Church flourished. But when Constantine recognised Christianity, the situation became changed; the sign of the cross was made the banner of the Roman Empire, and a number of laws were emitted for restraining heathen worship and promoting the Christian Church. This change brought about great dangers for both parties. It is not to be overlooked that the bishops at the time of Constantine, taken as a body, were too weak to withstand the encroachments of the temporal power, which assumed the form of benefits. We therefore find at once, that bishops were appointed by the *ipse dixit* of the emperor, in exactly similar manner as the officials of the empire and the prefects of provinces. The Eastern Church soon experienced the injurious results, when Constantius raised the Arian heresy to a dominant position.

It was a proper feeling that urged men to look about for a safeguard to protect the Church from such violence. They sought for it in the Primacy; and, indeed, the action of the great Roman popes of the Christian community did serve to promote independence and purity of doctrine. But now it became the duty of popes and bishops to recognise the independence of the temporal power in its own domain, just as decidedly, and to maintain the distinction between the two spheres, viz. ecclesiastical and civil. We know that this was not the case; on the contrary, two serious errors crept in. The popes accepted from Pepin and Charles the Great the dangerous gift of royal power and dignity, and they very soon claimed the possession of ecclesiastical state as a divine right and a necessity. At last they asserted that the temporal was altogether an emanation from the ecclesiastical power. Boniface VIII., in the bull "Unam sanctam," dated 18th November 1302, laid it down as an axiom, which every Christian was bound to believe under pain of forfeiting eternal salvation, that the temporal power was subject to the ecclesiastical: "Both swords — the spiritual and material—are under the control of the Church. The latter must be wielded for the benefit of the Church, the former by the Church itself. The former by the hands of the priesthood, the latter by the hands of kings and warriors, but under the guidance and with the permission of the priesthood. One sword must be subject to the other, and the temporal authority must submit itself to the ecclesiastical; the spiritual power ordains the temporal, and if it be evil condemns it. Hence, if the temporal power errs, it must be judged by the spiritual."

This bull was confirmed by Leo x. during his unfortunate fifth Lateran Council in 1517, just previous to the appearance of Luther.

The reaction followed, when, after the outbreak of schism in the Church, the Protestant rulers for their part took upon themselves the spiritual oversight, and usurped episcopal authority and functions.

Evil in both cases resulted. Whenever bishops desire to be kings, and kings desire to be bishops, divinely appointed ordinances and borders are displaced, and the consequences cannot but be disastrous.

Have not, as it is, the clergy more laid upon them than they are able to perform? But whoever takes upon himself matters which do not belong to his office, will inevitably finish by executing badly his own special and legitimate calling. Thus spiritual blessings languish, and, on the other hand, the people by no means obtain the blessings of a good government in worldly matters. Since the bishops became princes, the sons of princes wished to become bishops. Worldliness, want of spirituality, the usual vices of court life, gross offences and laxity, crept in, and led the Church to the brink of perdition. It has been seen from experience in the Pontifical States, and amongst us in the territories of German bishops, how wretchedly a nation is governed by prelates, even when they are filled with good-will and good intention. Poverty, ignorance, and indolence are at the present time in many places the characteristics of a population which has for centuries lain under sacerdotal rule.

When kings are bishops, this fact undermines the internal vitality of the Church in the most injurious manner. The entire mode and manner of direction becomes worldly, external, and spiritless. If the prince be a true believer, he protects and promotes correct doctrine; but in his hands it perishes and becomes a lifeless orthodoxy. For, as in the education and appointment of state officials, worldly wisdom is the main object sought for, so also in the case of ecclesiastics, only their acquirements, and but little if at all regarding their virtues or spiritual-mindedness, is inquired into. An affirmation or subscription of orthodox creeds is sufficient, and by this door hirelings and wolves obtain access to the fold of Christ. But in the other case, where the prince and his ministers are inclined to heretical doctrines, these soon strive for possession of professorial chairs and pulpits, meeting but little opposition. If in Byzantium it was impossible to guard against Arianism, as soon as it became the imperial court theology, so also in Protestant Germany rationalism forced its way in, and the ancient Christian traditions have nearly been overthrown, since the princes, their councillors, and consistories, and the university professors appointed by the princes, took up with rationalism.

How is it possible to justify, or even excuse, such evils on merely theoretical grounds?

The dependence of the temporal upon the spiritual power is supposed to be based upon the following grounds:— It is true that the civil authority is ordained of God; but its object, and the domain upon which it has to fulfil it, is of a subordinate nature to loose of ecclesiastical power. Temporal rulers have to protect carnal life, temporal possessions, and whatever else belongs to the perishable welfare of mankind. Ecclesiastical powers, on the other hand, have to care for the salvation of souls, for the better part of mankind, for their eternal welfare. Now the soul being of more value than the body, and as the latter must submit to the former and render obedience to it, so also, it is asserted, the temporal ought to submit to the spiritual power, and permit itself to be guided by it.

In the first place, we have here the duty of the temporal power conceived in too mean a spirit, for it ought also to deal out justice and law, to protect morality and respectability; on the other hand, the Church should not only distribute spiritual benefits, but also carnal. Withal the appointment and equipment of the Church is the more exalted; but it by no means follows, from the eminence of the duty imposed upon the one power, that the bearer of the minor commission is subjected to it, and is to serve as its handmaiden. The one commission, as also the other, is from God; the holder of the one as well as of the other is responsible to God, who is above all, and not to the authority which is co-ordinate. The most excellent pastor of souls is on that account no surgeon; and, if he be wise, he will be careful not to lay down rules for the surgeon, or in any way interfere with surgical treatment. It would be futile if he were to justify such an absurd action upon the plea that the soul is of more value than the body, and that the care of the soul is a more important matter than the care of the body.

In order to show that the power of the Pope, and his position as ruler of a country, is beneficial,—nay, more, necessary,—appeal is made to the fact that only thus, as a sovereign amongst the other sovereigns, is it possible for him to carry out his exalted office, to oppose with effect the mighty ones of the earth, and to assert truth and justice without fear. Hereupon we reply, the execution of such a commission is a matter requiring heroic trust in God. If such confidence dwell in a servant of Christ, he can fulfil his mission without a royal crown, ecclesiastical · state, army, or navy. When John the Baptist told Herod the Tetrarch the truth, when Paul laid down his testimony before Felix and Agrippa, when Ambrosius resisted the entrance of the Emperor Theodosius into the sanctuary, none of them possessed any of those appendages which are declared to be indispensable to the exercise of the temporal authority of the Pope; they all exercised a purely spiritual power. It is just that reliance upon God, without reserve of temporal power, which lends to the testimony of the servant of God for His commands, its true value and assures its moral effect. On the contrary, the greater the pomp and earthly panoply of the Pope became, the less moral power would his resistance to princes have. If a prince tells a prince the truth, there is no great merit in that. Besides which, if the possession of temporal power is to replace any lack of trust in God, the extent of the States of the Church as hitherto defined is much too small, and the patrimony of the Papal chair ought to be as extensive as the mightiest empire.

The theories with which attempts are made to justify princely power in church matters are generally wanting in distinctness. Constantine, evidently with the object of appeasing the bishops, termed himself the bishop or overseer over the external affairs of the Church (ἐπίσκοπος τῶν ἔξω της ἐκκλησίας). From this starting point the theory was developed by theologians of a *jus circa sacra*, not *in sacra*, which belonged to Christian princes. But it is difficult to grasp anything so uncertain and undefined as those two expressions are. With dangerous extravagance the title of high priest, ἀρχιερεύς, was accorded to the Byzantine emperors, which sufficiently pointed out their false position. When in the German Reformation the episcopate was unfortunately lost, the Protestant princes took over the exercise of episcopal functions,— naturally only as regards the discipline of the Church, and exclusive of sacramental offices, preaching, and the care of souls, which remained in the hands of ecclesiastics. Up to the present time no hesitation is felt in terming the ruler of the land, in Protestant church-law, *summus episcopus*, even if he belongs to another confession. The Consistories, composed of a mixture of jurists and theologians, were set up as organs of the royal will, and the most disastrous of church constitutions entered into action.

The present distinction drawn between the discipline of the Church and the ministry of ecclesiastical means of grace is utterly untenable, and is accompanied with disastrous results for the vitality of the body. In the Scriptures, and in ancient Christian history, we find no trace of such a distinction. A church discipline exercised without sacerdotal consecration, without any connection with the commission which Christ gave His apostles in the beginning, without any pledge of the indwelling of the Spirit of Christ, is and must be something monstrous. Protestant princes establish creeds, rituals, hymn-books, catechisms, and church ordinances, for their subjects; they select and appoint the ministers to their various grades and offices. They do all this, exercising thereby episcopal—nay, more than episcopal, apostolic—functions. If they are really empowered from above to do all this, why do not they consecrate the elements? Why do they relegate to others the celebration of the sacraments, the preaching of the word, and the care of souls? It is for this very reason that the discipline of the Church has become so very worldly, and her internal vitality has suffered so much; because the wielders of Church rule have been deficient of spiritual anointing and equipments; the consciousness of being amenable to Scripture and tradition and of responsibility to Christ was wanting. As soon as the ordering of the Church comes to be regarded and exercised as a portion of civil eminence and State control, the Spirit of Christ is repressed, and every possible opening is afforded for the entry of the spirit of the world. Again, if the temporal rulers are deficient of authority and equipment for the exercise of priestly functions, as they very justly feel that they are, whence do they derive the right to perform episcopal and apostolic actions?

Protestant theologians in Germany, feeling the untenable nature of the position, have on various occasions admitted it to be the result of necessity; they have compared the princely power in ecclesiastical affairs to a temporary roof erected over the dilapidated ruin of the Church. Intelligent princes have been brought to feel the oppressiveness of their position, like Frederick William IV., who desired to be relieved of this heavy responsibility, and to make over the direction of the Church to the proper hands again.

In England, where the various political and religious systems are most sharply defined, Henry VIII. was terribly in earnest in propounding the erroneous doctrine that the king was also head of the Church. Froude the historian, although himself permeated with that erroneous view, the so-called Erastian, has handed down to us a hideous picture of the tyranny of those times. Thomas Cranmer, led away by idolatry of royalty, saw in the supremacy of the king more than a necessitous expedient. When Henry VIII. died, Cranmer looked upon his commission as archbishop as at an end; he ceased to perform his functions, and applied to the new monarch, Edward VI., for a renewal of his powers. However curious and repulsive this procedure may appear, it was but the consistent putting into practice of a principle radically wrong.

The intermingling of the two powers has at all times proved itself to be a most dangerous matter as regards liberty, whether civic or of conscience. This is the result of indifference to divine ordinances, and preferring the inventions of man. Where can the oppressed and persecuted find a haven of refuge, if his bishop is also the ruler of his land, or if his king is at the same time his spiritual chief? A misuse of power is just as possible on the part of a bishop as of a king. It is well for us if we only have to suffer injustice from one, and are able to find an asylum and relief for our woes with the other.

Which of the two evils is the greater, and which the lesser—that the hierarchy be temporal rulers, or that an autocracy be the guide of the Church—depends upon the varied character of the times. If the hierarchy retains its severity, as in the Middle Ages—if the temporal power allows itself to be swayed by humanity—it may be that the ascendancy of princes is less oppressive and injurious than that of the priesthood. Providence overrules the mistakes of men, and causes even that which they have done amiss to be productive of good as well as evil. Now and again the royal power in the Church proved advantageous. This may serve as some consolation. But any justification of the Apap (the inverse of Papa)—as our old theologians termed the interference of royal power in church matters—is out of the question, and it will continue so until it can be shown that Christ ever said, "Herod, feed thou my sheep."

It is pleasant to be able to find, in the history of Christian States here and there, the basis of a healthy and proper relationship between these two powers. Such a bright spot in the constitution of the German Empire was the anointing of the emperor, if properly regarded in other respects. The anointing of a king or emperor by the hand of a bishop or pope must not be regarded as the impartation of royal or imperial power. A ruler is ruler, and has a claim to the obedience, respect, and allegiance of his subjects, even before he is anointed, and without that ceremony at all. He does not derive his power from the Church, nor from any ecclesiastical ceremony, but from his birth, or from election, from state contracts, from the laws, from the consent of Parliament, according to existing actual facts. The spirituality can neither detract from nor add to his power. But, in that he receives the anointing in the Church, he acknowledges that he requires, for the purpose of fulfilling his exalted duties, the assistance of the Divine Spirit and the grace which Christ alone can bestow. He seeks for it from the right source, and in finding it his position certainly does acquire thereby a more sacred character than before. There is imparted to him, and to his subjects, an assistance for the due performance of mutual duties. The Roman emperor of the German nation used to appear at his coronation in the robe of a deacon, and as such used to read the gospel in the Mass. In this manner his position as regards the Church was beautifully set forth. He is not a priest and not a bishop; he ought not to become one, and he ought not to wish to become one. But as the deacons were in the beginning set in the Church to be guardians of the poor, protectors of the widow, and stewards of the goods of the Church, and as laymen to lead the other laymen in a godly conversation, so also the Christian ruler should be a guardian of his people, a helper of the oppressed, a protector of the Christian Church against injustice and violence, and an example of Christian virtue to all.

The Episcopal Church of England has a heavy burden to carry in the royal supremacy. She feels her humiliating dependence upon the will of the Crown and Parliament. She is in a condition of restraint, which, it is true, in one respect assists in preserving her from error, but nevertheless does prevent her from making any progress towards perfection. Still, with all that, in her relations to the State a correct idea finds expression. The bishops have a seat and a voice in the House of Lords, but no minister of the State Church can be chosen as a representative in the House of Commons. This ancient provision is based upon wise grounds; hereby the relation of the Church to the civil legislature is more correctly expressed than in other countries. The clergy may not be chosen as representatives of the people. Thereby they are kept aloof from the turmoil of elections, and from a sphere of action in which their energies would be withdrawn from their proper functions. An ecclesiastic should hold aloof from the strife of political parties; he must not be mixed up in quarrels concerning questions of the day. He belongs to his congregation, he must minister to all, be a blessing to all, and he must therefore endeavour to gain the confidence of all, and have access to their hearts. In every congregation there are various political tendencies; a servant of Christ ought not, by insisting upon his own political convictions, to separate himself from any portion of his flock. He is protected from this danger if it is predetermined that he cannot offer himself as candidate for a seat in Parliament. If it frequently occurs amongst us that ecclesiastics take their seats among the representatives of the people, this neither promotes their spiritual office nor the civil legislation. But when, on the other hand, bishops take their seat in the Upper House, not by election and not temporarily, but in virtue of their office as life-long advisers of the Crown, it may be demonstrated to be proper. It does not denote that they are to take part in every political strife; but it does show that they ought to point out when a law, or any measure under discussion, is antagonistic to the commandments of God or Christian principles. They are qualified to do so, in virtue of their office, in a manner which no one else can, and it is meet and right that a Christian people should afford the servants of Christ, the representatives of Christian tradition, the opportunity of advising in weightier matters.

The Chorus in Greek tragedy is no idle looker on; it has a part to play and a place to fill, but its action is different from that of the other personages in the drama. The Chorus ought to occupy the position so beautifully described by Horace:—

> "The manly duties of the actor's part
> The Chorus should support; with all due care
> Fitting its language to the play's design,
> And uttering nought beyond. It is its role
> To patronize the good, and counsel them
> With loving words; to hold the proud in check,
> And furious wrath appease; to praise the meals
> Where temperance prevails; and sing the worth
> Of healthful Justice and of Law, and Peace,
> Safe with unbolted doors. And more than this,
> The Chorus is a faithful confidant,
> And wearies not of praying to the gods
> To scourge the haughty and console the sad."

The Chorus represents the religious element in tragedy; and, in fact, its bearing corresponds with the position which the representatives of religion should assume in society. It is the duty of Christian ecclesiastics also, when the people are excited by political passions, to calm them down, to remonstrate with the arrogant, to foster peace and not strife, to assist the suffering and oppressed with counsel and comfort, and to offer up petitions to Heaven for the greatest benefits of this life —for justice, unity, and contentment.

CHAPTER VI.

COMMON GROUND: EDUCATION AND MATRIMONY.

In the confusion of the present day, it is to be desired, as Franz von Baader teaches, that the two confused and intricately commingled powers would separate, in order to be reconciled and then to enter upon a proper relation towards each other. A careful definition of domain, and then a friendly compact between those who exercise authority on one or other of the domains—that is the proposition. This enunciation will probably be admitted by all parties to be nearly correct. But the difficulty lies just therein, in apportioning the field of action and functions to each. For there are domains common to both, so that in the same matter Church and State have each a duty to fulfil and privileges to exercise. Such are the education of the people and matrimony.

The Church as well as the State has an interest in the public education of the lowest as well as of the highest in the land. Both not only have a right, but it is the duty of each to strive after the spiritual well-being of the people by means of education. Children are born to parents, and upon them rests the responsibility, imposed by God, of their training and education. Whatever the civil local authorities, or the State, may do for the public schools, is an assistance rendered to the parents in the fulfilment of their duty. As a matter of course, the authorities are also primarily bound to train up as many intelligent men as possible for the service of the Commonwealth. Such instruments are all the more requisite, seeing that they have not only to care for the material, but also for the moral well-being of the people. Now, if the parents as well as the authorities understand their duties, there is but little prospect of conflict arising upon this field between the two parties. The duties of ecclesiastics in respect to public education are derived from the commission which Christ gave: "Teach all nations, baptizing them, and teaching them to observe all things whatsoever I have commanded you." Herein we have no authority for compulsory baptism or forced religious instruction; but when a nation, as such, accepts Christianity, it follows as a necessary *sequitur* that the spirituality shall take part in public education, and direct the religious portion thereof. Christian parents are in duty bound to impart the rudiments of religious instruction, to their children, themselves. When the pastor comes in to carry on and complete the instruction, father and mother should welcome him, and should endeavour to support his authority and to assist him in carrying out his office.

Just so should the authorities of a Christian people comport themselves. They may also care for elementary instruction in religion by the appointment of teachers, and then permit the spirituality to step in for the higher grades. They will take care to surround the position of an ecclesiastical religious teacher with dignity. They will provide that the whole of the rest of the instruction, whether elementary, middle-class, or higher, shall be maintained in harmony with the moral code of Christianity, and that Christian worship be looked upon with reverence. They are not necessarily obliged to go any farther. The State Church has no inherent right to claim the entire control of the schools, to determine the class-books, or to appoint the teachers.

If the entire oversight of the schools be accorded to the episcopate, as occurred in the Austrian Concordat, that is a voluntary concession on the part of the State, which must decide whether and for how long such an arrangement is beneficial. This decision ought to be arrived at by mutual agreement, and it is of the last importance to both parties that an amicable arrangement be come to; for nothing can be more dangerous than that the two authorities quarrel, and one seek to undermine the other.

The subject of matrimony holds a very similar position. It is primarily a union or contract between the betrothed couple. It is more important, more venerable, and more sacred than any other contract relating to property or mutual rights; but still, in its nature, it is primarily a civil contract. The ratification and confirmation of this contract ought to be sought for from the temporal authorities, as they have to care for morality and respectability and that the rights of inheritance are duly regarded; they have to prescribe the conditions under which a legal marriage may or may not be solemnized. Neither the temporal authorities nor the State can originate matrimony, nor can they conclude it—that is the office of the married couple; but the State can confirm it, thereby affording it a legal value, and guaranteeing the legitimacy of the children.

Seeing that the Christian feels himself bound to seek for the divine blessing upon every important step he takes, he will more especially recognise this duty in this, the most serious act of his life,—the completion of his marriage compact and the founding of a family. Hence matrimony ought, as Ignatius teaches Polycarp from Antioch, to be solemnized amongst Christians with the sanction of the bishop. The divine benediction, which Christ has committed to His ministers for distribution, should be imparted to it, whereby it obtains a holier sanction. Then the married couple are joined by a divine act; they are assured of that divine assistance and that measure of grace which they require for the fulfilment of their duties. The Christian who should despise the reception of this blessing would thereby deny his standing in Christ, and would announce the reprehensible determination of carrying on a life without God and without Christ, becoming a cause of offence to all to whom Christianity is sacred.

This distinction between the two aspects of matrimony as a civil contract and a Christian union is no new discovery. The very oldest church canon—that of the Greek Church—teaches that matrimony is, primarily, a moral compact, secondarily, a mystery or sacrament. It can only be solemnized as a Christian marriage in conformity to the commandments of God.

The divine word, and the ancient matrimonial code founded upon it, contain irrefragable conditions as to the degrees of consanguinity and affinity by marriage, within which no marriage is permitted; also regarding the indissolubility of the tie, so that neither of the pair during the lifetime of the other can enter into a new alliance. A marriage in which any one of these conditions is disregarded may be, if the civil laws admit it (whereby, however, they do not harmonize with the law of Christ), a valid marriage, so that the right of inheritance in the children is preserved; but a Christian marriage it cannot be, and a blessing in the name of Christ, who has forbidden such contracts, ought neither to be asked for nor granted.

In a Christian Commonwealth, therefore, a co-operation of both powers in this domain ought to occur. As soon as a nation, as such, has professed its belief in Christ, it is the duty of the legislature, in the interest of all Christian citizens, to bring the civil matrimonial code into consonance with the laws of Christ.

If, unfortunately, the various Christian confessions are not agreed as to what is the Christian code, there will remain for the temporal power no other resource than to come to an agreement with each separate denomination. Thus, too, it will be justified in allowing the Jews to live together according to their own matrimonial laws.

In this field, also, a definition of border is requisite. The ecclesiastics have no right to insist that the entire ceremony, in both parts, shall be handed over to them to perform. The civil ratification and the ecclesiastical benediction are originally two distinct acts. In Christian States they have been amalgamated, so that the ecclesiastic performing the marriage ceremony does also impart the civil ratification. In the one act that he performs, he ministers both as an official of the Commonwealth and as a servant of Christ. He imparts to the union not only civil validity, but also sacramental consecration. However wholesome and reverential this arrangement is, it cannot be said that any absolute necessity for it exists. If we suppose that, in the original compact between Church and State, it had been arranged from the beginning that every marriage should first of all be ratified by a State official, and then be solemnly consecrated in the Church by a minister of Christ, there would be nothing unchristian in that. But other considerations come into play when it is proposed to dissolve the union between the two acts which has so long existed, and which has taken such deep root in the national character. . Such a step is a critical juncture in the separation of Church and State, which must be the subject of a special chapter.

CHAPTER VII.

THE STATE CHURCH—FREEDOM OF CONSCIENCE—CHRISTIAN AND NON-CHRISTIAN TOLERATION.

The title of "State Church" is not a happily chosen one, for it brings too prominently forward her dependence upon the power of the State and the erroneous assertion that the direction of religious matters is a part of the business of the State. It is more to the purpose if we use the term National Church. When a nation as such has repudiated paganism and recognised the revelation of God in Christ, when the principal officers and the majority of the people have been baptized, it then follows as a matter of course that in such a country the Christian Church is placed in a position of security and respect. Then the keeping holy of the Lord's day becomes a national observance, and is established by law. The great Christian festivals become national holidays. In time of affliction, the whole nation unites to humble itself before God. Important transactions and joyful occasions, which concern the well-being of the country, are marked by divine services. The wielders of temporal power solemnly recognise that they owe their position to the mercy of God, and require His assistance for the proper exercise of their official duties. The influence which we have before described as being that which Christianity ought to exercise upon the laws and the government is rendered certain; and arrangements are made by which the servants of the Church and those of the Commonwealth work together harmoniously in those departments of this life which are common to both. And thus a National Church comes into existence. So far all is praiseworthy and of fair promise.

But if the Christian religion becomes a national matter, and the Church becomes the National Church, it is by no means a consequence that every individual member of the nation necessarily belongs to that Church. It is by no means implied that only Christians may be allowed to have civil rights. But so much is implied that the nation as a whole has accepted Christ and His laws, and that the Christian Church comprehends the whole country; so that the land is divided into bishoprics and parishes, and every inhabitant is afforded the opportunity of enjoying the blessings of Christianity and of procuring for his children the benefits of Christian instruction. This ecclesiastical organization, which comprehends the whole country, we term the old parochial system.

So far the setting up and consolidation of a National Church may be welcomed and recognised as one of the greatest blessings given by Heaven. The evil results of a dominant Church, which fill us with dismay, have not as yet become apparent. Want of tolerance, persecution, and cruelty towards those who are not Christians and towards those who are heterodox; lust of power, debauchery, and vice amongst the clergy; debasement of the Church of God to be an instrument of tyranny,—all these things are by no means necessary consequences of the erection of a National Church. The principle upon which a National Church is based by no means inaugurates such things. In modern and ancient times we have actual proof that such offshoots can be avoided or got rid of. Nevertheless, the very first step towards uniting the Church with the State is surrounded with peril. Misconceptions and mutual acts of violence are at hand. Friendly advances from the mighty ones, and recognition by entire nations, are more dangerous to the welfare of the Church and to true Christianity than persecution on the part of heathen State officials. Whilst Christianity acquires respect in the eyes of the world, and is decorated with worldly honours, it loses in integral worth. The days when Christian faith and life flourished were days of persecution. Even those periods of peace which periodically occurred, quite apart from any union of the clergy with the possessors of temporal power, acted in a debilitating and enervating manner upon the minds and conversation of Christians. Thus it was in those forty years (211–251), from the death of the persecutor Septimius Severus until the outbreak of the great persecution under Decius. Origenes complains that this period of peace had injured the spiritual life of Christians more than the previous misfortunes. The same degeneration took place during the period of repose between the reigns of Valerian and Diocletian (259–303); but the completely altered position of Christians under Constantine acted in an even more enervating and debilitating degree. If the confession of Christ is no longer combined with shame, loss, and persecution; if it, on the contrary, is productive of advantage and opens the way to preferment, it is impossible to prevent the intrusion of insincerity. At first unconsciously, but subsequently of set purpose, hypocrisy takes the place of former sincerity. A number of individuals are admitted to the communion of the Church in whom no heartfelt conversion has taken place, and in whom no trace of holiness of conversation is to be found. Heathen modes of life gain admittance; the ancient, severe church discipline becomes impracticable; there arises a Christian rabble of whom nothing was known in better times. In the living members of the Church, too, the holy fire of the Spirit is quenched. The favour of the mighty ones falls like a blight upon the entire nursery of the vineyard of the Lord.

Only an extraordinary measure of earnestness and temperance, of self-denial and reliance upon God, of firmness and disregard of the world, in the bishops and priests, would be able to get rid of the dangers accompanying the new state of affairs. Such a measure of the Spirit the bishops and priests of the time of Constantine and Theodosius ought to have had; but history unmistakably shows us how much all of them were lacking. Even at the time of the earliest Christian emperors, the evil burst in like a flood; it was the oppressive mid-day hour, when the servants of the Lord, whom He had set as watchmen in His vineyard, slept in lieu of watching, and when the enemy found a splendid opportunity of sowing, without fear of detection, a rich crop of tares.

The degeneration of the Orthodox Church in the East presents to us a fearful example for all future generations. Along with disregard of morality grew up superstition, and ancient pagan practices assumed Christian names. Together with a strictly orthodox, literal creed, Christ was in fact denied. Three hundred years after Constantine, there arose another power in the East, which, without presumption, we may recognise as the scourge in the hand of God wherewith the national Churches of the East which had become worldly were chastised. The victories of the Arabs, and later of the Osmanlis; the humiliation of the Christian Church under the rule of Islam; the extinction of the light in entire countries, as in northern Africa—such are the significant warnings that rulers and people, bishops and congregations, when they misuse the name of the Lord, will not remain unpunished.

Still, with all this, we have not mentioned the most serious evil. It is the application of violence for the purpose of enforcing acceptance of the Christian creed, and the persecution of those who refuse to believe, or fall away from the faith. These errors gained admittance even into the Eastern Churches. There the emperors issued orders for the baptism of their legions. The Grecian emperor instituted an inquisitorial process against the Pauliciani. Under a despotic government, such errors are easily taken up by the possessors of power; the fatal use of the iron hand granted to the temporal ruler is so easy in the domain of the Church, which ought to be kept quite free from it. Such are the consequences of improperly transferring the throne into the sanctuary of the Church.

But this error assumes a still more serious aspect when the altar itself is converted into a throne for the ruler, when the priests wield the temporal sword, whether personally, or when they by the application of their authority can influence the arm of the temporal power which holds the sword. Heavy is the yoke of a despot of this world; but heavier still, and less easy, is that imposed by a dominant sacerdotalism, when the priesthood have acquired full possession of the temporal and civil authority.

When the Germanic nations of the West were received into Christendom, more noble scions sprang up than were lost to her in the East. The Middle Ages, during which the Church and the world were united under a different form, was on the whole a more beneficial period. Noble princes, brave knights, heroic bishops, citizens full of independence and activity, the faithfulness of vassals, the childlike reverence for holy things, the poetic inspiration in the service of Christianity, the glorification of Christ by works of art, and especially in church architecture,—all such are characteristics upon which we, being members of a sinking race, may look back with reverence and regret. But who will deny that, at the same time, the disastrous commingling of spirit and flesh dims all the brightness of those times! That is the dark side of a period which, in many respects, is to be admired. Take one instance: how repulsive it is to find amongst the Crusaders a morbid mixture of religion and bloodthirstiness, of cruelty and prayer. The forcible compulsion of the Saxons to accept baptism by Charlemagne was bad enough; but that was a mere trifle compared with the system of persecution which Innocent III. organized when he instituted the Inquisition. Blindfold, the people in many places believed they were doing a work acceptable to God when they shed the blood of a Jew.

Thomas of Aquinum, the greatest theologian of that period, admitted that the Church had received no authority to compel Jews or heathen to accept the Christian faith; but asserted that she had power, and it was her duty, to use force against such as, having been baptized, had fallen away. The first proposition is correct; but, we are impelled to ask, why did not the ecclesiastics interfere, when the temporal rulers, lawgivers, and warriors endeavoured to compel the Jews, heathens, and Mohammedans, by threatening their lives, or by banishment and confiscation of their goods, to accept Christianity, quite contrary to the mind of Christ? The second proposition opens the door to the most egregious errors. Even actual falling away, as in the case of Judas, Simon Magus, and other heretics, which took place in the apostolic times, was not resisted by Christ or His apostles with temporal punishment, but with the sword of the Spirit alone. But in the Middle Ages the term falling away, or heresy, was understood to embrace every deviation from the doctrine and commands of the worldly Roman Church; by which theory the torch was placed in the hands of the episcopate for setting fire under the stake. It is a miserable subterfuge to say, in condonation, that the sentence of death was passed and inflicted according to the civil laws, not by the Church, and that therefore the blame is not to be laid at the doors of the representatives of the Church. Who was it misled the temporal rulers to the setting up of such laws? who was it insisted, under pain of excommunication, upon their administration of them?

The root and reason of all this lay deeply hidden in the history of the Western Church. How gloriously did the teachers of the Church, during the first centuries, defend freedom of conscience, and relegate the temporal power to the domain properly belonging to it! They had correctly designated the nothingness and worthlessness of an enforced Christianity, the hypocrisy and objectionableness of confession which did not come from the heart. They assigned to God, and to the Spirit of truth, the power of ruling men's consciences. Thus matters stood when the Christian Church was still persecuted. But after the persecutions ceased, a century had scarcely elapsed when the light of true knowledge disappeared from amongst that generation of Christians which had grown up in the deleterious atmosphere of an Established Church. The power of discerning the mind of Christ in such matters was lost. The folly and infatuation of the bishops, resulting from the favour and pomp of the empire, was so common that even Augustine, the most enlightened teacher of that period, became the advocate of the persecutions entered upon against the schismatics of his time, the Donatists. So far back into the past can the commencement be traced of a system of intolerance, which during the

Middle Ages grew up into a wide-spreading Upas tree.

Well might men hope that the Reformation would lay the axe at the foot of this tree; and not that alone, but that the noxious tree would really be hewn down. In fact, it was one of the first principles enunciated by Luther, 31st October 1517: "It is contrary to the mind of the Holy Spirit that heretics be burned." No one has testified so plainly as he did to the sacred right of conscience, which no commandment of men, nor dread of man, ought to rule. No one has asserted with greater power the distinction between temporal and spiritual, the separation of their respective domains, the independence of the civil authority resulting from its divine ordination, and the commission of the ministers of Christ to proclaim the gospel. It was possible at that time to hope for an efficient solution of the intricate knot. As a matter of fact, the existing evils were toned down, but no thorough cure was effected. The ancient Papacy was overthrown; but a new and perverted one arose, in that the Protestant princes, such as Henry VIII. in England, took to themselves the dignities attaching to the chief heads of the Church, and caused the spiritual power to be recognised as an attribute of regal dignity. Hence arose, again, the confusion of Church and world, and in England, at least, the old cruel intolerance. It is an honourable trait in Luther, and it is a proof of how thoroughly Christian his feelings were, that he never admitted it to be right to execute heretics, as even Calvin and Melancthon did.

The conduct of our Protestant princes in the orthodox ages was guided by the principle asserted by Lutheran theologians, and that was: "Kings and magistrates are set as watchmen not only over the commandments in the second table, which concern life, property, honour, and home, but also over the commandments in the first table of the law. They fulfil their duty, therefore, when they suppress a superstitious worship and take measures against heresy and misuse of the divine name." King Josiah, who extirpated all idolatry, was the model which noble Protestant princes, such as Duke Ernest the Pious of Gotha, zealously strove to imitate.

This theory did much good. The divine commission to princes, and their duty to care not only for the material but also for the moral welfare of their people, was thereby established. Hence emanated the wholesome stringency of those days against immorality, drunkenness, and luxury.

Still the above assertion goes too far, since it admits the ruling power to some fields that do not belong to it. If it looks upon itself as the absolute executrix of the divine commands, it will go too far; for these commands concern the inward parts, and call for the devotion of the entire man. But the ruling power has not to care for intentions and persuasions; it cannot punish any one for his thoughts. Just as little has it been commissioned to watch over the whole of private life; for instance, family worship. It has to order public life, and to protect and advance the welfare and moral progress of the nation.

The distinction between the commandments of the first and second table cannot be applied at all in this case. A Christian ruling power must assure to the people the sacred observance of the day of the Lord, as one of the greatest possible earthly benefits; and this is based upon a command in the first table of the law. On the other hand, it has nothing to do with the command, "Thou shalt not covet," which stands in the second table. Certainly a Christian government is bound to interdict, in agreement with the nation, the profanation of God's name, scoffing at religion, and the propagation of doctrines which undermine the moral law. But it will also be careful in discerning what is Christian or unchristian worship, true or false doctrine, not to be blindly led by narrow-minded theologians or hierarchs. This really was the case when Lutheran princes, in well-meant zeal, forbade the Roman Catholic forms of worship, and the forms of the Calvinists. As a consequence of the division of the Church, there arose the strictly denominational States; and thereby the evil of intolerance reached its culminating point, in that the penal statutes, which were intended to be fulminated against heretics of the Middle Ages, were now applied to Christians of other creeds, and in one State Protestants, in the other Roman Catholics, were persecuted. The Inquisition in Italy and Spain; the persecutions of the Protestants in France and Austria; finally, the thirty years' war in Germany, the cruel conduct of Louis XIV. and XV. against the Huguenots—all these were the horrible consequences of the false system.

In founding it, it had been said that, as heresy plunged men into eternal damnation, it was better to punish some with temporal pains in order to save many from everlasting torture—many, that is to say, such as would be led astray by the heretics if they were spared. But even supposing that there had been any question of a falling away from Christ, the principle contained a dangerously erroneous conclusion. A means condemned by God can never produce an effect which is acceptable to Him. In reality, the result of the intolerant system was the opposite to that which was expected and hoped for. Far from hindering the spread of erroneous doctrine and unbelief, the cruelties of the Inquisition, the religious wars and the dragoonades, are the principal causes of the modern apostasy from the sacred cause of Christ. When the ministers of the Christian religion commend such misdeeds; what ideas must arise as to the nature of the Christian religion generally, and what ill feeling towards its Founder! Can religion be capable of inciting to so much evil? By means of the stake, which, according to an inexcusable mania, was to ensure the salvation of souls, countless numbers have been hurled into the dark abyss of unbelief and doubt of all religion. It is not an ordinary debt of blood-guiltiness which we are all thereby liable for; it is the double curse of innocently shed blood and an accursed profanation of the name of Christ.

Voltaire and Rousseau, the false prophets of the philosophic century, took possession of this deadly weapon, which the servants of Christ had carelessly left in their way. The hideous hypocrisy of the French court,—where atheism and the vices of Sodom and Gomorrha flourished, and whence at the same time the persecution of the Huguenots and the execution of their preachers proceeded,—Portroyal destroyed, and thus a work of the Holy Spirit in the Roman Church was suppressed,—all these things were such crying evils, that unbelief, in that it opposed intolerance tooth and nail, seemed to acquire thereby a moral justification. Those who held the offices of Christian teachers had for centuries failed to insist upon Christian humanity, to protest against torture, the trial of witches, diabolical modes of execution, and persecutions in consequence of religious views; now, all such abuses fell into the hands of the unbelievers as a useful weapon. They insisted upon those ideas which ought long before to have been asserted in the name of Christ and His commandments; they set them up in their own names, in despite of the name of Christ, in the name of a worldly-mindedness devoid of Christianity. The results obtained in setting aside those dreadful abuses were trumpeted about as justifications and commendations of unbelief.

There arose in the public mind a doctrine, supposed to be wholesome, regarding a humanity apart from Christianity, which now, a century after the death of Voltaire and Rousseau, has proved a power capable of moving worlds. It dispossessed a number of evils, but at the same time it fostered new dangers for Christian nations; like an ill-selected medicine, which drives in an acute attack of illness, but at the same time weakens and poisons the whole system.

Christian or unchristian humanity? Christian or unchristian toleration? These are the questions. To discern between these two spirits, which are so easily to be mistaken for each other, that is the difficulty. At one time we find that patience, which springs from a disregard of all that is religious, exalted; and again we find Christian patience, regard for the convictions and conscience of one's neighbour, despised as tokens of indifference and lukewarmness. So great is the perplexity in this matter, that people hardly know whether the expressions "free-thinker" and "toleration" convey praise or blame.

The two different kinds of toleration arise from perfectly different principles and notions, and have no internal connection, although they may coincide in many outward details. Non-christian toleration regards all religion with indifference. It looks down with supreme contempt upon any one who has any anxieties about the salvation of his soul, the honour of God, and the commandments of Christ. It inquires coldly and contemptuously with Pilate: "What is truth?" There is no such thing as truth; why should people trouble one another about differences of views on religious subjects? Is there any one still so weak in intellect as to lay any stress upon special doctrines, or upon a special form of worship, leave him to the enjoyment of his folly. It says with Voltaire: "Why should not the Huguenots sing their Psalms in bad French, as well as the clergy read their office in bad Latin?" Itself indifferent about divine matters, and careless of eternity, unchristian toleration boasts, like Frederick II. of Prussia, that, "In my country every one can go to heaven his own way." It says with the Turk, who looks on with apathy at the conflicts of the Christian parties ruled by him: "It is all the same whether dog bites pig, or pig bites dog!"

Such is the feeling upon which non-christian toleration is based. However much we may value its principles, it certainly has no stability. It takes up a position which cannot long be maintained; for out of indifference towards religion there arises hatred to it, and toleration becomes at last the most cruel intolerance.

Christian toleration assumes a different tone. Christ does not wish to have any hypocrites amongst His followers. God finds no pleasure in forced devotion, but in free-will offerings. He detests unbelief, but there is nothing He detests so much as hypocrisy; a form of worship consisting of ceremonial only, a prayer of the lips in which the heart is not concerned, He despises. His sacraments and blessings may only be administered to such as are inwardly prepared for and capable of receiving them. Hence Christ used for the introduction of His kingdom no violent means, by which only a lying assent can be called forth, but the word of truth, holy conversation, and those miracles which were not punishments, but sheer works of mercy. When many of His disciples went back and walked no more with Him, He made use of no arts of persuasion, much less of compulsion, but said to the twelve, "Will ye also go away?" He placed before them the free option of remaining with Him or of leaving Him. When Judas had completely forsaken Him, joining himself to His enemies, and came to deliver Him into their hands, He said, "Friend, wherefore art thou come?" and restrained Peter, who had drawn his sword, from committing acts of violence. The apostles followed His example, and employed no force against heretics; as St. Paul says, "The weapons of our warfare are not carnal, but spiritual." When they exercised church discipline, it did not occur to them to appeal to the temporal arm for aid, and to call for the infliction of civil penalties. Such means of persecution Saul had at one time employed, when he was still a Pharisee and an enemy to Christ; but ever since he had received the mind of Christ in himself, he exercised discipline in a different spirit. He pronounced the sentence of rejection or excommunication, and trusted in God that He would confirm it in the conscience of the sinner. He expected that Providence, by means of chastisements inflicted without human aid, would bring the foolish-minded to their senses, and, if possible, still save them.

When the inhabitants of a Samaritan village refused accommodation to Jesus and His disciples because they were Jews, and were at the time engaged in a pilgrimage to the temple at Jerusalem, James and John wanted to call down fire from heaven to punish them, as Elias did; but Christ forbade them with the words, "Ye know not what manner of spirit ye are of."

So that Christ has nowhere given us authority to exclude such as do not believe on Him, on that account, from the benefit of civil rights. It is completely contrary to His intentions that we attempt to convert others to His paths by treachery or intimidation. Such were the principles of the Church in her best days. The words in the gospel, "compel them to come in," which were later on so much misused, were understood to mean a compulsion by the power of truth, holiness, and charity. By such means was Christianity spread abroad amongst the nations by the apostles, and those who walked in their footsteps.

Christian faith is a matter of the heart and of free conviction. The conscience may not be forced; it must be enlightened by the word of truth. Men have to declare the truth; it is God's affair to lend their words power. The conscience is sacred, and even an erroneous faith must be spared and respected. The worst harm one can do a man is to bring him to a confession and form of worship which his inward monitor denies. Decency of conduct requires that we respect the various convictions of others; and even when one is obliged to regard them as erroneous and dangerous, still we must presuppose the individual to possess probity of mind and intention. In a time of confusion like ours, and after that the matter of Christianity has been placed in so bad a light by its own representatives, it becomes all the more our duty to confront such as hold erroneous views with patience. Let them be told what great danger their souls are in, but do not allow their civil honour to be interfered with. In a still higher degree is it fitting that the representatives of the various Christian denominations meet each other, not only with forbearance, but with respect, so that we may not treat with disrespect that which others reverence.

If any one, owing to his religious convictions, comes into conflict with the requirements of the authorities, Christian rulers should carefully consider the matter ere they introduce violent measures of compulsion, or compel such subjects to emigrate. It is true, a despot usually hates such as appeal from his demands to their consciences, or their duty to obey God's word and commandments. Why was it that the faith of the Calvinists in France was constituted so heinous a crime? "They have embraced a religion which is displeasing to the king!" This was considered sufficient reason to persecute them to the death. The despot will not allow of any independent conviction beside his own. If he comes across such, he does not rest until he has seduced the persons to deny their convictions and to commit some act contrary to their conscience. It has been often said, that despotism destroys the character of mankind. It is so, and the reason is, because it stifles conscience in the subject, uproots the consciousness of responsibility to God, and thereby pollutes and destroys the fountain of all virtue and moral power.

Therefore one ought, in the name of Christian toleration, to call upon all in authority to honour conscientious subjects and to learn to value them! If there are such as willingly offer up earthly advantages, spare them, for you will not find any better subjects than they. The faithfulness which, according to the measure of their knowledge, they display towards God, will also lead them to fulfil their duties as subjects to you, in such matters as you have a right to command them as their temporal ruler. Rejoice that there are some who have a conscience, and whose conduct is regulated by higher motives than mere fear of man and by a straining after earthly advantages.

Constantius Chlorus, the father of Constantine, when he was in Gaul, had not publicly acknowledged the Christian faith. One day he called upon his officers, of whom he knew that they too were inclined to Christianity, either to sacrifice to idols or to leave his service. Some declared themselves ready to obey the will of their chief, whilst others avowed their intention to resign their position. Before the sacrifice was consummated, Constantius revealed his true intention. He dismissed such as had no fixity of purpose, and retained in his service only such as were true to their convictions, considering that men who would betray their God would have no compunction in betraying their earthly ruler also.

Modern history has confirmed the fact, that the oppression and driving forth of such subjects as are convicted of no other crime than that they cannot agree with the dominant ecclesiastical system for conscience' sake, brings a curse upon nations and upon the reigning family. The national misfortunes with which France has been so constantly chastised must be, partially at least, referred to the iniquitous oppression of the Protestants and the so-called Jansenists. Spain, Italy, and Austria also suffer from the disastrous consequences of similar acts. The fact of offering an asylum for refugees who have left all for conscience' sake has brought much benefit to England and to Prussia. Such a policy is not only commended by worldly wisdom, it is also crowned with the blessing of Heaven.

True toleration, based upon Christian principles, found its first expression in England. After that the nation, under the Tudors and the Stuarts, had been compelled to drink the bitter cup of intolerance to its dregs, Cromwell granted toleration to all kinds of Protestant worship. To the Independents belongs the honour of being the first who seriously maintained the principle of religious liberty. Cromwell allowed the Jews to build a synagogue in London. William Penn and his Society of Friends were even more consistent in their requirements. At last, under William III., the principle of toleration gained a complete victory; and since then it has gone on by degrees doing away with disabilities.

Every newly-acquired political liberty is a great advantage to a people of solid principles and character. The fear of God and Christian morals are pledges for the proper use of freedom. If these conditions are wanting, every new degree of liberty is an acquisition of dubious value. Unhappy Germany, who in her better days, when she was distinguished among the nations for her fear of God, domestic virtues, decency, faithfulness, probity, and sense of justice, enjoyed no political freedom, no liberty of religious action! But when in 1848 these advantages, so long withheld, came into her possession, one may say it was too late. The postulates required for a beneficial employment of liberty had already been too much damaged. It was unjustly said, We are not ready for freedom-! On the contrary, the time when we were ready for and worthy of it seems to be already passing away. Our liberty has not come to us too soon, but too late!

Hence, also, the toleration and freedom of worship, which has at last been granted, assumes rather the form of a humane indifference to everything divine, than a respect for the rights of conscience.

It is not long since that we were obliged to do battle with the injurious action of the old system of intolerance. Before the last revolution in Italy, matters were carried so far that in Tuscany, the best governed of the Italian States, officials were obliged annually to send in at Easter a certificate of confession and communion! No medical man dared to visit a patient more than three times, unless during the interval the sick person had sent for a confessor. Under Frederick-William III. of Prussia, all officials were commanded to celebrate the royal birthday by partaking of the sacrament. From the just indignation at such things emanated the resolution of the German Parliament that no one should be compelled to attend any religious ceremony.

This was one of the fundamental rights which was then assured to the German nation; and, as a matter of fact, the principle has since then been carried out in all parts of Germany.

If in ancient times, during the spread and introduction of Christianity, no one was compelled to receive baptism, it was because people desired to win others to Christ by the power of divine truth alone. But when a modern Parliament enunciates that principle, it is to be feared that thereby a disinclination for all religious actions, and the desire to get rid of all allusion to God in public affairs, is shown to be the influence at work, along, perhaps, with other more noble motives which certainly may still exist. Nevertheless, the principle asserted is in both cases the same, and is right in itself. The liberty allowed by it is taken advantage of by those who wish to separate themselves from Christ, and that is a pity; but that very liberty is an advantage to real Christianity, and it is to be hoped that the latter will gain in sincerity, sterling qualities, and power amongst its adherents under the influence of the principle.

CHAPTER VIII.

THE EMANCIPATION OF THE JEWS.

OWING to the existence of the Jews in the Roman Empire, a great duty was imposed upon the Christian Church, when her persecution ceased, and she herself took part in the framing of the laws and the conduct of public affairs. By the proper, or improper, manner in which she treated the Jews, she was obliged to manifest whether the heads of the Church, notwithstanding the change of their position, had remained true to their former opinions or not.

Up to this period, Christians had, so far as we know, kept themselves free from the sin of hating and mocking at the Jews. The first persecution of the Christians had originated with the Jews, but the Christian community had learnt from their Divine Master to love their enemies, and to intercede for them. Paul, who suffered so much from the Jews, could say: "I love them for the fathers' sake; and I bear them record that they have a zeal of God, but not according to understanding." This gentleness of mind existed also in the fathers of the Church, and it was increased and strengthened by the hope of an eventual conversion of the Jews to Christ, which is positively foretold in the records of the Old and New Testaments. Of this hope Augustine was still able to say, that it was "frequently reflected upon in the hearts and in the conversation of the faithful."

When, for the first time, owing to the laws of the

Christian emperors, a Commonwealth was to be ordered upon Christian principles, it may well have been justifiable to forbid heathen forms of worship, for they were radically unclean, and in most cases combined with morally objectionable exhibitions and actions. But where was any cogent reason found for Christian rulers to suppress the worship of the synagogue? Christ Himself had taken part in the solemnization of it; and if indeed no Christian creed was to be found in it, still it is in all its parts worthy of respect and morally clean. The disbelief of the Jews in Christ is certainly a sin in the sight of God, but not a crime which could be recognised by an earthly tribunal. We Christians ought to cure them of this unbelief, but by persecution we render the disease incurable. The hope of an enlightenment of the Jews at some future time depends upon their experiencing from us Christian, that is to say, just, noble, and benevolent treatment.

The laws of the Christian emperors were at first temperate; after the time of Justinian severe measures were adopted, and the Jews fled from the Byzantine Empire.

Into those laws the noxious folly crept in, that it was high treason for any one in the Empire to profess a different faith from that of the Emperor. The severity of the old heathen rulers against such as despised the worship of the idols of the land was now turned by Christian rulers against the Jews, because they did not believe in Christ; and this occurred without the ministers of Christ, so far as we know, in any way raising a protesting voice against it.

In the empire of the Visigoths, in Spain, the bishops had an opportunity of making their influence more strongly felt than in Byzantium. After that King Reccared [A.D. 588] had accepted the Christian faith, and incorporated it with the law of the State, a number of laws were published against Jews and heretics, in which the intolerant and evil spirit which later, after the expulsion of the Arabs, culminated in the Spanish Inquisition, was clearly betrayed in a remarkable manner. Those laws were the commencement of a sacerdotal tyranny, for which the ecclesiastics of the West were to blame.

Whilst the severe enactments against the Jews increased, the hope of the future conversion of Israel decreased in equal measure. Men did not any longer see in them the blood-relations of Christ, whom we ought to win over to Him; the people whom we have to thank for the spiritual endowments which have come to us; the heirs to a divine promise, which will still be fulfilled to them. Men saw in them only the murderers of Christ, forgetting that *we* have no right to punish the children for the sins of the fathers, and that Christ had prayed for His murderers. Christian rulers and ecclesiastics foolishly imagined that the time had come when they were to rule this unhappy nation with a rod of iron.

In the Roman Empire of the German nation the Jews occupied a peculiar position. They were the body-servants of the sacred Roman Empire—a band of slaves, with whom each successive emperor could deal as he pleased. As in those times everything was arranged according to corporations, the Jews also existed as a corporation, enjoying their own laws. But they had no claim to legal protection; and hence it was that their lot during the Middle Ages was subject to such varied vicissitudes, dependent upon time and place. For a short time they would be allowed liberty to follow their business, amass riches and influence at court, and so on, when suddenly the fierce hatred would break out again against them. If they had practised usury, and attracted the cupidity of their neighbours by their acquisition of wealth, it was very easy to excite the wrath of the populace by fearful accusations. They were said to have murdered Christian children, defiled the host, or poisoned the wells. There is hardly a single town in the German Empire where the Jews were not subjected to murder, fire, and rapine.

The very fact of their being slaves was their protection against complete extirpation; for the emperor could not desire to lose his property.

The persecutions in Spain were even more systematic and cruel. There, during the worst times, under Ferdinand the Catholic, one of their Rabbis addressed the Christians thus: "We are a blessed and at the same time an accursed race. You Christians wish at present to extirpate us; but you will not succeed, for we are blessed. One of these days you will do all you can to exalt us; but that, too, will not succeed, for we are accursed."

The immeasurable weight of crime which Christians have heaped upon themselves by their unchristian treatment of the Jews has not yet been expiated by the Reformation, nor by the changes introduced with it. It is true that a nobler state of mind became then apparent. In that the rights of all were more carefully respected, the Jews also found more security and protection. Yet it was a long time before the consciousness of our duty towards the people of Israel became at all clear. Luther, who was in other respects averse to the persecution of those who held a different creed, distinctly advised that the synagogues should be burnt and the Jews compelled to take up some kind of manual labour, and that their daughters should have spindle and distaff placed in their hands. Luther, who in other respects held so firmly to the text of Scripture, lost all hope of the conversion of the

Jews, which he had himself distinctly mentioned in the first edition of his Homilies. Such portions of Scripture as Romans, chap. xi., which seemed to have any tendency to favour the nation, were to be construed quite differently; the heart of a Jew was, as Luther said, as hard as iron, stone, or the devil.

Thus, even after the Reformation, there was a vast, uneffected task left undone. Modern governments have taken the solution in hand; they have emancipated the Jews in their own way, but whether this is the right way is still a question.

It was by no means a Christian feeling, but rather an unchristian, which had the most effect in producing the mighty change which took place in the treatment of the Jews. However lamentable the admission may be, it must be made. Their fetters were broken more owing to the influence of a false system than of an increase in true enlightenment. The growing indifference of Christians to their own religion, the estrangement of men of education from Christ, and, finally, the illusive idea of a humanity without Christianity, have exerted the greatest influence in this matter, and on that very account the altered treatment of the Jews has assumed a false, nay, even a dangerous tendency.

Owing to the divisions in the Church, owing to the causes of offence afforded by the clergy, owing to the religious wars and the alternating oppression inflicted upon each Christian sect in its turn, there had been called into existence that departure from Christianity which was first constituted a system by the freethinkers in England, under the name of Deism. The Deists were ashamed of the appellation Christian, and were of opinion that it sufficed to hold to faith in God, without any regard to Christianity. This idea, which was suppressed in England, but was then carried over by Voltaire and Rousseau to France, and disseminated there with the greatest success, could not do otherwise, when applied to the region of politics, than promote the entire equality of the Jew with the Christian. The Deists and their successors saw in the Jews like-minded brethren. If in many instances the Jews had nothing to do with the matter, still it pleased the Deists to annoy those who believed on Christ by extolling and favouring the Jews, who denied Him.

Here, again, the representatives of this false system were aided by a change on the part of the Jews; the ancient Sadducean unbelief raised its head again amongst them. Spinoza took it up with a truly fearful boldness of thought and coldness of heart. As in Germany, the entire change of feeling assumed a milder form and an ideal tendency; so also did this revival amongst the Jews, after it had been planted on German soil in the celebrated Moses Mendelssohn. Lessing started with the usual idea of the Freemasons, that the various religions were only different phases of one and the same faith, eternal in its nature, but never attaining to perfect development during the existence of time. In "Nathan the Wise," Judaism, Christianity, and Mohammedanism are compared and placed on a footing of equality; and yet, with a spice of malice, Christianity is characterized as the least good of the three.

Thus everything was prepared for the assertion of equality for the Jews in the State and in social life. It only required a forcible disruption of the old system, and the new, which was already there, took its place. This occurred in the French Revolution and the assertion of the rights of man. Since then the emancipation of the Jews, and their participation in all civil rights and privileges, has formed part of the programme of the modern party of progress throughout Europe.

The raising into importance of the dignity of man, the insisting upon the rights which emanate from it, was a well-founded and necessary revulsion against the remnants of slavery, bondage, compulsion of conscience, the various forms of legal disability, and the too sharply defined distinction of classes. It was in itself a holy postulate that the Jews, after being so long humiliated, should be assured of humane treatment, and that they should be granted liberty and respect for their religion. We may heartily rejoice at the liberty which they acquired in Poland and Holland, in England under Cromwell, and in Austria under the Toleration Edict of Joseph ii., 1781. But with the French Revolution, postulates of a very different nature were insisted upon. It was reckoned amongst the rights of man that every one had a right to take part in the government, and to make the laws of the place in which he lived and paid taxes. To deduce such a postulate from the rights of man is a palpable mistake. The distinctions existing between nations, and their partition upon the face of the earth, is a fact ordained of God, just as much as the distinction between the degrees of age or the difference of sex. Every nation has the right, and it is its duty, to form itself into a well-ordered commonwealth; but whence arose any obligation to allow every stranger who has accidentally settled in the land to take part in the framing of the laws or the government. A man may live happily and respected in a foreign land as a guest, without possessing the slightest claim to a participation in the government of the country.

In the law of the Old Testament, the Jews were bidden to love the stranger: "For ye also were strangers in Egypt, and the Lord loveth the stranger." This duty is incumbent upon us also, and in every Christian State the Jew should meet with benevolent treatment —as strangers. The same law impressed upon the Jew: "Thou mayest not set a stranger over thee (as king) which is not thy brother." Just as little do the rights of hospitality, which strangers ought to enjoy, confer any right to participate in the government. The Jews have even less claim to such right amongst us, seeing that they have forfeited the same at home, in their own land. If the providence of God has not permitted them to rule in their own country, whence do they acquire a right to behave as rulers in ours?

The lawgivers of a Christian State may, in admitting the Jews to civil rights, go a long way without any question being raised in the name of Christianity. How much or how little liberty may be granted them is not an ethical, but a national question; and the national interests must be protected against them, as against every other stranger. To define the amount of concession may and ought to be left by theologians in the hands of jurists and statesmen.

The assertion of modern Jews, that they are no longer strangers, but that in matters of birth and feeling they are German, French, and English, etc., that their fatherland is here, and that they seek no other, is not to the point; for with them religion and nationality are most intimately connected, in that their religion makes it their duty to hold fast to their nationality, and to the hope of returning to their country. One stands or falls with the other. If they really wish to abnegate their nationality, they ought to recognise the higher and more perfect religion of Christianity, and enter the Christian Church. Only when they have done this, have we any pledge that they are in earnest about the abnegation of their special national interests.

Even in the present day, there exists an unmistakable antipathy of natural feeling between the Western nations and the Jews. It is a curious coincidence, that those very politicians who have inscribed the principles of nationality in the largest letters upon their banners, should, in the most self-contradictory manner, fail to see this anomaly, and pave the way for the rule of the Jew.

The religion of the Jews, in its present form, has this peculiarity, that it causes its professors to approach us, and at the same time removes them far from us. They are related very closely to us, and we can, in many things, make common cause with them. They recognise the personality of God, the Almighty Creator; and this admission alone is at present, for all who hold fast to it, a bond of union. They hold the ten commandments, upon which all social morality is based. They respect monogamy; and from the days of their ancestors all domestic virtues, such as family affection, conjugal fidelity, obedience and reverence to parents, have been handed down, wherein they even excel the majority of Christians of our time. And yet it is just their religion which divides them from us. They are, according to the divine ordinance, a separate people; they are preserved for a future purpose, and maintained in their segregation. This segregation is intensified by their continued non-recognition of Christ. That which is the most sacred matter to us, they regard with horror, and their conscience, however erroneously, calls upon them to avoid any community of religion with us.

These are the reasons against their complete incorporation into a Christian commonwealth. The faults of their national character now would not militate against their emancipation. For these faults, which, it is true, showed themselves amongst them under the ancient Roman Empire, their tendency to usury, to base and deceitful modes of gain, have been increased by continued oppression on the part of Christians. Just such faults have been fostered amongst the Grecian Christians under the Turkish rule. In England, where the Jews for the last two centuries have experienced a nobler treatment, these faults appear in a minor degree, and the well-to-do Israelites, in a general way, enjoy respect and confidence there. It is true their usurious spirit and growing wealth threaten us with serious dangers; but these must be combated not by a return to the former exceptional legislation against the Jews, but by a revision of the whole economy of our national system.

The unconditional equalizing of the position of Jews and Christians has become an accomplished fact in most of the European States since 1848. In Prussia it was asserted in the constitution of 1850. In England about the same time, under Sir Robert Peel's ministry, their admission into Parliament was permitted, with the concession of a form of oath consistent with their creed. No office under Government, save that of Lord Chancellor, is theoretically closed to them. This exception was maintained because the Queen is required, in matters of conscience, to seek the advice of the Lord Chancellor. At present a Jew is Master of the Rolls.

This equalization of the position of the Jews has been productive of disadvantage for us, and even for them; for us, because the entry of men who are not Christians into our legislative assemblies has produced a breach in the Christian State. In most of these assemblies throughout the Continent there reigned already so unchristian a tone, that no speaker could refer to the words of Christ and the commandments, without calling forth a storm of reproach and scorn; and yet the Divine Word and Christian doctrine still remained in force, so to say, as an authority which could be appealed to. But this authority is called in question by the introduction of men who deny Christianity; and it is to be feared that the last remnants of Christian spirit will be driven out of our Parliaments, and the words of Christ will no longer be looked upon as the utterances of the supreme Lawgiver, but only as sentences like those of any poet or philosopher. If the arrangement cannot be altered, at least in all cases where questions regarding Christian institutions arise, regarding questions which are common both to the State and the Church, such as matrimony and national schools, or regarding the privileges of the different confessions, the Jews should refrain from voting. Such reticence has lately been exercised, with a tact worthy of respect, by the Roman Catholics in the Prussian Chamber of Deputies during the consultations regarding the internal constitution of the Protestant Church; but, unfortunately, no such modesty has as yet been displayed by the Jews.

The present emancipation promotes the dissolution of Judaism. For if the Jews amongst us held as faithfully to Moses and the prophets, and the whole of their religious traditions, as is still the case with their brethren in the East, in Russia, Hungary, and Poland, they would not ask for emancipation, but would repudiate it; for with equal privileges the Jews must also assume equal duties with other citizens. But such duties introduce a conflict with serious requirements of the Mosaic law, such as the law of the Sabbath and forbidden meats. For a real Jew, to be required to perform military service, or to go through exercises in the use of his arms on the Sabbath, would be unbearable. He would rather give up all idea of emancipation, and determine to emigrate. It is not long since that the Rabbis of the ancient faith expressed themselves distinctly opposed to the innovations of the so-called reformed Jews in France and Germany. By the latter, German forms of prayer have been introduced in lieu of the old Hebrew ones. They have set up organs in their synagogues (with Christian organists!

because the playing of an organ on the Sabbath is forbidden as a form of labour). They have imitated the Protestant confirmation of children, accompanied by the recital of a creed and benediction. All such things the orthodox Rabbis repudiate. In like manner, a real Israelite would consider the marriage of a Jew with a Christian as a thing to be scouted. But for the very same reasons, all Jews, who hold to their ancient belief, ought, far from asking for emancipation, rather to decline it in the form in which it has been presented to them.

Modern arrangements tend, in that the Jews accept them, to the rapid ruin of the ancient Israelitic spirit. Our governments have long promoted unbelief amongst the Jews, partly from ignorance of the consequences of their measures. The Rabbis have been obliged to acquire in the Universities a certificate as to their general knowledge. Such men come from the Talmud schools. That is usually their sole preparation. Then they are suddenly plunged into a totally different atmosphere, which they are not able to breathe. They attend the lectures on philosophy, and become acquainted with worldly systems which are quite foreign to religion. Their belief in the Talmud breaks up, and with it their belief also in the Old Testament. For a Christian theologian who finds himself in such a mental conflict there is, if he takes the matter seriously enough to heart, help and advice. There is such a thing as Christian philosophy, and a philosophical Christian theology; paths of reconciliation are open, and in such a case Lord Bacon's saying is still applicable: "A superficial knowledge of philosophy leads away from God; deeper draughts at the same fountain lead back to Him." But a Jewish theologian is in a much more unfortunate position. He is not capable of digesting philosophy; he can only accept unbelief. A philosophy which could lead him back to a faith in the Old Testament without the intervention of Christianity, he cannot find anywhere. The doctrines of the Talmud, however, contain but little which can satisfy a thinking mind. Thus the synagogues are provided with Rabbis who have made shipwreck of the faith of Moses.

Modern unbelieving Judaism is a source of corruption to the people of Israel, and it is also a thorn in the side of Christian nations. Wherever we find tradition and all that is sacred denied, scoffed at, and reviled, we are sure to find the irreligious Jewish *literati* in the front rank. With their faith they have also abandoned their country; nothing is sacred to them. They find a pleasure in destruction alone. Whilst everything else is going to ruin, they still dream of a Jewish rule in the future—the last distorted and corrupted remnant which remains to them of their ancient faith.

It is difficult to decide which has done the other most harm, whether the unbelieving Jew has injured the Christian, or unbelieving Christians have injured the Jews most. But this much is certain, that when, in the German press, an impious and irreligious tone prevails, this may for the most part be ascribed to the Jewish element. In this respect matters are quite different in England; even in France, the newspapers observe a more dignified bearing, with regard to the things which are sacred to a Christian people, than in our country. The majority of the papers are either written by Jewish men of literature, or are at least written to the order and in the pay of Jewish capitalists.

Matters have arrived at such a pass, that a Christian government ought to respect and seek to uphold the few remnants of ancient Judaism which still exist in

Germany. The antagonism to the synagogues which existed in former ages was principally based upon the fact that, in the Talmud and certain prayers of the Jews, there are revilings and curses directed against Christ and Christianity. But we may reasonably hope that, with a nobler treatment, this sinister hatred of Christianity on the part of the Jews would disappear, as appears really to be the case in England.

"You will some day seek to elevate us; but you will not be able." This prophecy is, according to the present state of affairs, apparently contradicted, if we only regard the enormous power of wealth the Jews possess, which daily increases, and which is tangibly appreciable in all classes of life connected with this enterprising and pretentious nation, who have been so long enslaved and have at last regained their freedom; but the end has not yet come. The ancient hatred of the Jews has not yet died out; it has only assumed another form. Notwithstanding all that is being said about humanity and equality, it is just those who make use of such language that are imbued with and retain the old antipathy. When the day of terror comes, when Socialism and Communism will for a short period be allowed to gain the upper hand, we shall then see of how little use this pseudo-emancipation has been. When the great raid upon possessors of property breaks out, it will probably be the Jews who will be the first to suffer.

CHAPTER IX.

SEPARATION OF CHURCH AND STATE.

The cry for disestablishment and the separation of Church and State is daily becoming louder, and is being raised on all sides. In this cry the representatives of the most antagonistic views combine. On the one hand, we have those who wish to see the influence of religion upon civil life put an end to as soon as possible; on the other, we have those who are honestly seeking after the kingdom of God, and who hope for a period of energy and effectiveness in the Church, as soon as she shall be relieved of the oppressive bonds which the temporal power has laid upon her. Let us for the present consider such hopes as not forming part of the question; one thing is certain, that the separation may be desired upon very estimable grounds, viz. the disapproval of the inherent untruth with which the entire system has until now been infected. For the National or State Church would fulfil her duties and carry out her pretensions, only if every minister were filled with the Spirit of Christ, and every member of the State Church, whether man, woman, or child, led a Christian life—if all acts of worship, whether public or private, were performed with inward conviction and joyful self-dedication by all who took part therein; instead of which we meet at every turn a monstrous distinction between the Christian faith and the actual position of affairs. It is true that here and there pleasurable exceptions exist; but, taken all in all, there is no question of the fact that, measured by the standard of the word and example of Christ, both high and low, minister and people, fall very far short of what is required of them. In the services of the Church, lukewarmness or indifference is palpable; on the spiritual life of the best Christians there seems to brood an incubus, which must be ascribed for the most part to the general condition of Christendom. Under such circumstances, a feverish desire for freedom, spiritual reinvigoration, and a higher tone of activity in the Church, is very justifiable.

Towards the attainment of this desire, as men hope, the act of separation between Church and State is to conduce. Then we should find sincerity and truth taking the place of hypocrisy; zeal would spring up in lieu of lukewarmness, and activity in place of lassitude. Then it might be possible to reassert the discipline of the Christian Church, which has fallen into such decay and disuse. It is true that, in consequence, fewer would bear the appellation of Christians, but those few would do honour to it.

With such expectations English Dissenters were and are imbued. Vinet, the most noble and eloquent of the advocates for the separation of Church and State, gave himself completely up to such a hope. The Scotch Free Kirk, which arose from the mighty secession in 1843, has inscribed that motto upon her banners. And finally, a portion of the highest churchmen in England would be glad to see the Church disestablished, upon the plea that the Episcopal Church would really begin to flourish, were she set free as in the United States of America. But are such hopes and aspirations really based upon any foundation? and would not the advantages which may be anticipated be overborne by disadvantages and dangers which have not been sufficiently considered?

Let us first obtain a clear conception of what is meant by a separation between Church and State. Is it a clear definition of, and distinction between, the spiritual and temporal power, followed by a friendly compact between the two, by which each, unhampered by the other, and yet mutually co-operative, may strive to attain their common aim, the spiritual and moral welfare of the nation? No, that is not what is meant. Is it that gentleness, patience, and mutual respect shall be reciprocally exercised by the adherents of the various religious creeds? No; this again is not separation between Church and State. Rather, it is insisted upon that the State as such, that the nation and its leaders, shall acknowledge no Christian creed and have no religion. Religion, and especially Christian faith, is to be looked upon as a purely private affair, affecting the individual alone, and such religious societies as may set themselves up. The Christian Church is regarded as a private association, with which the State has nothing to do. Christian religion is no longer to have any recognised position in public affairs; it is relegated from the sphere of national life to the chamber of individual feeling, and is to be exercised only in private assemblies, where similarly-minded persons may meet together. The State, as such, is not to assert any recognition of God and of Christ; it is not to avow a knowledge of any Word of God to which it must submit. The State is atheist.

Let us first attempt to realize what would be the result of such a condition of affairs as regards the rising generation. Countless numbers who at present still enjoy a Christian training would then be deprived of it. Many parents are so careless that they would not impart to their children any baptism, any religious instruction, or any confirmation, unless usage, the customs of society, and the feeling of respectability connected with those two impelled them so to do.[1] Many of us who are blessed with Christian faith would not have attained to it, but would have grown up in a heathen condition, unless those beneficent influences of usage and public custom had come to our aid. If all this is taken away, we may apprehend that a generation will grow up in which the majority will arrive at a condition of estrangement from God and barbarity, which has hitherto been looked upon as exceptional. This apprehension arises from the already apparent indifference of many; it is increased by the unfortunate fact that the German nation especially, in consequence of centuries of tutelage, is not accustomed to self-assertion either in political or in religious matters. People have been led into bad habits by a system under which a paternal Government cared for everything, and considered itself bound to arrange every detail of life. Anything which is not promoted by the authorities is disregarded, so long as necessity does not compel it to be undertaken. Under such circumstances, to commend the separation of Church and State, to strive after it, and to aim at tearing asunder all bonds which still connect the two, is to assume a grave responsibility with regard to the juvenile population whose welfare is confided to us.

Protestants especially should weigh these considerations; for the Roman Catholic Church, and the people adhering to it, are better fitted to stand such a trial. The influence of her clergy is great, her organization is compact, the traditions of her independence are well authenticated; whereas in German Protestantism all these advantages exist only in a very slight degree.

---

[1] Since the above was written, baptism has been rendered non-compulsory during the six months previous to Christmas 1875; and it has been statistically asserted that one-third of the infants born during that time in the city of Berlin have not been baptized!—*Note by Translator.*

The great example to which all the advocates for a separation between Church and State in the more ancient States of Europe point, in order to recommend their theories, is that of the United States of America. They assert that there a rigid separation exists, and that there experience has shown how well it works in religious as well as civil matters. The zeal and activity of the various Christian parties, as there exhibited, might be well taken by us as an example worthy of imitation. At the same time, there reigns a spirit of forbearance and mutual recognition; whereas the State is completely free from those ecclesio-political strifes from which Germany is at present suffering, and by which her future is so gravely threatened. There is much truth in this; and why should we not desire to see these advantages transplanted to German soil? Yet there remains a twofold question to be raised,—first, whether the separation of Church and State would assume the same form; secondly, whether the same favourable conditions upon which those advantages are based exist also among us.

There the separation is so complete that the State does not interfere with the religious affairs of the various societies. Freedom of worship is once for all firmly established, and religion is no affair of the legislature, whether in Congress or in the individual States. But although no established religion exists there, the Americans, as a people, are a Christian nation. No law compels the adoption of the Christian faith; but Christian customs are in the ascendant, and custom always has been more powerful than law. It is usual for Congress to be opened and prorogued with prayer, and on these occasions leading ministers of the various denominations are alternately called upon to officiate as chaplains. In all the States of the Union one Christian institution, and that the one which has most influence upon the national life, is inviolably maintained, namely, a rigidly strict observance of the Lord's Day; and this not only by the sanction of custom, but also by law. Many usages exist which—as, for instance, the tendering of an oath—solemnly recognise Christianity. It is a common occurrence that preachers and missionaries, as recognised agents for the public welfare, receive free passes to travel on the railways and steamboats.

The seven States of New England form the historical basis of the great Republic, which is washed by three oceans; and those States were founded by the Pilgrim Fathers, those faithful heroes, who, during the reign of James I. and Charles I. of England, emigrated thither. They left their country because they were dissatisfied with a Church which had become worldly, and because they were thrust forth by a corrupted and tyrannical court, as at a previous period the citizens of Phocæa, in Asia Minor, migrated in order to escape from the tyranny of the Persians, and to found for themselves a new home beyond the seas. The Pilgrim Fathers sought to find a home in the New World, where they might live in peace and liberty; they did not seek for liberty in order to escape from the laws of God, but rather that they might be able to conform their lives to the word of Christ and serve God without hindrance. Like genuine Puritans, their chief object was to put in practice a purely Christian national life. They succeeded in so doing to an extraordinary extent. To the present day the States of New England, if we regard the social evils of New York as the exceptional accompaniments of all great cities, are the paradise of America, as regarded from a religious and moral point of view. Pennsylvania was also founded with the same objects. Such precedents produced an effect upon the subsequent development of the States, and imparted to them a similar impress, although less clearly defined, and weakened by foreign elements. Even on the occasion of their severance from the mother country, although that proceeding cannot be legally justified, still a powerful element of Christianity pervaded the movement. The French, as a nation, made their Revolution with the Bible under their feet. The Americans made theirs with the Bible in their hands. Hence, in the case of America, the necessary conditions existed for the maintenance of a Christian national life, which is strong enough to hold its own without assistance from the temporal power, and to maintain its position without the patronage of the State. There every man is accustomed to be independent; he knows what he believes in, he knows what he wants to do. He stands up for his religious convictions, and is prepared to make further sacrifices for religious purposes. Such a people is capable of making a good use of unrestricted liberty of worship. In such a case, advantageous results may follow from a separation of Church and State.

But who will take upon himself to assert that the same advantageous conditions exist, and to the same extent, in Germany? Give us the Christian national customs of the Puritans; give us the benefits of the celebration of the Lord's Day, which have been so earnestly insisted upon by Calvinists, Scotchmen, Englishmen, and Americans; make the dominant tone of the press and of public feeling to be that of respect towards Christian religion; in a word, give us an energetic people, conscientiously believing in its creed, then there would be but little mischief to apprehend from a separation between Church and State in Germany.

This separation would infallibly assume a different form amongst us, less resembling that of the American

Republic than that which existed during the short period of the first Republic in France. We have already gone so far on the road to apostasy that a complete severance of the State from the Church, and the relegation of Christianity to the domain of private life, would be the first step towards the setting up of the tyranny of Atheism.

The theory of the separation as proposed by Vinet deserves closer consideration. The chief point is the doctrine restricting the temporal power to interference in purely temporal affairs. But the defenders of this separation admit, that even those may not be ordered without regard to moral principles; that the State must be moral, and be a supporter of morality, although not of Christian but of social morality. The latter is supposed to be capable of existing independently of the Christian faith, and without any regard to it. The component parts of this social morality are, according to Vinet, threefold—namely, Security, Property, and Decency. As soon as men come together to lead a social existence and form a community of citizens, it becomes necessary to protect the life and property of each and every one. For this object some authority is called into being, that is the task with which it is entrusted by the community. The State is an institution for mutual assurance; such is the contract upon which it is based, and authority or government is only the agent set up by the body of insurers to see that the object of their association be carried out. Niebuhr remarks, that amongst Latin nations the doctrine of a natural state and a social contract still prevails; whereas we have returned to a deeper apprehension of what a State is. Vinet's example is quoted as a confirmation of this remark. Still he certainly did ennoble that deplorable theory, and thus arrived at better conclusions than its exponents usually do. He introduces as the third component of social morality, decency and respectability. But in this very fact may be seen how impossible it is to separate social morality from the source of all genuine morality, which is the Christian religion. In the States of heathen antiquity, this third element was very slightly realized; in the course of time it was almost entirely obliterated, and no power on earth was capable of saving and restoring it but Christianity alone. Only a Christian people, and a government which admits its allegiance to Christ and His commandments, will be able to put into practice social morality as Vinet calls for it. Separated from Christianity, such morality will prove to be as unstable as Deism, which always degenerates into Atheism as soon as left entirely to its own resources.

Somewhat different is the theory under guise of which in our day the complete dissolution of the bond between Church and State is called for. In order to reconcile us to the loss of those supports which have hitherto sustained the fabric of the State, we are referred to the majesty of the law and the respect shown to it. This is said to suffice; and that the State, based upon the law, can still subsist though deprived of the assistance of the Christian Church.

There is something grand and majestic about a State in which the law is not only made known, but is also observed; where it is applicable to all, even the highest, and where it is regarded with respect by all. That was a fine saying of Demaratus to the Persian king, when the latter wondered how it was that the Greeks had not a despotic government, as the people of Asia had: "They have a king whom they all obey," was the reply; "that king is the law." Respect for the law is not only *a* political virtue, but it is *the* political virtue. It comprehends all that makes a good citizen; it is the fundamental principle of all national welfare. It constituted the strength of Rome; it is the secret of England's power. That people will do well whose rulers look upon a law once entered upon the statute-book as inviolable, amongst whom every man knows that transgressing, or even circumventing the law, is a mean and disreputable act. A mournful state of degeneracy has set in when people become accustomed to the promulgation of a number of laws without any serious intention of putting them into execution!

Theologians are quite right when they draw a distinction between Christian and civil righteousness. Respect for the law comprises, and is, real civil righteousness. Of that there is no question. But the question is, whether this respect can continue to exist when separated from Christian religion, and whether, as must be the case, it can under such conditions be propagated and invigorated in one generation after another? If there is any saying which is entirely consonant with our reason and with history, it is this: The law itself requires a sanction from above, in order to take root in men's dispositions; and respect for the law only acquires a true basis and proper consistency when it is derived from a regard to higher superhuman and supernatural power. With regard to subjects upon whom the majesty of the law imposes burdens and restraints, this fact is self-evident. The idea of God as ruler of all, omniscient and just, furnishes an impulse and vigour to the observance of the law even when it may be difficult for us, and in cases where no human being would discover or punish the trespass. In a word, in order to respect the law a conscience is necessary, and in order to have a conscience one must believe on God. If faith is wanting, there can be no conscience, and without it no respect for the law. This was the case in Rome. As the fear of the gods disappeared, respect for the law was lost too; the ancient Roman fidelity to an oath fell to the ground, and oppression in the provinces, and impious attacks upon the constitution of the country became matters of everyday occurrence. Upon the ruins of the old republican virtue, there sprang up a fabric of barbaric, inhuman imperialism. In England this sublime feature of the national character, respect for the law, has indisputably its origin in the Christian faith. Nelson's famous signal before the battle of Trafalgar, "England expects every man to do his duty," produced at the time such an effect, and it still produces the same, because it is a quotation from the explanation of the ten commandments contained in the Church Catechism, and because it awakens the most sacred reminiscences in every member of the Anglican Church. This sublime consciousness, that God is the original and final source of all law, and that obedience to the law is obedience to God, was transplanted by the Pilgrim Fathers and the English emigrants to the soil of America. It is no abstract, cold, and dead idea of the law, but this religious respect which forms a basis for all that is great and good; which basis, too, still exists in the United States, along with all the corruption and lawlessness which has crept in and multiplied in modern times. Do those who talk about a State without religion really mean to assert that even an irreligious people can be virtuous, righteous, and happy? If they have not lost all knowledge of human nature, together with their loss of faith, they will be constrained to say with Voltaire, "If God did not exist, it would be necessary to invent Him." It is not the Christian State, but the State devoid of all religion, which is Utopian.

In America we have, under extraordinary conditions, the abnormal spectacle of a State devoid of religion and a religious people. But we may be sure that, in our case, if the State became devoid of religion, so would the people too. The social evils from which the American Republic suffers would become rampant among us—such as, want of obedience and respect on the part of children towards parents and teachers, irreverent treatment of religious subjects on the part of sectarian teachers, avarice and deceit practised under the cloak of religious zeal, judicial corruption, and a spirit of lawlessness.

The complete separation which our Ultras strive after, would, when put to the test of experience, be found an absolute nonentity. If the State wished it ever so much, it could not become completely neutral in matters of faith and religion. Every State requires some guarantee for the fidelity of its civil and military officials in the administration of justice; it requires a pledge for the truthfulness of witnesses; it obtains both by requiring and accepting an oath. Without some solemn, religious assurance of fidelity and truthfulness, the objects of the administration could not be attained. In the face of the unreliability and deceitfulness of mankind, we are obliged, as a last resort, to order an appeal to the Omniscient, Almighty, and Just God. "An oath," as the Bible says, "is an end to all strife." Without it, we could not arrive at the end at all.

Let us try to realize how the ideal State of our opponents would succeed in such a case. In India the following scene not unfrequently takes place. In some criminal proceedings a witness is called upon to give evidence, and upon the tenor of what he says depends to a material extent the verdict of the jury. The judge asks him, Who or what do you swear by? Are you a Hindoo who swears by the water of the Ganges? No. Are you a Parsee who swears by the holy flame? No. Are you a Mussulman who swears by the Koran?

No. What are you, then? I am nothing. He must be dismissed, and his evidence is of no avail in a court of justice.

The Atheist cannot take an oath, but neither can he require one to be taken. This is the necessary result which would obtain in a State devoid of religion. If a judge, or any other official, were to proceed to administer an oath on behalf of the State, the reply not only of the Atheist, but of any one who chooses, might be: " How dare you ask me to assert my religious belief? The State has nothing to do with religion; such a requisition is diametrically opposed to the principle of a complete separation between the civil and religious departments."

Thus, then, the indispensability of an oath proves that even the most modern State cannot do without some connection with a higher world, some dependence upon the latter—that, in fact, it cannot do without reverence for God; but this implies a belief in God, and a profession of that belief. Thus it will be found necessary, at every step, to recall into the sphere of national life that religion which had been thrust out. Oaths, and the necessity for their continuance, are, as it were, the link which connects the State with the unseen world, however much men may strive to break asunder this union.

The expectation of those believers who hope that by such a separation their own spiritual life would be strengthened, and the Church, although more contracted in its dimensions, would spiritually flourish, is, on a more careful consideration, found to be very doubtful. A thoroughly sickly organization is by no means improved by the mere fact of an amputation being performed. If no healthy vital powers exist, the operation endangers life. It is true that we all require a renewal and reinvigoration of our Christian faith and conversation; but that is an operation of the Divine Spirit; it can only reach us by means of some purifying and life-giving act emanating from Christ. If this be wanting, even the enmity of the world and persecution of Christianity will be unable to produce any good effect. It is a mistake to suppose that, on the separation of Church and State, the fulness of the Spirit would incontinently come upon believers. Even in lands where this separation exists, we hear bitter complaints of the lukewarmness, want of unity, and worldliness of religious communities. If a sick man has lain for a long time upon one side, he hopes to find relief by being turned over upon the other; but if his wish be gratified, he soon becomes as uneasy as before. The same mistake is made by those who expect, by a separation, to find the Church healed of her infirmities.

It is not this separation, nor the disappearance of Christian religion from the laws and national proclamations, that can bring us any good. The nation, as such, must have a conscience as much as every individual must. This conscience of the community finds its natural expression in a Christian profession by the nation; it derives from such a constant public testimony fresh strength and nourishment, which it, like all other living organizations, stands in daily need of.

Those praiseworthy things which we observe in the United States—such as liberty of conscience, zeal in religious undertakings, mutual forbearance among the various denominations, peace between the temporal power and religious communities—are not, as is supposed, necessarily the results of a separation between Church and State; they may all exist and flourish in the presence of a firmly-established, reverently-surrounded, and lawfully-protected National Church.

The proof of this is Great Britain. Just as in that

realm the great political problem has hitherto found the most perfect solution, so, too, has the great ecclesiastical problem. A firmly-established National Church, combined with freedom of conscience and of worship; such is the arrangement which is most satisfactory, which we should desire for ourselves, and which we should strive after.

CHAPTER X.

THE LAWFULNESS OF TAKING AN OATH IN A CHRISTIAN COMMONWEALTH.

In the face of the many religious sects and individuals who object on principle to take an oath, as contrary to the express command of Christ contained in the gospel (see Matt. v. 34), it may be advantageous to enter more fully into the question. Christ says (see Matt. v. 33-37) : " Again, ye have heard that it hath been said by them of old time, Thou shalt not forswear thyself, but shalt perform unto the Lord thine oaths : But I say unto you, Swear not at all; neither by heaven ; for it is God's throne : nor by the earth ; for it is His footstool : neither by Jerusalem ; for it is the city of the great King. Neither shalt thou swear by thy head, because thou canst not make one hair white or black. But let your communication be, Yea, yea ; Nay, nay : for whatsoever is more than these cometh of evil."

An oath is a solemn recognition of God, Almighty, Omniscient, and Just. There is a distinction between the oath required of a witness in cases where a fact or facts are being deposed to, and a promissory oath which is to regulate our future conduct. In both cases we call upon God to witness to the truth of our assertions ; we imprecate His judgment if our words be found to be untrue. Hence perjury is the most grievous abuse of the divine name, the gravest insult to divine majesty, a calling down upon ourselves of divine and temporal punishment; for God will not permit His name to be taken in vain.

Oaths occur in sayings ascribed to God Himself on weighty occasions, in solemn moments. "By myself have I sworn," says God to Abraham (Gen. xxii. 16, 17), "because thou hast done this thing, and hast not withheld thy son, thine only son: that in blessing I will bless thee, and in multiplying I will multiply thy seed as the stars of heaven." On the occasion of the installation of the Son of man in His eternal priesthood it is said, "The Lord hath sworn and will not repent, Thou art a priest for ever after the order of Melchizedek" (Ps. cx. 4).

"Men verily swear by the greater: and an oath for confirmation is to them an end of all strife" (Heb. vi. 16; comp. Ex. xxii. 10, 11). There is a divine ordinance in human communities by which strife may be put an end to, whereby justice may be done, peace assured, and life and property protected. This is the duty which has been committed to all authorities from above, and they have to carry it out in a world full of untruth, lies, and deceit. Hence they require an oath. They must call for one in serious matters, in order to assure themselves of the truthfulness of evidence, the fidelity and trustworthiness of their servants and fellow-labourers. There must be a last resource, and this can only be found in a solemn appeal to God, the Judge of all men. Nothing less will suffice, and any one who takes a true oath upon the requisition of the authorities assists them in fulfilling their calling.

Christ found that, with respect to swearing, degeneracy and misuse had crept in amongst the Jews. Assertions upon oath were customary in common life, as is here pointed out, and in Jas. v. 12. Want of truthfulness in conversation was widespread, and it could not be said of many, as our Lord said of Nathaniel, "Behold an Israelite indeed, in whom is no guile!" At the same time the Jewish nation respected and feared the name of God. Hence arose the custom of introducing asseverations on oath into daily conversation, in which asseverations, however, the name of God was avoided. This and that was asserted by heaven! by earth! by Jerusalem! or by the speaker's own head! This evil habit was succeeded by a still more evil doctrine, which was meant to serve as justification of it. "Whosoever shall swear by the temple, it is nothing; but whosoever shall swear by the gold of the temple, he is a debtor. . . . Whosoever shall swear by the altar, it is nothing; but whosoever sweareth by the gift that is upon it, he is guilty." Our Lord strongly opposed such distinctions (Matt. xxiii. 16–23); and hence we deduce from His language that there were scribes who maintained that if only the name of God were not expressly used, the truth of the assertion made was not of great importance; that it sufficed if oaths made in the name of God were kept sacred. We mention here, as a fact which reflects credit upon the Jews, that such excuses for untruthfulness cannot be found in the Talmud. The testimony which Christ bore against such was not borne in vain.

Christ appeared and did away with solemn asseverations in common intercourse. Christ required that His disciples should always act and speak under a sense of the omnipresence and omniscience of God. We are answerable for everything that proceeds from our lips: "For by thy words thou shalt be justified, and by thy words thou shalt be condemned" (Matt. xii. 37). Hence the disciples of Christ ought to be distinguished by the perfect sincerity and simplicity of their language: "Let your communication be, Yea, yea; Nay, nay; for whatsoever is more than these cometh of evil." The serious "Yes" and "No" of a Christian man should have, for all such as know him, the weight of a solemn asseveration.

So it is in the Christian Church. "Yes," solemnly enunciated and spoken in the presence of God, serves in baptism and at ordinations (in England during the marriage ceremony) in lieu of an oath. In ancient Christendom it was looked for that the authorities should accept the simple "Yes" and "No" of a bishop or priest, and assign to it the same weight as an oath.

In the meanwhile the authorities constantly require from us Christians, and even from the servants of the Lord, an oath, when evidence is to be given or fidelity promised. We swear when duly called upon, and do so with a full knowledge of the sanctity of an oath; we look up to God, the just and omniscient, giving Him the honour. We do this with a good conscience, because Christ has not forbidden it.

It is true that there are many earnest and well-meaning Christians, worthy of all respect, who are of opinion that Christ forbade this also. We honour their conscientiousness and fidelity to their convictions, but cannot agree to their interpretation of the passage; for, in the first place, we note that Christ in His prohibition only quotes the forms of asseveration in use in common conversation: By heaven! by earth! by Jerusalem! by one's own head! Such are not judicial forms of expression. Then we also observe that, at verse 39, where He says, "Resist not evil," He evidently stipulates for the administration of justice. Brethren are not to requite injury for injury, nor reproach for reproach; but the Government is to punish the evil-doer: it does not bear the sword in vain, and God has committed that office to it. This commission from above Christ did not do away with, but recognised.

Hence also in this case He does not gainsay the right and duty of the Government to call for the assistance of an oath in the execution of its commission, as that alone makes an end of all strife among men, and is for confirmation.

Unfortunately, the language and conduct of Christians in general have not been such that the authorities should look upon our Christian calling as anything very special, or that they should be satisfied with our simple "Yes" and "No."

The times of the apostasy have come, and godless men have sprung up, who do not hesitate to say— inasmuch as they declare that "there is no God"—that an oath, an invocation of God, is a meaningless ceremony; and on that ground they object to take an oath. It will eventually come to pass that the reverential taking of an oath on convenient occasions will be looked upon as a proof of and testimony to the Christian faith.

As amongst the Jews abuses had been introduced, so also amongst us Christians. Nothing is any longer held to be sacred, and amongst other things an oath. But we must not countenance such desecration; we ought rather to raise our protest against it. In courts of justice, even in trifling cases, an oath is tendered and taken with indifference. The grave responsibility of the act is overlooked, and the consequences upon the consciences of the people are most disastrous. The number of oaths taken is one of those things which is corrupting the social state; and he would be a benefactor to mankind who would get rid of this evil, so that an oath should only be required on emergent occasions, and surrounded with grave ceremonial. Political oaths are recklessly called for, carelessly taken, and wickedly broken. Public opinion in this respect is so utterly at fault, that the disregard of political oaths is looked upon quite as a matter of course; and yet this misuse of God's name does bring upon us His judgments.

The abuses in ordinary conversation amongst us assume a different form to what they did amongst the Jews, and are of a worse kind. The Jews avoided calling on the name of the Lord in vain. With us it is a prominent and evil habit to call thoughtlessly upon the name of God and Jesus on every slight occasion. How our Lord Jesus Christ looked upon this is not open to any doubt. He did not come to do away with the law, but to fulfil it; and that law says, "Thou shalt not take the name of the Lord thy God in vain; for the Lord will not hold him guiltless that taketh His name in vain." If we take the name of the Lord upon our lips unnecessarily, the foremost evil consequence is, that our prayers lose their efficacy, and no answer is vouchsafed to our invocation of the divine name. Christians ought to render themselves remarkable by the fact that to them the name of God, the word of God, prayer, the Lord's day, and all the ordinances of God, should be especially sacred.

CHAPTER XI.

THE POSITION OF A CHRISTIAN STATE TOWARDS SCHISM IN THE CHURCH AND THE VARIOUS SECTS.

THE bond between Church and State, between the temporal and spiritual power, could be simply and peacefully arranged if the temporal government had only to deal with one undivided Christian Church. When, in the early times of the Middle Ages, the Teutonic tribes, with their dukes and sovereigns at their head, embraced Christianity, those heads of the people had to deal with one body of clergy, which was not split up into parties; there was only one doctrine in the Church, only one form of worship, one harmonious whole. The office-bearers could explain what they required. The rulers knew with whom they had to do, from whom they had to learn the law of Christ, and whom they had to consult in order to bring their own actions and the laws they promulgated into accord with the divine command. As a matter of fact, the Christian bishops in the empire of Charlemagne obtained a position which nearly corresponded to that which was normal and to be desired. They did not exercise any temporal power, they had nothing to do with the conduct of government; but they had a place in the councils of the king and of the nation, and could make their voices heard. If any one of the mighty ones of the earth attempted to set himself above the divine law, the bishops could remind him of his Christian calling and Christian duties. But the relations were disturbed and the bond of peace destroyed when arrogant emperors forcibly interfered with the affairs of the Church, and when Roman bishops, ignoring their calling, stretched out their hands to grasp temporal power, desiring to wield both temporal and spiritual swords, asserting that the temporal was only an emanation from the spiritual power, robbing princes of their thrones, and releasing people from their allegiance to their rulers. In the face of a ministry which raised such pretensions, it became difficult to rule, difficult to uphold a Christian Commonwealth. But since the Reformation fresh obstacles have been added. The presumptuous fabric, whose apex was intended to reach to heaven, was broken down, and the language of the work-people confounded. An earthquake rent asunder the mighty city, schism in the Church became an accomplished fact; and from the date of the Reformation, Christian princes found themselves face to face with two sets of ministers, two ecclesiastical parties, of which each declared itself to be the only true one.

Now, when in a nation either one or the other of these has a considerable predominance, and the ruler himself subscribes to such party from conviction, the matter becomes somewhat less intricate. In such cases it is still possible for a National Church to exist and to maintain satisfactory relations with the State, —as, for instance, in England, Scotland, and Sweden, where Protestantism predominates; or, on the other hand, as in those countries which are nearly exclusively Roman Catholic. Germany was divided into two nearly equal parts. For a long time it was held to be impossible that public worship should be conducted in any one territory both in the Protestant and Roman Catholic form. Not only were the Roman Catholic princes convinced of this impossibility, but Luther also believed that such a state of things would lead to civil war. Grotius, the Dutchman, was of the same opinion. In the Protestant countries of the north, public Roman Catholic worship was not permitted. This idea of the incompatibility of a dual form of worship with the welfare of the State was the cause which led to the pernicious principle in the German Empire, that the territorial ruler should decide as to what the religion should be, whether the National Church should be Roman Catholic or Protestant. Gustavus Adolphus was the first who, after his conquests in Germany, proclaimed the principle, of which they had no idea in Sweden, that both forms of worship should be recognised, and should co-exist with equal privileges. This theory, then unheard of, was preached by the court chaplain, Fabricius, from the pulpit of Saint Anna, after the Swedish king had taken possession of Augsburg.

In the peace of Westphalia it was still insisted upon that the ruler and his subjects must be of a similar faith. Only when Frederick II. of Prussia had conquered Silesia did a numerous Roman Catholic population come under the sway of a Protestant ruler. In the electorate of Saxony, on the other hand, a royal family which had become Roman Catholic ruled ever since 1697 over a Protestant people. When, after the storms of the Napoleonic period, Germany was again subdivided at the congress of Vienna, the various creeds were as little taken into consideration as had been the case under Napoleon. Twelve millions of Roman Catholic subjects were handed over to Protestant princes.

The opponents of a Christian State, well knowing the difficulties which must arise from such a state of things, asserted that it was no longer possible to set up such a Commonwealth. As people are not contented with an individual who simply avows himself to be a Christian, and refuses to belong to any particular denomination, so too they would not listen to the proposal for having a Christian State, it must also have some distinctive creed; but seeing that, owing to the intermingling of the various parties which had gone on all over Germany, this would bring about endless strife, there was no alternative left but to set up an undenominational, and hence—here we have the fallacy—a Commonwealth devoid of religion.

Not to be devoid of religion, but to be Christian; not to be denominational, but to be catholic, is the object which at present should be the aim of the State. Just as much as the denominations could exist side by side in the German Empire, so too can they in each territory: such is the experience of two centuries; that is what has been taught us by history, which has overleaped all those ancient prejudices. We have been allowed to enjoy a peaceful community of life under one Government, and as citizens of one country.

The Government can and ought to hold fast to its Christian calling, and fulfil the same without regard to the denominational schisms amongst the people. It can do so—it can, by an impartial demeanour towards both parties, maintain the Christian character of the legislation and of the Government, for the simple reason that the strife of the creeds does not affect that aspect of Christianity which has a decided influence upon the State. The strife does not concern the moral law, nor the decalogue; but it is the fact of upholding the moral law which imparts to the State its Christian character.

This fact is recognised by the Protestant party. Equality of civil rights for the Roman Catholics as well as Protestants; the capability of Roman Catholics to fill all offices of State, even in a Protestant State; equality of support and equality of protection for both forms of worship, are acquisitions which, it is to be hoped, no Protestant will ever again permit to be called in question. One cannot be certain of a similar liberality on the part of the others. Pius IX., in his *Syllabus Errorum* (77, 78), has disapproved of granting permission to any other form of Christian worship in Roman Catholic countries, even immigrants of another creed should not be allowed to celebrate their form of worship openly. These are unfortunate premonitions, although better views amongst that party are not yet quite extinguished.

The reason which, in a State where all creeds are upon the same footing, leads to a similar recognition of both denominations, is not indifference to religion, nor the contemptuous notion that it is folly to lay any stress upon religious questions, but rather an arduously acquired insight into the nature of the Christian Church, in consequence of which the ancient sectarian brusqueness is smoothed down.

In holy baptism we are incorporated into Christ, and are constituted members of His Church. Baptism with water, in the name of the Father, the Son, and the Holy Ghost, is the one proper Christian and effective baptism, which may not be called in question or repeated. Such is the ancient Christian doctrine, such is the doctrine taught by the various Christian Churches; God has so graciously overruled matters, that in this matter of baptism unity still is maintained. Here we have a safe point of departure. As is asserted in the Nicene Creed, there is only one Christ and one baptism; so also are we all baptized into one Church, and the authorities have a right—nay, more, it is their duty—to regard every baptized person as a member of the one Christian Church, and to treat him as such. As assuredly as the Jews, notwithstanding the divisions which exist amongst them, are still one people in consequence of their lineage, and must be treated as a nation, so too we Christians, notwithstanding the divisions and denominations amongst us, form one religious community, one Church. Further, however much the Christian ministry may have ramified and become involved in strife, it does as a matter of fact form a unity; they are the servants of Christ, whom He has set over His large household. The ministers of the various denominations participate, though in various degrees, in that commission made over by Christ to His disciples, whether it be as priests or as preachers. Hence the authorities do well in recognising the ministers, without regard to their denomination, as servants of Christ, and in protecting them. Now there exists, no doubt, the unspeakably mournful fact, that one portion of this ministry has anathematized the other, and that this latter has replied with a rude and exclusive bearing. If the authorities, in this matter of strife, do not take the part of either side, and do not allow this excommunication to form any basis for their conduct towards either party, such a proceeding cannot be blamed for its indifference. Even supposing the anathema to have any value, those who are anathematized would still have to be regarded as Christians; for in the Christian Church a ban or anathema, even when properly employed, has not the power nor is it intended to separate the individual to whom it is applied from the body of Christ, nor to deprive him of his Christian standing, but is only intended to improve, heal, and save, as a means of Christian discipline. But this ban, which thus hovers between the denominations, has, it is true, been uttered by men, but has never been ratified by Heaven. Of this we are convinced by the manifold experiences of the last three and a half centuries. Had the anathema been confirmed by God, the guilty party would long since have been brought up for judgment; truth and Christian virtue would have disappeared, the Divine Spirit would have withdrawn from them, and have left nothing but a plain strewn with corpses. Still such is not the case. If the real condition of a Christian nation be examined, whether it be Roman Catholic or Protestant, we shall find an equal amount of piety and of the fruits of the Spirit in either case. It is palpable that the ministry and the worship are in both cases accompanied by a divine blessing. It is evident that a Christian Government does right in maintaining and protecting the existence of both. The faithfulness and mercy of God have evidently cared for both; should not the attitude of a Christian Government try to do likewise?

The researches of science, since the Reformation, have also not been in vain; they have contributed to the peace of the Church. Whilst passionate decisions and bitterness of feeling have disappeared, owing to depth of research and calmness of reflection, old misunderstandings have been discovered, and a path cleared for their solution. It was seen in the mirror of history what grievous mistakes had been committed on both sides at the time of the separation, so that each does well to modify its judgment upon the other. In the Holy Scriptures, and from ancient Christian records, it is evident the Church once possessed a conformation which none of the present systems exactly represents, and that in her bosom truths were compactly united which now show themselves, here and there, scattered amongst the various denominations: we see that, in the sects, many gifts come to light, and that they are confirmatory and supplementary to each other. The two great parties, Roman Catholic and Protestant, have not only human permission, but also one derived from a higher source, to exist side by side; and that, too, in the hope that some day a perfect reconciliation and reunion will be brought about.

For there can be no doubt that the present condition of division is one of suffering, humiliation, and desire. Healing of the wounds and restoration of unity, is what all should earnestly strive for, for the sake of the glory of God, the salvation of souls, the advancement of Christian national life and a Christian State. When Germany, exhausted by the terrible war, attained to rest at the Westphalian peace, it was well known that the arrangement of tolerance, which was based upon schism, was only a temporary agreement, a provisional scheme until better times should come, a transitive arrangement until unity of faith and worship should be restored,—until men should agree on the subject of religion.

Such is the firmly established civil law in Germany. It is the fruit of the bitterest quarrels. And all parties should unite in hoping that this equality of position and similarity of treatment of both confessions may be permanently upheld; the more so, because during the last two centuries experience has shown such parity to be beneficial.

The monopoly which, in a strictly denominational State, the dominant ecclesiastical party possesses, has always reacted in an injurious manner upon its spiritual and vital powers. Self-contentment and pride, indolence and diminution of zeal, are the evil consequences of uninterrupted and exclusive possession of power. Free competition, which may in other matters be attended by some disadvantages, exercises in religious, as also in scientific matters, advantageous effects. The universities would become lethargic if every subject were to be in the hands of a single professor. The juxtaposition of the Roman Catholic and Protestant religions moreover, under equally auspicious conditions for mutual activity, excites a noble competition. For this reason the general condition of the Roman Catholic theology, ministry, and people in Germany, is so much more favourable than, for instance, in the Latin countries of Europe or in South America; because here constant intercourse with Protestantism, and the need of maintaining its position by spiritual pre-eminence, have advanced the spiritual and religious life. In the same manner, the proximity of the Roman Catholic Church has benefited Protestantism. Wherever the latter has found itself in a minority, as opposed to the old Church party, it has displayed more earnestness and more faithfulness to tradition than in the large Protestant States, where it appears to have gone steadily on to dissolution.

Our State Church in Germany is twofold; the Roman Catholic and the Evangelical divisions enjoy simultaneously the coveted position of an Establishment, and ought to do so. But when under such circumstances smaller Christian communities come into existence, it would be unreasonable to claim for them either subsidy or support from the State, or a similar position to that of the State Church. Still it is beneficial, and one of the duties of a Christian Government, to allow to smaller and newly arisen Christian communities perfect freedom of worship and the enjoyment of equal civic rights.

How ought the powers that be to comport themselves towards the so-called sects? The attitude which a State devoid of religion assumes towards these will be very different to that assumed by a Christian State based upon parity. The former will, under the pretence of perfect indifference, contemplate with secret satisfaction the dissolution of the existing remains of a national Church, and promote such dissolution in an underhand way. Atheistical partisans, who, under the cloak of religion, seek to destroy all religion, will be treated with respect and forbearance. For a time, but certainly not for a continuance, the same indulgence will be extended to decidedly Christian endeavours. The general tenor of the law in such a State will be that all sects are to have perfectly free scope for their activity, provided that they do not come into actual conflict with any specific law, and that even then the transgression of that law shall alone be taken notice of, whereas in other respects the spread of the sect shall have free play. Essentially different is the aspect of a Christian State based upon parity; whereas it compels no one to attend any religious ceremony, or to profess any religious creed contrary to his own convictions, it certainly does not, blindly and without discrimination, or irrevocably, grant to every existing or subsequently arising sect permission to constitute itself as a body corporate, and by means of public assemblies and lectures to disseminate its principles. It will reserve to itself the right of examining such principles. A Christian Government will look upon it as its duty not to shrink from the trouble of carrying out such an examination. Centuries ago the Mennonites and the Moravians underwent such an examination in Germany, and proved themselves to be deserving of liberty of worship and full civic rights. The former sect owing to their Christian virtues and firmness, the latter owing to the blessings showered down upon a work of Christian charity, proved to be a blessing to the country. Similar confidence ought to be shown to the Methodists, on account of their untiring zeal for the salvation of souls and for the moral elevation of the people. Doubtless old Lutheran communities possess a sacred claim to recognition and protection. If any new appearances of a similar kind should spring up, the examination which the authorities have to submit them to is not so much dogmatic as moral; for every Christian, and especially the Government of a Christian State, has a right to decide in questions of Christian morality. Wherever the principles of a sect are at variance with the moral law, whether in respect to matrimony, or obedience to authority in worldly matters, or property, the Government has a right to interfere, and to prevent the dissemination or putting in practice of such principles. The real difficulty lies in such cases where the doctrines of Christianity, but not the moral law, are denied. Here the permission or prohibition of forming such sects is not a question of right or wrong, but of State expediency. Blasphemy against that which is sacred to a Christian nation is, in a well regulated State, an offence punishable by law. If injurious attacks upon respectable individuals or whole classes of society are punishable by law, certainly revilings against that which is sacred to Christians at large are even more so.

Liberty of discussion within certain bounds is always more wholesome than authoritative suppression. In England the Unitarians, who deny the Godhead of Christ, have been allowed to form separate communities. In Germany, where this permission was denied them by the existing law, like-minded persons, that is, the Rationalists, found their way into the professorial chairs and the pulpits of the Protestant Church. The result was that over in England such men have been productive of much less harm than amongst us.

The entire course which the Legislature in Great Britain took with respect to Dissent, as also the general political development, has been a more normal one than amongst us. There, privileges have been gradually ceded to the sects, and have been subsequently enlarged and increased; whereas here, an exceptionally long period of oppression and restriction was suddenly followed by an excess of liberty and freedom from restraint, which certainly approximated very closely to endangering the Christian Commonwealth :

> " Dread the slave who breaks his chain,
> Not the freeman's honest claim."—SCHILLER.

In England, the advantageous effects of this wiser mode of treatment have long been apparent; the Christian creed of the nation as a whole has been protected, the uprightness and truth of individual character has been advanced. What the State Church lost as regards the number of her adherents, has been amply made up to her by the exciting reaction produced by the free Churches and sects, whose existence, proximity, and restless activity have been a constant admonition to the ministers of the State Church to distinguish themselves by education, morality, and fidelity to their calling; and whilst completely abstaining from compulsory measures, to keep their congregations together by the bonds of charity, conviction, respect, and pastoral care.

The condition of all Germany may be likened to a mixed marriage between a Catholic and a Protestant; and the unhindered co-existence of these two great parties has been productive of great advantages to each. In like manner, a beneficial influence is to be expected when the chief parties in the Church see smaller Christian sects in unrestricted activity around them. For here again the fact is, that every party worthy of the appellation Christian owes its origin and existence, its power and influence, to some verity which until then had been repressed or not sufficiently recognised. It should be the object of Christian statesmen to recognise in the so-called sects such complementary truths as may serve to impress upon all the fulness of the Christian life and Christian doctrine. It is on this account worthy, and the interest, of a Christian Government to respect and recognise such communities.

CHAPTER XII.

THE POSITION OF A CHRISTIAN STATE TOWARDS THE PRETENSIONS OF THE PAPACY.

IN Germany, the tolerant and yet Christian State was firmly established. Between the two creeds there existed on the whole a peaceful competition. The battles which took place were for the most part fought out with spiritual weapons. Each party knew that in all essential points their rights were secured. The ecclesiastics on both sides exercised what influence they possessed upon public instruction; and, as regards matrimony, acted according to the principles which obtained in their denominations. Conflicts with the temporal authorities, such as the strife anent mixed marriages in 1837, were transitory episodes. Mutual toleration went so far that in many places the mutual use of one place of worship existed without disturbance. The most remarkable sign of this happy state of peace was the existence of Catholic theological professorships under a Protestant *régime* in the preponderatingly Protestant universities of Tübingen, Bonn, Breslau, and Giessen. These professorships, as also those filled in the same spirit in Munich, Wurzburg, Freiburg, Munster, and other places, advanced and cultivated Christian knowledge by the side of Protestant theological chairs; the noblest representatives of which theology may be said to have been such men as Möhler, Hirscher, Klee, Döllinger, and others. When in those happy days one happened to be thrown in contact with the representatives of Catholicism, they gave one comforting explanation of those appearances in the Roman Catholic Church of former times which gave the most offence. The claims of the Popes during the Middle Ages to a judicial power over kings and nations, and their allegation that the emperor was only a vassal of the Pope, that the Pope could depose kings and give away countries—all these, as we were told, rested upon no divine ordinance. It was a transitory extension of power, which princes and people pandered to. It was a departure from the true Christian principle. These claims have died out, and we need not expect that they will ever be revived. The whole of this abnormal development has passed into history. At the time of its occurrence, it produced some beneficial effects, too; but those days will not return. When the question was raised as to how the principle of persecution stood,—whether the present hierarchy had renounced it, whether it was really looked upon as wrong to have employed forcible and cruel measures against individuals of another creed, whom they wished to bring by such means into the Roman Church,—we were given the consoling answer that that was now all over; that better times had come; that those persecutions were the result of too much intermingling of the temporal and spiritual matters; that the separation of both was now an accomplished fact; that now civil rights were firmly established, and hence no relapse into such measures need be apprehended. There is only one assertion wanting, and that we have never heard that party make, viz. that such things were in themselves and in all ages detestable and wicked, and that such acts should be distinctly repudiated, detested, and repented of. We have known bold champions of liberty of conscience who have belonged to the Roman Catholic Church; as, for instance, Count Montalembert.

In Belgium and in England a school of such appeared to spring up, who were good Catholics, and at the same time advocates of freedom of worship.

Any one who lived through those times looks back upon them as upon a pleasant summer's day, and cannot help looking forward with deep anxiety at those dark clouds which have risen upon the horizon of the latest politico-ecclesiastical disturbances.

How did matters ever reach such a point? Those dangerous principles of the supremacy of the spiritual over the temporal power, of the right of the Church to award temporal punishments, and to call upon the temporality to punish heretics, have, it is true, been repudiated by all enlightened theologians in countries where parity of religion existed, but have never been officially denounced from the Papal chair, or formally declared to have been done away with. In no Concordat have the rights of Protestants to a celebration of their worship been formally recognised. On the contrary, we are frequently reminded, by suspicious assertions coming from Rome, that although at present it is not proposed to press for the practical carrying out of those principles, still the right was reserved, under a different combination of circumstances, to revert to them. It is true that well-instructed Catholics would not be bound by such assertions; for the ancient genuine system still existed in full power, by which in questions of faith and morals not the Papal chair, but a general council, had the power of deciding. It was known that the promise of the support of the Holy Spirit, who should lead them into all truth, was made to the apostolic college, and not to any individual bishop separate from the rest.

During the protracted pontificate of Pius ix., the horizon has become clouded over, and the whole aspect of affairs has changed. The official organ of the

Papacy, the *Civiltà Catholica*, has for the last twenty years been promulgating a totally different theological system, which contradicts the ancient genuine episcopal system, the principles of the Gallican Church, and the ideas of the greatest Roman Catholic writers of our century. The theology of the Jesuits became predominant in the highest places. In the year 1854 Pius IX. created a most dangerous precedent, when he alone, without his Council, proclaimed, as a truth necessary unto salvation to be believed, the dogma of the immaculate conception of the Virgin Mary. There followed, under Papal authority, the publication of the *Syllabus Errorum*, in which it is true that, on the one hand, many mighty and seasonable truths were published; but, on the other hand, the two principles were repudiated, either that Protestants had any claim to freedom of worship (Prop. 77, 78), or that the Church possessed no temporal power and had no right to employ force (Prop. 24). These are denounced as errors. But thereby we have two assertions, having enormous bearings, set up as truths: "No rights for Protestants; but, on the contrary, a right of the Roman Catholic Church to employ force." In these few words we have, as in an egg, that monster, persecution and religious war, which is the most wicked of all wars. Still, one might have left Pius IX. and his theologians to hold their own opinions, whilst comforting oneself with the reflection that the conscience of a Catholic Christian is only bound by the revealed truths contained in Holy Scripture and apostolic tradition, without reference to any other doctrines and opinions. According to the really Catholic system, the Pope is capable of error, and should in such cases be set to rights by the General Council. But the final step has been taken upon this fatal road. The Curia succeeded in procuring from the Council of the Vatican, on 18th

July 1870, the declaration of the dogma that the Pope was infallible in his official decisions, and that such decisions were of themselves unalterable, but not in consequence of the consent of the Church ("ejus modi definitiones ex sese non autem ex consensu Ecclesiæ irreformabiles esse").

This is not the place in which to relate how it came about that matters ever proceeded so far that the bishops, in countries where both confessions were on an equality, in which especially religion and theology flourished, were able to bring themselves to agree to this disastrous conclusion. No ecclesiastical theory of such wide bearings has ever been proclaimed. If the present Pope possesses infallibility, his 267 predecessors have also been infallible. In that case none of the claims, officially and solemnly made by them at any time, have grown out of date. Then we have still in force what Bonifacius VIII., at the summit of ecclesiastical pretension, taught the whole Church in his bull *Unum Sanctum*, issued from his throne, that the whole creation was made subject to the Pope, and that it was necessary unto salvation to believe this. The paragraphs of the *Syllabus* which Pius has proclaimed are no longer matters of private opinion. Any one who has accepted the Council of the Vatican as his guide, must accept all those statements, together with the consequences thereto attaching. The ancient foundations of faith are overthrown, since men have dared to raise the question of "new dogmas;" for a dogma—that is to say, a truth necessary unto salvation, and revealed by God—can only be that which has been proclaimed in the Christian Church from the beginning. Nothing new can ever be raised to the position of a dogma; and a real dogma cannot be anything new, but must be old and original. A new dogma is, to a properly taught Christian, about as incomprehensible an article as wooden iron or a round square.

If, then, this *Syllabus* is to be looked upon as the legal creed of the Roman Catholic Church,—if we are really to understand the twenty-third proposition as it stands, that the Popes never have exceeded their powers,—then it is easy to explain the excitement and resistance which has been called forth in both rulers and nations. People were impressed with the idea that in Rome a conspiracy was being concocted against all the civil authorities of the world. The tremendous danger was not concealed from our bishops. The Archbishop of Munich-Freising did well to send a document to Rome, begging that, in order to pacify the governments, an official explanation should be issued, declaring that the new decrees were not intended to renew and confirm the Papal supremacy in worldly matters. How easy would it have been for Pius IX., and how beneficial to the whole Christian world would it have been, to issue such an explanation! The threatening storm might yet have been thereby set at rest; but the explanation was never vouchsafed.

Hence it comes that the new Papal decrees have created a new position for the civil powers. In such countries as the United States of America and Great Britain, where the Roman Catholic Church exists only as a private society, the promulgation of the new dogma may be regarded as innocuous, because those to whom it was addressed lacked both power and opportunity to carry it out. It may be, too, that in Roman Catholic States these principles have not at once openly asserted their destructive effect. Where a Concordat exists, they may be allowed to rest for a time; but in States where the two creeds are on a par, where the Roman Catholic and Protestant Churches both have the privileges of State Churches, and have mutually to co-exist, the situation is a very different one. There we cannot be surprised to find that friendship has cooled down, mutual confidence has disappeared, and that the strife concerning the legitimate bounds of both parties is carried on on the common domain.

In that the civil power in Germany conceived itself to be challenged by the Papal claims, and felt insulted by the non-recognition of its ambassador, it proceeded at once to issue such laws as seemed called for. Without any consultation with the opponent, it was considered expedient to concert protective measures, not as a matter of mutual agreement, but in accordance with one-sided conclusions. The civil power considered it wise and just to confirm these measures, with the concert of a parliament in which the Roman Catholics formed a minority. Throughout the whole territorial possessions the sphere of action of the ministry should be as much restricted as possible, and a mighty counterpoise of worldly influence should be set up. It is true that the principle is still supposed to be in force, that the interior economy of the Church is to be managed by the Church, and that external matters are to be arranged by the State. No interference with religious matters is said to be intended. But seeing that the question at once arises, "What are interior and what external matters?" the sole decision has been relegated to the temporal power. Each of the two belligerents has stretched out its arm to the uttermost, in order to command as much of the battle-field as possible.

Hence we have, in reply to the claims raised in Rome, a set of laws issued, which the bishops, who are faithful to their instructions received from Rome, refuse to recognise. The ministers are obliged to undergo a course of study at the universities, and to submit to a State examination. The temporal power is to be informed of their appointment, in order to exercise a power of veto. The national schools are placed under lay inspectors. Civil officials are to register births and marriages; baptism and marriage by the Church are matters of option, and the State no longer requires any certificates of baptism or matrimony.

Each of these new measures calls for particular consideration.

As regards the appointment of the clergy, such a co-operation of the civil authorities as is required at present in Prussia exists, in many States where the two creeds are on a par, and especially where the Government is Protestant, as a recognised right. Therefore it is scarcely possible for the bishops to define this as anything *per se* opposed to divine law or divine order; on the contrary, if a Christian Commonwealth be once established, such a co-operation may be deduced from the principles of the primitive Church. Certainly not from that idea of a temporal power before which everything must bow, but from the principles upon which the rights of a Christian community are based; for, according to the usages of the primitive Church, the people too, or laymen, had a right, before the ordination or appointment of a minister, to express their wishes or raise objections—in fact, to have a voice in the matter. In a State where both creeds are on a par, the civil authority is regarded by both as a member of the Christian Church, bound to represent the laity, and to speak up for them when required. If, therefore, the civil power demands that she shall be made acquainted with all the ministers who are to be appointed to public positions, in order that she may have the right to object, there is nothing in such a demand that exceeds her legitimate rights. If, then, it be not the matter, but the manner of introducing this claim which is objected to, the solemn assertion of it may well be justified. But it is difficult to comprehend how men will be able to justify their endeavours to embitter the strife by actual resistance and non-compliance, thereby endangering the entire spiritual good of whole dioceses. It is incomprehensible why, upon this very point, which has led to the arrest of several bishops, no peaceful instructions have been issued from Rome.

The demand that the ministry ought to enjoy the benefits of a university education, and exhibit the same in their after lives, is based upon commendable motives. Unfortunately, the bishops in Germany have for one generation done all in their power to withdraw young clerics from the universities, and to isolate their entire education. They have done what they could to bring about the complete vacation of theological professorships in these institutions, which actually represented the existing peaceful coalition of Church and State; they wanted to have, in their lower and upper seminaries, the entire control of the education and instruction of ministers. We are afraid that they did not keep before them a proper regard for the welfare of the Church; they did not consider what would be the mournful results of producing a ministry utterly estranged to the general tone of the nation, narrow-minded in its ideas, and not in harmony with, incapable of assisting, and without influence over, the educated portion of the nation, which has passed through the public schools.

The advantage of the Reformation, irrespective of any shortcomings which attached to it, consisted in the fact that an attempt was made to combine Christian piety with true education; and to a great extent, if not perfectly, the attempt succeeded. The most striking example of this union of piety and mental education that we know of was Melancthon. The conflict between the traditions of the Church, which were mixed up with so much superstition, and the newly sprung up classical education, had assumed a very decided tone in Italy, and threatened Christianity with the greatest spiritual dangers. This evil was opposed by the Reformation of Luther with mighty results; and at present, again, just such a disturbance is going on now throughout the world. Modern science, like the elegant Epicurism of the Italians during the fifteenth century, is devoid of, and alien to, Christianity. But we must not incontinently reject all that is true and justifiable in scientific, æsthetic, and political developments, or keep such things from the knowledge of ministers and people; we ought rather to digest them, and, by true education, combat false knowledge. It is not sufficient to keep the people in ignorance, and the clergy, by the entire bent of their education, in narrow-mindedness—an endeavour which at best cannot be for ever successful, and which, in consequence, paves the way for a still greater apostasy from Christianity. That which the best of our contemporaries justly long for is a lively and real unity of religion and scientific advancement. To realize this is a portion of the duty of the clergy, and especially of the clergy in Germany.

Seeing that the community—nay, more, every educated Christian—has a right to expect from the spiritual guides, in whom we and our children are to confide, at least an approach to the fulfilment of this task, unquestionably Christian authorities have a right to demand that nothing shall be left undone which may conduce to educating the clergy who are to occupy public positions, recognised by the State, into such men. The requirement that Roman Catholic ministers as well as Protestant shall have undergone a course of university education is *per se*, and so far as it goes, justifiable. It is so much to the interest of the Roman Catholic Church that it should be so, that it is difficult to understand whence comes the opposition. One would think the opportunity of acquiring such an education would be regarded as a benefit. It is only to be regretted that the requisition has been made too late, and that it was not in force during the whole of the past generation. We should be in a different position now; the Roman Catholic ministry would not have lost so much of their influence and respect, if the young theologians had not been, as was the case, withdrawn from the professorial chairs—if, instead of having ministers who have been educated in Rome, or within the narrow limits of the ecclesiastical seminaries, we had pupils of Sailer, Möhler, Hirscher, or Leopold Schmid, we should probably have avoided much of the present ecclesiastical confusion. Certainly the desire of the bishops to have their students under the protection of an earnestly Christian discipline is highly commendable; but such discipline can, and should, go hand in hand with a university education.

The national schools belong to the State, but at the same time they belong to the Church. This principle is open to many modes of arrangement, without in any way causing the Christian character of the schools to suffer. When both powers act in harmony, it is almost immaterial whether the oversight of the school is committed to an official of the temporal or of the spiritual estate; still less does it matter whether the school-inspector is a layman or a priest, if he only possesses the personal qualifications required for his office. Even the complete separation of the school from the Church—so that religious instruction is given by the ministers of the different denominations, just as other subjects are taught by the appointed masters —can take place without evil results, if a Christian people and religious activity, Christian families and faithful ministers, have to be dealt with. Such is the experience of the Old Catholics in Holland, where the above separation exists.

But who can shut his eyes to the danger with which the cessation of ecclesiastical school inspection is fraught amongst us? It is true, that in the towns it would still be possible to find laymen fitted for the office of school inspectors; but in the country the pastor is the natural school inspector, and, as a rule, the only man competent to fulfil the office. What security can the superintendent of schools have, seeing that he only inspects village schools once a year, that the master is not immoral, a drunkard, and cruel? The pastor of the place, if only he be to a certain extent faithful to his duty, becomes acquainted with the shortcomings of the master, and has the means at his command of counteracting them. This relationship is now at an end. If the separation of the school from the Church is really insisted upon, the pastor, if he does enter the school at all, will now come and go like the gymnastic or singing master. He will no longer be the one person by whom every one, pupils as well as teachers, is to be taught what is Christian truth and what is Christian conversation.

The position of our schoolmasters is, as it is, inclined to lead a man, especially if his scientific acquirements are not great, to form too high an idea of his own profession and capacity. Greater independence, and release from all ecclesiastical oversight, can only tend to increase the temptation. Besides which, the Protestant communal life in Germany is so weak, and the Christian family life so imperfect, that if the Christian element be eliminated from the public national schools, there is but little prospect of its being replaced by those powers. It is to be hoped that we may not ere long have to experience, even more than at present, how true the cutting speech of the old Duke of Wellington was when he said, "Instruction without religion makes only clever devils." Switzerland, whose development in many points has outrun ours, shows us, in those cantons where the school has been emancipated from the Church and the schoolmaster from ecclesiastical oversight, the bitter results which, in a time like the present, cannot be avoided in any such arrangement.

In concluding a contract of marriage, to keep the civil and ecclesiastical ceremonies apart is in itself not antichristian. We cannot agree with those who see something profane and derogatory in civil marriage, as laid down in the Napoleonic code. Where this arrangement exists, the Christian should not only bear and comply with it, but heartily respect it also. But the practical question which arises in Germany is totally different. Ought we to divide that which by habit and law has come to be looked upon by the majority, from time immemorial, as one act? Any change in such matters is accompanied by disintegration. Our country-people in particular are extraordinarily tenacious of ancient customs, and feel injured and molested by any innovations. It is this very feeling upon which is based the maintenance of so many traditions amongst the peasant class. Take away these ideas, and that class will rapidly degenerate into barbarism and brutality.

With the separation of the civil and ecclesiastical acts in a marriage contract, the latter is naturally left to the option of the parties concerned. Now men may say what they please, the common man understands or misunderstands—the result in both cases is the same—this optional treatment to be an invitation and challenge, on the part of the authorities, to him to set aside the ecclesiastical act as something quite superfluous, and by a contemptuous disregard for it to break away together from the Church and Christian customs. We observe in our antichristian literature an endeavour to bring about an exclusion of all reference to divine interference in the national as well as in the individual career. If it be intended to cause such tendencies to permeate into those strata of society which do not read newspapers and antichristian literature, and who still with a certain *naïveté* cling to Christian customs and convictions, then the means employed are the best that could be devised. It would be difficult to find any other measure which would go so deep. There are many who will not let it be said to them in vain, "You may commence your married life without God, without prayer, and without benediction." The impression created will be all the worse, because the invitation comes from a direction which, notwithstanding all the lawlessness which exists, is still looked upon by the people as the highest authority—namely, the temporal government.

If the civil marriage contract is introduced, another threatening prospect is opened up to us. The civil and ecclesiastical marriage laws will diverge, and by this change the former will not be improved, but, on the contrary, will deteriorate. Pseudo-humanity will diminish the number of impediments now opposing certain unions, and divorce and re-marriage will be facilitated. The divine word teaches us to look upon marriages between uncle and niece, nephew and aunt, as unholy, being incestuous; Christ says, "Whosoever shall marry her that is divorced, committeth adultery." Such unions, legalized, confirmed, and commended by the State, will become more numerous; and public morals, proper feeling, and the public conscience will thereby become more and more blunted.

It is the greatest reproach men have hitherto been able to bring against German Protestantism, that it has undermined the sanctity of matrimony, and that Protestant ministers constantly consecrate in Christ's name those unions which He forbids. In Protestant marriage ceremonies the formula is repeated, "Death alone shall part you." After a time the parties can obtain a divorce, and coming again, require and obtain the benediction of another, therefore adulterous, union, when the pastor will again declare, "What God hath joined together, let no man put asunder." If the introduction of the civil marriage does produce any good, it will be that Protestant ministers can no longer be compelled to solemnize such marriages, and they will have a good opportunity of thinking over the command of Christ, of weighing their responsibility before God, of striving to set up truly Christian marriage laws, and of putting an end, in this matter at least, to the desecration of the sanctuary and the misuse of the divine name.

We find ourselves in the unwonted position, that Roman Catholic ministers and ecclesiastics appeal to the sacred right of freedom of conscience against the latest ecclesiastico-political laws. It is they who appeal to the words of Saints Peter and John, who, in reply to the prohibition of the Sanhedrim that they should not preach the gospel, said, "We must obey God rather than men." As a matter of fact, the present ruling tendencies do threaten liberty of conscience. It is true that such is not the intention of our leading statesmen, but, upon the course which they now pursue, they will find that to be the result. Men propose to solve, with the power that is resorted to in war, the spiritual problem of how the temporal and spiritual powers are to comport themselves to each other. The clergy will not depart from the instructions which they receive from their bishops and from Rome; then they are deposed and exiled. Others are called in to fill their places, and for the communities there remains none but the cruel alternative either of turning their backs upon the sacraments, or of receiving them from the hands of men whom they cannot for conscience' sake regard as legitimate ministers of Christ. We hear already, in parliamentary speeches and elsewhere, a tone assumed, in which we can detect disregard for, and contempt of, conscience.

Where it becomes a question of the moral law and of the recognition of eternal truths, we must all take our stand and follow the teachings of an enlightened conscience, even if it cost us our lives. The battle of truth and progress to better things must from time to time be fought out in this manner. Without the principle, "We must obey God rather than men," there can be no martyrdom and no truly religious life; every hope of a better future state depends upon the existence of such a feeling.

Only those who dare to obey God rather than men have a fulcrum which is beyond the reach of this world; they alone are in a position to overcome the world, and to preserve mankind from sinking into a moral "Slough of Despond." But in our public assemblies we hear every appeal to such a principle termed presumption, hypocrisy, and rebellion, and cried down. Those who make such speeches, and impute to us high treason whenever we oppose any act, and at the same time appeal to our consciences, would seem to assert that they have no conscience. Those who take offence when we speak of a duty towards God and Christ which takes precedence of all other duties, are open to suspicion that they themselves believe in no other God than the temporal power of the moment; and their speech calls to mind in a solemn manner the cry of the Jews, who, when Pilate set before them Christ as their King, exclaimed, "We have no king but Cæsar!"

But still, in all justice, we must not silently pass over the fact that the Roman Catholic party certainly do on occasion employ that ancient and sacred principle inappropriately. It may only be applied to a case in which a divine command, or a divine commission, is called in question. The case is different with ecclesiastical arrangements which have been set up by men, ecclesiastical prohibitions which may be altered or to which exceptions may be made, or ecclesiastical privileges and exemptions which are not based upon God's word. The canon law consists, for the most part, of human devices. Now herein lies the misfortune, that, in consequence of the latest tendencies of the Roman Church, the utterances of the Pope are to be clothed with divine authority, seeing that he claims to be in all ecclesiastical matters infallible, hence the sole judge. To make all Papal instructions without exception count as divine commands, leads to a misuse of the divine name. In order to give men's commands more weight, the divine commands are detracted from, and, by an injudicious appeal to the conscience, the sacred right of liberty of conscience is made an object of doubt and suspicion.

Far be it from us to employ the usual reproaches regarding the obstinacy of ecclesiastics. Even an erring conscience should be respected and spared. We may regret that any one should allow his conscience to be swayed by unfounded ideas, and thereby injure himself. But we may not despise him; on the contrary, if he were to do violence to his conscience for the sake of temporal advantages, he would become unworthy of our respect. Any act which a man does in opposition to his religious convictions, and to his own conception of the divine commands, is a sin; for he thereby runs the risk of insulting God. Such acts destroy the character of a man; for it is to be anticipated that, in cases where it really becomes a question of the divine commands, he will disregard the precepts of God and his own conscience.

Tyranny over the conscience is by no means an element in a Christian Commonwealth; on the contrary, respect for the conscientious opinions of its subjects is one characteristic of a Christian government.

Such is the disastrous movement to which Pius IX. gave the first impulse. His object was something other than the Christian State; he wished to produce the Papal State. Whilst, however, he fails in setting that up, he is doing his best to overthrow the Christian State. For whither must the conflict in which our Government and our bishops are at present engaged lead? The situation is becoming unbearable, the injury inflicted upon the Christian portion of the nation incalculable. Both parties are equally obstinate. If matters continue as they now are, it must end in a complete disruption of Church and State. This is what will eventually be the result of the Papal claims. That which the opponents of a Christian State and legislation desire—namely, that all confession of Christ shall disappear from public affairs, and that religion shall be made a purely private matter, which is what enlightened statesmen do their best to prevent, as being mischievous—is being hurried on by the irreconcilability of the claims on both sides. It is like an unhappy marriage, where, in lieu of living together in constant quarrels and annoyance, a separation *a mensa et thoro* is looked upon as the lesser evil. But those who suffer most from such a separation are the children; just so will it be when it comes to a separation between Church and State, the rising generation will be most severely affected by it. Both authorities should support and exalt one another. By their united influence, justice, morality, the fear of God, and every other good feeling, should take firm hold of the national feelings and character; but we are now reaching that terrible condition when the two authorities countermine each other, and thereby destroy where they ought to edify. It is as though the enemy of all that is good had crept in, and used his influence to urge on against one another the two powers which God has ordained for the welfare of mankind, in order to make each destructive of the other.

By his decree, Pius IX. has shaken the fabric of the whole Church. The mistakes that were made at Rome during the sitting of the Council could not remain hidden from the world. Leibnitz, in the seventeenth century, said that every mistake made by the Church would be laid hold of by atheism as an argument in its own favour; and this has been the case. Owing to the proceedings in Rome, all ecclesiastical authority has received a blow. Amongst educated men in Catholic countries, unbelief is making huge strides. Public opinion is daily losing its respect for the servants of Christ. Pius IX. has—and this is admitted even by the Protestant party—damaged Christianity in every country.

A bad look-out! A real contract of peace between imperial and sacerdotal power is hardly possible, in consequence of the Vatican Decrees; for they call the rights of the temporal power in question, and are incompatible with the entire legislation of Germany. An armistice would still be possible; for experience has shown that the hierarchy knows how to pause in carrying out the principles involved, and has, under certain circumstances, shown itself to be very pliable.

But even for an armistice such as we hope for, it is a necessary preliminary that passion be put on one side, and that a disposition be shown to listen to the wishes and proposals of the other party. We cannot decide on which side, at the present juncture, the disinclination to come to an understanding is greater or less. But if on the one hand we have Christian bishops, and on the other Christian statesmen, neither should wait obstinately for their opponents to advance, but should themselves make advances with a view to mutual explanation, thereby practically showing forth their Christian character, and their care for the welfare of the Christian nation committed to them, which really ought to be the common object each is striving for.

Abraham and Lot allowed their herds to pasture upon ground common to both; and there was a strife between the herdmen of Abram's cattle and the herdmen of Lot's cattle. Now, if both had insisted upon their entire rights and nothing less, and if possible seized possession of the whole country, peace could never have been established. But Abraham did not act thus. He could not bear a state of war. He set an example, which should be followed by Christians under similar circumstances, in that he said to his brother's son: "Let there be no strife, I pray thee, between me and thee, and between my herdmen and thy herdmen; for we be brethren."

CHAPTER XIII.

THE DUTY OF A CHRISTIAN COMMONWEALTH WITH REGARD TO THE WORKING CLASSES.

For a Christian State there exists a duty which the heathen State never attempted to perform, which it did not even recognise—namely, to afford protection and assistance to such as have no possessions, or who have fallen into poverty. This serves as an excellent touchstone, whereby to test how far a Christian State has become a reality amongst us.

In the law under the Old Testament, this duty was kept in view. The law contains a number of humane ordinances, which cannot be found elsewhere in ancient legislation. On the original parcelling out of the land, every family was granted a freehold. If any one, owing to circumstances, was obliged to part with his freehold, he could not sell it out and out, but retained a right to redeem it. If a Hebrew was compelled by want to sell himself as a slave, he regained his freedom at the commencement of the seventh year. In the year of Jubilee, at the end of seven weeks of years, in the fiftieth year, every man returned to his possession, and thereby the poverty from which he had in the meantime suffered was removed. It is true that this remarkable provision of the year of Jubilee never came into operation, according to the Talmud; but it shows what the intention of the Almighty Lawgiver was, and what should be the object of a Christian nation: to guard against the formation of an impecunious class.[1]

Rome, that Paris of the ancient world, is the spot where a class of villeins similar to those of our day was first formed, after the fall of the Republic and the decay of ancient laws and virtues. During the time of the emperors there spread all over Italy this social evil of a sharp line between wealth and poverty. There were manors upon which one rich proprietor ruled over 10,000 slaves.

In the Christian States of the Middle Ages, it is true that a heavy load of bondage and dependence weighed upon the lower classes; but still there was no misery amongst the masses, and there was no impecunious and helpless excess of population growing up. Slavery was hard to be borne, but it possessed some alleviating features amidst its debasing ones, seeing that it was to the interest of the owner to maintain and protect his property. As Bensen shows in his *History of the Proletarians*, the peasants, the manufacturers, and the bondsmen of the Middle Ages were not real villeins. As yet money payments were not prevalent, and the natural exchange, that is to say, the payment of wages in kind, served to prevent the direst misery. It was towards the end of the Middle Ages, owing to the abuses and avarice of the higher classes, that the condition of the peasantry in Germany became unbearable, leading to the risings of the lower classes since 1493. They were put down then; but it was only long after, and by slow degrees, that the complaints of the peasantry were attended to and their burdens removed.

The modern villein class first arose in Paris, which had already, during the Middle Ages, had its revolutions of the beggars, and in the large commercial

---

[1] Or, as they were termed in Norman English, "villeins."—*Translator*.

towns in the south of France. Next to France, England became the place where industry on a large scale was carried on, where the agglomeration and power of capital was first felt, and a class of labourers produced, who, having no possessions, live from hand to mouth, but may be numbered by millions.

It is well known how it came to pass that this mighty evil has spread itself all over Europe. Free trade, the discovery and perfection of machinery, the enormous intercourse of nations, the increasing excess of population, the indifference of governments and legislators, want of Christian feeling in the upper classes, —all these agencies have co-operated in this matter.

It was in vain that Bacon, in his *Essay on Seditions and Troubles*, warned his readers that the agglomeration of capital in the hands of the few, and the simultaneous increase of poverty, must bring about insurrections, and that it was the duty of the Government to prevent such evils by wise laws. At present the danger of a social revolution surrounds us like a rising flood, which threatens society with destruction. In a Christian State matters ought never to have come to such a pass. But as the case stands, we are liable to the same reproach as our ancestors, that one of the highest duties of a Christian people and a Christian government has been neglected. Here we have a common sin, which all we who belong to the middle or upper classes have a share in. Respectability, comfort, and wealth are all, if not exclusively, at least for the greater part, the result of accumulating the products of labour. Others have worked for us, and have received too little reward for so doing, whereby we enjoy the fruits of their labours. Our hands are not clean. All our possessions are sullied by something, which causes them to be open to the biblical term applied to earthly possessions, "Mammon of unrighteousness." At present, care for the working classes and the solution of the so-called social question is of more importance than all political quarrels. In comparison with it, all talk about forms of constitution is mere chatter. Herein lies the great task for our statesmen and legislators; and, so long as it is not set about in an earnest manner, we have no right to talk of a Christian State, or to speak of our much vaunted jurisprudence as a reality.

Upon the soil of such an unwholesome condition of society as described above, there sprang up, first of all in France, the curious, wide-spreading trees of Socialism and Communism. They assume, in respect to political economy and jurisprudence, the same attitude as heresies do to the Church. They must be tested, disproved, and disallowed; nevertheless, every heresy serves the purpose of bringing to mind some truth, either at the time neglected in the Church, or else half forgotten by her; and it is her duty not to disregard this truth or to smother it, but to bring it prominently forward, and to put it in its right light. Thus, too, it is part of the chief duties of science in our day not merely to reject Socialism, but, whilst combating it, to bring to light the truths and neglected duties which it contains and of which it reminds us. A just appreciation of social heresies, a diligent search for the cause of their origin and their development, and a careful discrimination between what is right and wrong in Socialism, what is wholesome and what to be rejected in it, is one of the most necessary intellectual labours of our time. Towards the solution of this problem two authors of our nation have contributed much—Lorenz Stein, in his *History of the Social Movement in France*, 1850; and Frederick Schäffle, in his work upon *Capital and Socialism*, 1870. It makes us ashamed to feel that a nation which possesses so much that is excellent in its literature on the subject should have lagged so far behind as regards any practical action towards the solution of the difficulty.

With these two authors we so far agree that it is not sufficient simply to condemn Socialism, but that, in order to guard against social revolutions, we must pave the way for social reforms, for the furtherance of which all the component parts of the State are called upon to co-operate and assist.

Socialism has arisen from the sufferings entailed by modern society. "An enormous mass of misery forms the basis of our much lauded civilisation;"—thus speaks one of the noblest of Socialist writers, Winkelblech. "By means of researches carried on during many years, and conducted with scrupulous conscientiousness, I found the extent of suffering to be great beyond expectation. Everywhere I was confronted by poverty, amongst those who undertake work, as well as amongst the workers; amongst those of the people who stand highest in intellectual culture, as well as those on the lowest step of the ladder; in the foci of luxury, such as large capitals and commercial towns, as well as in the cottages of villagers; in the fertile plains of Belgium and Lombardy, as well as in the sterile, mountainous districts of Scandinavia. I found that the cause of it did not lie in nature, but in our own institutions, which are based upon principles of false economy."

Who can refuse to see that Count St. Simon and Charles Fourier were actuated by the most humane motives, and that during a whole lifetime they made the greatest sacrifices in order to bring about a cure of those evils? As to the serious errors in which they were at the same time entangled, they shared in common with the whole revolutionary age during which they lived. They were governed by mistaken views with reference to liberty, equality, and the rights of man; but they differed from the victorious political parties of their time, in that they deduced with greater boldness and more acutely consistent train of thought the final results of such ideas. They, too, were infected with the insane idea that in social matters man was capable of raising an edifice upon new foundations, of effecting a new creation.

Yet we must not forget that such desperate efforts were caused by the unfathomable corruption existing in the ancient state of affairs. The kernel of all Socialism and Communism, the actual heresy in it, is the denial of all rights of property—as Proudhon said, "La propriété c'est le vol." Yet this perverted statement would probably never have occurred to any one, had not at present a perverted idea of the rights of property existed in society. It is an idea which may with justice be termed atheistical. The proprietor looks upon himself as a sovereign, who can do as he pleases with his own. In the Mosaic law, it was laid down as a fundamental principle that the land of Canaan belonged to Jehovah. It was committed to the landlords as a loan from God. Just so the Christian who is in possession of this world's goods should not look upon himself as a sovereign, but rather as a steward, who is bound to employ these goods agreeably to the will and according to the directions of the original owner, who is God; and to recollect that, at the end of his earthly career, he will have to give an account of his dealings to the supreme Judge. But the intention of God in entrusting temporal riches to men is that which is described by Paul when he says to Timothy, "Charge them that are rich in this world that they be not high minded, . . . that they do good, that they be rich in good works, ready to distribute, willing to communicate." When the well-to-do have forgotten their responsibility and neglected their duties, when they take their stand upon the rights of property like a wild beast with his prey between his claws, gnashing upon every one else with rage for fear they might want to have a portion, this does not justify the heresy of Socialism, but it goes far to account for it.

It is true that, according to the divine commands, the property of our neighbour is inviolable, and this may be expressed in the words, "Property is sacred." But they are the grossest hypocrites who are always crying out about the sacredness of property, and will not hear of anything else being sacred. First of all, they assist in overthrowing every other sacred thing; and then, when their pockets are touched, those are suddenly to become inviolable. The rights of property are sacred, but so also is poverty—that is to say, those who suffer want have a sacred right to the pity and material assistance of the possessors of property.

It is quite true that God has said, "Thou shalt not steal"—nay, more, "Thou shalt not covet thy neighbour's house, nor anything that is his;" but He also has said, "Thou shalt not oppress the poor and needy, neither shalt thou keep back his hire, lest he cry against thee unto the Lord, and it be sin unto thee."

Christianity sanctions no injury to property, whether caused by the violence of an individual or by the legislature at large. If the property of one individual is attacked, the property of all is in danger. For this very reason, it becomes impossible to guard against every abuse and hardness of heart by laws or authoritative commands. The State, whether it be a monarchy or democracy, will never be able to do this; hence arises the necessity for another compensating power, and such an one exists. It consists in the moral responsibility of the well-to-do classes to be charitable and benevolent; it is the appeal to men's consciences; it is the proclamation of the moral law, of the divine promises and threatenings, to all who are endowed with power, influence, or this world's goods, which has been committed to the servants of Christ.

If we examine Fourier's system closely, we cannot fail to be astonished at the complete ignorance and disregard of one of the chief elements. Christian faith, with the internal peace which it brings with it, is surely of considerable importance when treating of the happiness of the individual or of the nation. Upon this point, or regarding any substitute for it, Fourier does not say a word.

Socialism, combined with estrangement from God, produces in the masses the most fearful results that we have been permitted to feel the effects of in modern times. It calls forth the most mighty and at the same time the most dangerous passions. Proud self-sufficiency, intense hatred towards the better-to-do and more fortunate classes, inextinguishable hatred to all authority which obstructs the realization of Socialistic ideas, are looked upon by the uneducated, social-democratic mass as virtues, and welcomed by the leaders as levers for the execution of the catastrophe. If the great political desires of a nation are accomplished, the whole of the revolutionary fire concentrates itself as it were upon this one point, the social question, and burns away the more fiercely. When the third French Republic in 1871 went over into the reign of terror of the Commune, we had set before us a beacon, revealing to us what we have to expect from social democracy.

As compared with Socialism in France, that in England seems temperate and considerate. The powerful unions of workmen in England do not strive for that which is impossible and unreasonable, not for the abolition of property and dissolution of family ties. They do not expect, by means of violent revolution, but by legitimate means, to attain to everything that can be desired for the improvement and happiness of the working classes. The practical sense, the political education, the clearness of ideas, respect for the law, and the opportune introduction of wholesome legal measures, the relatively healthy general political condition of the community, all serve to account for this gratifying fact. It was there that the right of combination amongst working men was first fully recognised; there, too, tribunals for arbitration already exist which have done much to decide in cases of dispute between employers and workpeople.

We, on the contrary, in Germany, appear to be drifting towards the same goal as France. The same part which French infidelity played in European literature, appears, we regret to say, to have been taken up in our days by German infidelity; and it shows itself in Socialist periodicals, such as the *Volksstaat* (People's State), in its worst, corrosive, poisonous form. Whereas the social revolution is knocking at our doors, we have hardly taken the most preliminary steps for setting our house in defensive array by wise and humane arrangements. On the contrary, as if to accelerate the process of destruction, we have cancelled the laws against usury, and abolished the hours for closing places of refreshment, that last legal restraint upon intemperance.

We constantly hear it asserted that, "There is no such thing as a social question; there is no difficult problem waiting solution; there is no danger!" Incomprehensible blunders, so to say, whilst the horizon is banked with the lowering clouds of the portending storm! Many are still impressed with the foolish idea that freedom of intercourse would of itself get rid of the evils, and at last bring about a peaceful ordering of society. What marvellous inconsistency to expect assistance from free competition, that is to say, from the very principle which has conduced most to plunge us so deeply into our misfortunes.

Others, who see the storm brewing, content themselves with observing that a resolute government, with the military at their disposal, would always be powerful enough to crush any insurrection of villeins, as was the case in Paris during June 1848 and in May 1871.

We may certainly expect that the arrangements which Socialism proposes will only endure for a short time. The natural order of things in society, which is opposed to it, will soon take effect again. The crisis will pass away, like the Peasant War of 1525; but it will be worse than that was, and worse for both parties. Those who hug themselves with the idea of the military power shooting down Socialism, and disposing of it with bayonet thrusts, forget what is implied by a day of terror setting in, when the Almighty takes away the courage of kings and looses the girdle of the mighty ones. When those in authority are once overcome with the feeling that God is fighting against them, even the military force upon which they relied becomes powerless in their hands. Only a monster can thoughtlessly and foolishly omit to take such measures as might still be capable of partially warding off so great a misfortune. If charity does not impel us to do so, common sense and the instinct of self-preservation ought to. Social revolution is like the Sibyl, who came three times to King Tarquinius, and each time with increasing and more difficult requisitions. Who knows but what it may be the last hour for Germany in which it is still possible to bring about an understanding, by mutual concessions, and thereby to divert the flood into a regular channel? Or is it really to be, as we have occasionally had examples in history, that only a few individuals will recognise the danger and the duties arising therefrom; but that entire classes, impelled by selfishness, refuse to listen to words of wisdom, and, rather than make the necessary sacrifices, will assist in bringing about their own destruction?

Let the teachers of political economy measure their strength with this great question of social reform; here we have only space to touch upon the ethic points which arise in considering the notion of a Christian commonwealth. We have to do with moral principles. And we may mention the following as duties which ought to be fulfilled in a Christian community:—To support and encourage working men's associations; to promulgate penal laws against manufacturers, and other employers of labour, who are guilty of an inhuman penuriousness towards their workpeople; to pave the way for an international factory law, by which similar usages may be introduced into all European countries; to prohibit unconditionally Sunday labour; for the temporal powers, the ecclesiastics, and free societies, to co-operate towards the carrying out of an intelligent system of relief for the poor.

Protection and encouragement for the associations of working men has become a duty which can no longer be neglected, now that the ancient guilds have disappeared. The individual is helpless against capital and the large factories. The association of many working men into a company for the formation of and for carrying on business on their own account, and with a fair share of the profits, is the most obvious, natural, and expedient means of help. The co-operative movement in England has already begun to bear much rich fruit there, prompted as it has been by noble men of the higher classes, as for instance Maurice the divine, and Ludlow the lawyer. The system proposed by Schulze-Delitzsch is similar, but it wants that beneficent element of Christian principle which those men were able, in England, to combine with the movement. But it is in very few cases possible for the working men to bring together the necessary capital at the commencement. Here it is that the duty of which we speak steps in. Not, as Lasalle asserts, a duty of the State to make a present to the working classes of fifteen millions of pounds, by an Act of the legislature, thereby robbing the other classes of so important a portion of their property; but it is a moral duty, incumbent on all who are possessed of means, to offer their capital at a moderate rate of interest for such purposes, and, by a generous disregard of a portion of their income, to do a permanent benefit to the impecunious classes and the whole social system. Victor Amadeus Huber, that noble friend of humanity, has incessantly urged upon us this duty, and fulfilled the same so far as it lay within his means. The same duty which is incumbent on the individual possessor of capital, is also incumbent upon our civic magistrates and large landowners, to further such undertakings. Whoever has an opportunity of furthering this work, either with material or mental assistance, let him lay to heart the saying which Huber selected as a motto for one of his publications: "Therefore, to him that knoweth to do good and doeth it not, to him it is sin."

Another duty lies completely within the province of our legislature — that is, to establish severe laws against the grinding of workpeople by the factory owners. Our Trade Regulations of 1872 contain some good provisions, but the punishments laid down for the infringement of the same are much too slight. And how about their being put into execution? Children of twelve and thirteen years of age are to be employed, at most, for six hours in any factory. But what happens? Parents, impelled by poverty and blunted in their consciences, agree that their children even at that age shall work for twelve hours, and no measures are taken to put a stop to it. That is what we suffer from in Germany, that laws are being constantly passed without any real intention of enforcing them. Happy England! where the laws for the protection of the working man are energetically put in force. There the factory inspectors, appointed by Government, occasionally walk suddenly into the workrooms, five minutes after the appointed time for leaving off work. If they find workpeople still employed, the employer is so severely punished that he has no desire to expose himself to such a thing again by any more infringements of the law. A short time ago, the English newspapers reported a case where a milliner had allowed her sempstresses to work until midnight. The excuse was that a bridal outfit had to be completed by a certain day, but it availed her nothing. She was punished all the same. In Germany, cases occur which cry aloud to heaven, and no punishment is inflicted upon the transgressors. In lucifer match manufactories, when the necessary provision and care is not taken, there occur cases of that most fearful of all diseases, phosphoric necrosis of the jawbone, in which the life of the patient can only be saved by the excision and complete removal of the lower jaw. When accidents occur through machinery, at the inquiry it is too often admitted as an excuse that the workman contributed thereto by his own negligence. An anonymous surgeon, in the *Allgemeine Zeitung* (General Newspaper), has described all these matters from his own experience, and with the pathos of a truly humane heart, in an article suggesting the necessity of a State medical department; but where do we see any sign of help being afforded?

What is the real reason that in Germany we have no efficient factory laws, and that at the same time such good laws as do exist are not put in force? If we put the question to such men as are in high places, the final excuse to which they have resort is, the impossibility of competing with neighbouring countries. It is said, if the hours of labour were to be further restricted by law than they already are, if the overworking of women and children were completely abolished, and the law of rest on Sunday were to be strictly enforced, our native industry could not compete with the factories of neighbouring countries where such stringent regulations do not exist. Then, again, the injury of our manufactories would react to the disadvantage of our working classes. These, then, are the true reasons why no Continental State of Europe will be the first to make a commencement. The question is somewhat similar to that of diminishing the standing armies, which no individual government will undertake to do, unless all the others do the same.

What is to be deduced from all this? Certainly not that the requirements of humanity, wisdom, and justice should remain unfulfilled. It is shown to be the duty of each of the European powers to strive after the setting up of an international, harmonious, general law, which must come into force everywhere at the same time. This idea is not a new one. About twenty-four years ago, Daniel Legrand, a manufacturer of Steinthal in Alsace, a pupil of Oberlin, undertook a journey to all the capitals of Europe, in order to lay before the various governments his draft of such an international factory law, in order to beg for a consideration of the same, and to procure the adoption of initiatory measures which might precede general action. His Christian feelings allowed him no peace, and he made great sacrifices for the attainment of this noble end. He was possessed of the practical experience requisite for preparing such a draft, and the memorials which he sent in are most probably still to be found in Berlin, Vienna, St. Petersburg, Paris, and Turin. The only effect of all his propositions was a number of civil speeches, and nothing more.

During the lapse of these twenty-four years, the need, the danger, and the responsibility have considerably increased. We may say the last hour has come in which such large and beneficial measures for the liquidation of the old debt, and diversion of social revolution, can still be undertaken with any prospect of successful issue. Meanwhile, Providence has assigned to the new German Empire such a position that our imperial Government is called upon, above all others, to take the initiative in this matter. Whoever plays first fiddle in the European concert, ought to recognise it as a duty too to give the keynote for so wholesome an undertaking. The highest honour of a Christian emperor consists in being a protector of the oppressed, a helper of the wretched, a saviour of the sinking ones, a father of his people; and in this case he might be more than a father of his own subjects,—he might be a father and benefactor of all the weary and heavily burthened people throughout Christendom. If at the present time a general congress is being convened for determining normal rights in war, why should it be impossible to hold a congress for the preparation of a general law for the protection of the working classes?

The next duty of a Christian State is the upholding and carrying out of the celebration of the Lord's day. The celebration of the first day of the week, and of the resurrection of the Lord Jesus Christ on it, is a religious duty for a Christian man; it is an unconditional duty, which is based on its own grounds, without any regard to the beneficial effects upon the individual, or upon the community, which result from its fulfilment. Just as it is impossible to conceive a Christian family who do not celebrate the Lord's day, so, too, a Christian nation. Such an one, by the public celebration of the Lord's day, professes the Christian faith, and without such celebration it cannot acknowledge Christ. Without such celebration the Christian State is not a verity. As, in the days of the old covenant, Israel was recognised to be the chosen people of God by its keeping holy of the Sabbath, so also ought Christians, Jews, and heathens to see by our celebration of the Lord's day that we are a Christian nation, the people of God under the new covenant. As a matter of fact, the early Christian emperors did recognise the necessity and the duty of caring for the celebration of the Lord's day by means of imperial laws. Constantine and Valentinian I. forbade all work, Gratian and Theodosius the Great forbade theatrical shows, on the Lord's day. The Capitularies of Charlemagne also coincide with the above.

Certainly the manner of carrying out these points during the Middle Ages was most faulty. When, in the sixteenth century, the recognition of so many abuses and the desire to get rid of them was awakened, it became necessary, as a chief element in any real reformation, that the sanctity of the Lord's day should be recognised in the national life and in the public service. Calvin and his followers were most earnest in endeavouring to fulfil this duty. And this is the one especial point which must be conceded to be the prerogative of the Reformed Church party, that in it, more than anywhere else, an attempt was made to conform the life of the people to the commandments of God. This was what was to be admired in the mother Church at Geneva, the Christian discipline and strict morality which pervaded public and private life.

Thence the care for the celebration of the Lord's day was conveyed to England and Scotland, and from Great Britain it was carried across to America. In those countries it still exists. In Germany, unfortunately, the matter was not earnestly taken up; and whatever did exist in the old Lutheran times, as regards a strict observance of the Lord's day, has disappeared during the subsequent periods of lukewarmness and decline. Even amongst the Reformed Church in the Palatinate, in Switzerland, and in Holland, the ancient discipline has disappeared. At present one must admit that both portions of Germany, the Protestant as well as the Roman Catholic, are equally guilty of this grievous sin of the desecration of the Lord's day. Work in the forenoon; pleasure in the afternoon and evening; the scandals of the following Saint Monday; the weekly markets, which in Bavaria have been altered so as to fall on a Sunday,—a disgrace to any Christian national life; the undiminished traffic of posts and railways, when even the heavy good strains are not excepted,—an abuse which robs hundreds of thousands of human beings of their day of rest; the special excursion trains on Sunday,—all these matters are a grievous sin which lies at the door of our country, forming a fearfully practical contradiction to our much lauded Christian German State.

It is futile to urge that the celebration of the seventh day is only a Mosaic command, which we are permitted to disregard. It is true that the Mosaic law contains a number of precepts which, although given by God Himself, still in their literal acceptation had only a transitory significance. But here we have to do not only with a commandment given on Mount Sinai, but with a fundamental law of God, given by the Creator of the world for all people and all times. In that the consecration of one day in seven is immediately connected with the creation, Holy Scripture holds up to us the command to celebrate this feast as the oldest of all laws. Just as marriage is based upon an originally divine revelation and institution, so, too, is the consecration of the holy day of rest. It is indissolubly connected with the nature of man and the welfare of the human race. This command is at once a natural and a moral law, the transgression of which entails its own punishment in its effects both on the natural and spiritual life of man. The Christian festival which commemorates the resurrection of the Redeemer has a higher sanction than the Mosaic, and is productive of a richer spiritual blessing. Far from its being the case that the Christian may disregard this ordinance, he brings upon himself more evil, and incurs a greater responsibility, by its infringement.

Bitter experience teaches us, if we will only look around, what are the results of that desecration of the Lord's day which is so rampant amongst us. As often as the festival recurs, with its celebration in divine worship, with its cessation of earthly toil and worldly amusements, it is a witness to the fact that man does not live for this world alone, but was created to enjoy a higher life. If, during the six following days, he has to labour to procure his earthly food, he ought to employ the whole of the first day in rejoicing in his eternal and heavenly calling, and in storing up some spiritual treasures for the ensuing week. The day of the Lord is to him an earnest and precursor of the future kingdom of peace. If amongst a nation the celebration of this feast is established by law and by custom, without exception or any possibility of infringement, all are impressed with the exhortation to reverence; Christian morals and the fear of God obtain thereby a hold, which nothing else, no invention of man, could replace. Immortality and the eternal destiny of man are the basis of all religious feeling and morality. Upon these the dignity of man and of the Christian rests, and true civilisation emanates from them. Any one who denies the eternal destiny of man, thereby placing him on an equality with the beasts of the field, aims at the overthrow of all civilisation, and would lead us on to barbarism.

What is the desecration of the Lord's day but the denial of our heavenly calling and Christian dignity? In that the highest earthly authorities, the temporal powers and legislature, sanction and assist in the profanation of the Lord's day, they treat men as mere carnal beings. They permit the employer of labour to treat his workpeople like animals, and to work them to death. This is nothing less than a practical denial of the dignity of man. We are, in fact, told there is no necessity for you to strive after eternal life. Who can be surprised if, after such a practice has gained the upper hand, the theoretical denial follows? If, at the present time, that hideous folly, that murderous heresy, of man being only a more highly developed animal, makes progress on all sides, we must admit that the desecration of the Lord's day prepared the way for it.

This much at least should be clear to every statesman, that it is impossible to retain a nation at a high moral standing, if it is not induced and coerced to devote one day of the week to higher interests. In the meanwhile, even disregarding for the moment the prejudicial consequences to religion and morals, the curse of Sunday labour is making itself felt in respect of the health and length of life of the poorer classes. It is a fact that in Paris, amongst the working classes, a grandfather or a man of more than fifty years is rarely to be found; and this premature exhaustion of the vital powers is to be imputed, to a great extent, to the fact that the day of the Lord is misused, partly in labour, partly in intemperate enjoyments and amusements. It is a disgrace to the elected representatives of Christian principles and traditions, that the Socialist Proudhon was the one to stand forward as champion of the necessity and wholesomeness of the celebration of the Lord's day.

Thus, then, the mass of those who, by undertaking laborious work, serve society, has a sacred right to expect from society that it will procure for and secure to them the undisturbed enjoyment of the weekly day of rest. This right is based upon the spiritual and the bodily welfare of the working and serving classes. To secure this right is one of the chief duties of a Christian government, legislature, and administration. Although it may be anticipated that, owing to the present low standard of popular morality, many would make a bad use of the complete rest on the Sunday, still that in no way interferes with the duty of the Government to respect the divine institution, and to permit the possibility of every one enjoying the fulness of the blessings which attach to it. This would therefore be a principal feature in the international law which is required for the solution of the social question.

In so serious a matter no irresolute or half measures are of any use. Unfortunately, in our imperial Trade Regulations of 1872, such were considered sufficient. In the factories, Sunday labour should only take place in urgent cases, and with the free consent of the workpeople so employed (sec. 105). But the self-interest and avarice of the employer will never want for an excuse to call some piece of work urgent. The general practice in our factories is well enough known. Repairs to machinery and cleansing of pipes, tubes, etc. are simply postponed to Sunday. It is true they might be executed just as well on Saturday or Monday, but the profitable employment of the factory must not be interrupted for even a quarter of an hour. That is termed urgent. The least diminution of the profits of the master is considered a much greater evil than interfering with the day of rest for the working man. As to the free consent of the employed, it is thus: A portion of the workpeople, owing to the pressure of poverty and in consequence of a want of Christian principle, are glad of the wages earned on Sunday; but the others, who would gladly go without, dare scarcely, when it comes to their turn, refuse to work on Sunday. Owing to their dependent position, they fear lest the master, or the superintendent, or the work-master would make them suffer for so doing on the first opportunity. Thus those paragraphs of the Law are absolutely void, and leave untouched the mountain of abuses which they were intended to get rid of. How far godlessness may be carried on the part of those who have the power, may be deduced from a fact which occurred in a town on the Baltic. There exists in that spot an enormous trade in timber. The logs are partially sawn up, partially rough hewn, for export and for shipbuilding. As these labours were carried on on the Lord's day also, the numerous workpeople sent a deputation from their number to the owner of the establishment, with the ingenuous petition that he would be pleased to excuse them this, as God might punish them for so doing. The reply which they received from the wealthy man ran thus: "I am your God."

The objections which will be raised to the proposals which are about to be laid before the German Parliament, for the assurance of the celebration of the Lord's day, may be easily foreseen, but they may be also very easily combated. It will be said that the loss of income in various trades, as well as the incomes of the postal and railway service and other public undertakings, would be too serious, the welfare of the State and of the people would suffer too much. To this we reply, that the community has as many duties to fulfil as an individual. The latter is told to work for six days, and to rest on the seventh, in full confidence that God will bless the labours of the six days, thereby procuring for him all that he requires for sustaining his life. Six days of work, with a blessing from above, are worth more to the Christian than seven working days without such blessing. The representatives of a Christian nation ought also to allow themselves to be guided by such a conviction. When it becomes a matter of reverencing a divine command, men must not allow themselves to be too much swayed by considerations of temporal disadvantages. The former must be enforced, even though no promise were attached to it. But in this case there is such a promise, and the experience of many can confirm the fact of its having been fulfilled. There is no instance of a man having closed his business on a Sunday, in obedience to the divine command, who has been in consequence brought to ruin. Let an instance be brought forward if such be known. On the contrary, there exists a noble example before our very eyes, which proves as clearly as the sun at noonday that the celebration of the Lord's day is practicable for a whole nation, and not only that it is not injurious, but that it produces beneficial results. It is the example of Great Britain. There the law of the realm is still maintained, all workpeople rest, the theatres are closed, no public amusements take place, no letters are delivered, and the railway traffic is confined to a few passenger trains. In the expectation that the Lord's day will really be devoted to the service of God and family edification, and will be spent quietly, but at the same time recognising the fact that the hard-working man must have time for physical recreation and re-invigoration, and for wholesome pleasures, places of business and workshops are closed on Saturday at one or two o'clock in the afternoon. Care is also taken that on Saturday opportunity shall be given for excursions into the country, and for returning again on Monday morning in time for the commencement of work. Besides this, the working man has, in the course of the year, several days of rest instituted by the civic authorities, such as Whitsuntide and the Bank holidays. As the Jews as well as others are bound to obey the laws of the State, and because they still observe the Sabbath, they are obliged to close their houses of business for two days in the week. But England and Scotland certainly are not sunk in poverty, and this one example is sufficient to confute any preconceived ideas of the impossibility of a national observance of the Lord's day. For those who look below the surface, the manner in which Sunday is kept in one of the populous cities of England makes a deep impression. In Scotland, we grant that in some cases the matter is carried to excess; but such instances are no disproof of the beneficent working of the system on the whole. Unchristian, carnal, and pleasure-seeking men, it is true, do not know what to do with themselves on an English Sunday. They complain bitterly of its deadly weariness. We cannot help their complainings, for the fault lies in themselves, and not in the arrangement. Nothing would be more senseless than to disturb a wholesome institution, thereby setting the welfare of the whole nation at stake, for the sake of appeasing the dissatisfaction of such persons.

Not only has the strict observance of the Lord's day brought no disadvantages with it, but rather it is one of the chief pillars upon which the happiness and prosperity of England are built. One is reverence for the law; the other is the observance of the sanctity of the Lord's day. These two fundamental principles are connected one with the other, and react one upon the other. Reverence for the law, that source of all civic virtue and political greatness, requires to be based upon religious grounds, and to have its origin in the fear of God; and these are the very feelings which the observance of the Lord's day calls into prominence and strengthens.

In England all the elements necessary for a social revolution are present, so numerous is the body of the working class, so perceptible is the inequality of wealth collected in the hands of the minority, the upper ten thousand. But England has been, and will probably long be, spared any such convulsions. Socialism itself is there more intelligent and more temperate than amongst us. In addition to other wholesome arrangements, the observance of the Lord's day is one of the things that protects England from a downfall. If this were removed, the ship of the State would be irresistibly hurried along to destruction. If Socialism is to be overcome, if Germany especially is to be protected against social revolutions, depend upon it that this is not possible unless the State be Christian.

Heathen antiquity knew nothing of a governmental relief of the poor. The authorities and the bulk of the community knew nothing of the duty of charity. Public benefaction, and care for those who were suffering in any way, was first called into existence by the Christian Church; and yet the Mosaic law had preceded it. The people of Israel had been told to release their brethren from debts at the end of every seventh year, "to the end that there be no poor amongst you." When the harvest was gathered in from the field or the vineyard, the ground was not to be gleaned by the owner, but something was to be left for the poor and needy. When the Sabbath year came round, that which grew spontaneously was to belong to the poor; besides which, in every third year, a tenth part of the produce of the fields was to be given for the benefit of the poor, the widows, orphans, and strangers. The Israelite was not permitted to take any interest from his brother. The working man was not to be kept waiting for his wages, but they were to be paid to him in the evening. All injustice or hard-heartedness towards the needy was threatened with the disapproval of God.

The duty of mercy towards the poor and suffering of all classes was, by the words and example of Christ, confirmed, more deeply implanted, sanctified, and extended beyond the limits fixed by the Old Testament. The Christian community, filled with the spirit of Christ, carried out this duty, and we find that its execution was secured and regulated by two divine institutions. The first-fruits of all sources of income were voluntarily and gladly brought by believers and dedicated to the Lord; deacons were chosen and appointed, in order, in the exercise of their wisdom, to assist the poor out of such funds belonging to the Church. This much we gather from the New Testament. Somewhat later the principle appeared in ancient Christendom, that, of the first-fruits or tithes thus brought up, at least one-fourth belonged to the poor. But the fathers of the Church repeatedly enjoined, that if the ministers could support themselves, or if a time of special need occurred, all the revenues of the Church, even the holy vessels and other treasures, were to be applied to the relief of necessity. Out of these beginnings sprang, in the Middle Ages, all those undertakings and foundations for the relief of the poor, which, noble as the cathedrals of those days, are deserving of our admiration; but, at the same time, it was an unfavourable change which caused the office of deacon—a lay and not a priestly office—to fall into desuetude, and allowed the relief of the poor to fall, for the most part, into the hands of the clergy.

Since the Reformation there has gradually crept in —and not only in the Protestant, but also in the Roman Catholic States—a secularization of the goods of the Church. In proportion as the temporal authority assumed the care and distribution of the property of the Church, so also did it incur the responsibility of relieving the poor. According to the calculations of Sir Archibald Alison, the English historian, the property of the Church which has been secularized for the last 350 years, would, if it were now available for charitable purposes, suffice to alleviate the pauperism and misery which exists in all Europe. So much the more does it behove our governments to make the most strenuous exertions in that direction.

Even setting aside the fact of the property of the Church having passed into the hands of the State, it is the duty of the Government to care for the poor— first, on the ground that it is a Christian government, and its duty is to take part in the common duties of Christianity; secondly, because it, to a certain extent, has taken up the position of the office of deacon in the primitive Church—as, for instance, the emperor, as head of the Roman empire in the German nation, was looked upon as the head deacon of the Church.

In this matter, too, experience has taught us how wrong it is that both powers, spiritual and temporal, should go their own way, without regard for each other. Like education, the relief of the poor is a common field, which both must labour in with their united strength. Only in the case of such co-operation —in other words, only in a Christian State—can the gigantic task which is in this matter set before us be even approximately solved. Wherever the relief of the poor rested entirely in the hands of the clergy and the cloisters, much was truly done to relieve necessity; but at the same time laziness and alms-seeking were encouraged, and the poor were in no way encouraged to be active and self-reliant. To this day the consequences are visible in those districts of Germany which were formerly ecclesiastical domains. Nowhere else do we find so ignorant, unthrifty, and helpless a population. That is the result of a purely clerical relief of the poor.

A similar example of purely secular relief of the poor is before us. In England, rates and poor-laws have been introduced, and the effect is as follows:—No man is obliged to die of starvation; every one has a right to claim admittance into the workhouse of his parish, erected and maintained for him at the expense of the State. But the arrangements in the workhouse are such that a residence there is terrible, and one can understand how many unfortunate beings prefer death from starvation to "going into the house." The workhouse is like a prison. If a family is compelled to go there, man and wife, boys and girls, are separated, and each placed in the division of the establishment to which they belong. The option of leaving is at any time free; but this option affords small comfort, for any one who has been in the workhouse is ashamed of the fact, and does not easily resume a position amongst his fellow-citizens. Finally, the whole arrangement is productive of the following disadvantageous effect upon the rich and well-to-do, that they, if not disposed to be kind-hearted, stifle all appeals to their conscience by the reply that, having paid their poor-rates, their duty at least has been done. No one need suffer from hunger, for the workhouse is always open to him.

In Germany another course is pursued. In our towns the relief of the poor is in the hands of the police. Out of the funds which the community collects, weekly relief is distributed by the civil authorities. It is true that, as a rule, the minister of the parish, as is only right, has a seat at the board for the relief of the poor; still the distribution of the relief granted is a civil matter, and it is a common complaint that little or no advantage or blessing seems to accompany this police relief. The gifts produce, as a rule, no moral effect at all upon the recipients. Most of them receive such gifts without an atom of thankfulness, without being conscious of any obligation to make an effort to raise themselves above requiring such assistance; it is looked upon as a provision which the community is bound to make for the poor. Discontent and grumbling is not an uncommon concomitant of the receipt of eleemosynary assistance.

In addition to this relief by the police, a good deal is effected out of means supplied by the Church, voluntary associations for the exercise of Christian benevolence, and many individuals carry out works of charity without any one else being made aware of the fact. But, so long as these various modes of relief act independently of each other, the whole system for the relief of the poor is injured by being thus split up. Cunning fellows enjoy, at one and the same time, the advantages of all. Owing to a want of organization, the means collected are squandered with little benefit. Every one must admit that our relief of the poor proceeds upon no organized system. If such existed, fewer would receive relief, but then such as did could be materially assisted.

The problem which has to be solved is simple

enough: to relieve want, and yet not to encourage idleness; to stretch out a helping hand to the needy, and at the same time to excite their sense of honour and duty; to afford an opportunity of earning something, however little, to such as are capable of labour; to prevent a misuse of alms and reckless squandering of them; to awaken in the hearts of those who possess nothing the hope of gradually putting something together, and thereby to induce in them habits of contentment and saving. Where shall we find this problem solved? Not in the one-sided clerical relief of the poor during the Middle Ages; not in the relief of the poor by the civil authorities as in more modern times; but only where that relief is considered the duty of the diaconal office. The diaconate is the link which is now-a-days wanting. So long as it existed, the distribution of material aid was combined with moral religious influences and support. A bond of union was formed for the two elements which should here work together, —practical knowledge, and a sanction from above.

In the present day there are splendid means available for the realization of the Christian diaconate. At various points arise truly wise suggestions, and undertakings containing much real truth, which should be promoted, welcomed, and imitated. The "Cité Ouvrière," in Muhlhausen, perhaps stands at the head of the list of such undertakings. V. A. Huber founded, in Berlin, the Co-operative Building Society, which, being contented with a low rate of interest, supplies the working man with wholesome dwellings; which dwellings, after a term of years, by a regular payment of rent, become the property of the working man. Gustavus Werner's establishments, in Reutlingen and other places in Wurtemberg, are a standing proof of what Christian love, combined with an active spirit, can do. The proposals of the Countess Butler-Heimhausen, to found colonies of poor people, in which the adults should find employment and assistance, and orphan children should be provided with instruction, are well worthy the consideration of our magistrates and provincial authorities. But the employment of such means, and their proper organization, is not to be expected so long as Church and State remain inimically sundered and are mutually repellant. Our only hope lies in a reconciliation between the two—in fact, in a Christian Commonwealth.

Finally, let us be allowed to call to mind how well adapted Christian doctrine is to bridge over the chasm which exists between these two sections of society, those who have means and those who have none, and to assist in the healing up of this deep wound.

In the light of Christian truth we recognise society as an organization, and the distinction of classes as something necessary and ordained of God. The differences existing in mental power are not a matter of chance or of human invention. Just as the different bodily capabilities with which we are born, and which cannot be reduced to a level of uniformity by any power or dexterity of man, are assignable to the providence of God, so too is the variety of our position in society. It is agreeable to the will of God that well-to-do people and needy ones exist side by side and are dependent upon each other. As, in the vegetable world, all plants do not attain the same growth, but trees, shrubs, and grasses are all different, so too the all-ordering eternal Wisdom has ordained certain grades in society amongst men. The rigidity of demarcation between those grades, the indifferent and hostile attitude of the various members of the organization towards each other, come of evil, and must be got rid of. So also hatred between nations is a sin, and yet the distinctions between nations are ordered of God.

We must quite disabuse our minds of those erroneous ideas of social position which in our days are being disseminated, and which appear to be countenanced by the introduction of universal suffrage. In them society is looked upon as a mere aggregate of similar atoms, a mere numerical entity, something like a heap of sand. Under such circumstances, it appears very distasteful and very unjust, to the individual who has to work hard for very little emolument, that another should have little to do and many enjoyments. What is the good of equal political rights without an equality of wealth and means of enjoyment? No wonder then, that, as soon as the fear of God is got rid of and the light of faith is extinguished, Communism, with all its extreme consequences, should spring from such premises. But did not Menenius Agrippa, the Roman, when he brought back the discontented poor who had gone out to the holy mountain, set forth a more correct and profound doctrine regarding society, in comparing it with the human body, in which the various members have different functions, by which they serve one another and support the welfare of the whole organization? The description given us in the Bible of the Christian community agrees with it, and civil society too is just the same.

Still there remains the oppressive harshness with which, owing to the faults of men, the various grades of society are separated; and with that is connected a constant temptation for the lower classes to indulge in discontent, murmurings, and violent attempts to right themselves. But Christianity sheds a ray of comfort into this gloomy region of life. Christ Himself assumed the form of a servant, and thereby reflected honour upon the position. He did not come to be waited upon, but to serve and to give His life a ransom for many: "Though He was rich, yet for our sakes He became poor, that we through His poverty might be rich." Hard and menial labour, which, according to the ideas of the heathen world amongst the Greeks and Romans, was despicable and assigned to slaves, has acquired respectability through Christianity. Many members of the early Christian communities were slaves, and most of such were the property of heathen masters. Paul addresses these serving men, who had no rights, no protection, and no position, in those wonderful words: "Servants, be obedient to them that are your masters according to the flesh, with fear and trembling, in singleness of your heart, as unto Christ: not with eye-service, as men-pleasers; but as the servants of Christ, doing the will of God from the heart; with good will doing service, as to the Lord, and not to men: knowing that whatsoever good thing any man doeth, the same shall he receive of the Lord, whether he be bond or free."

It is a verity which is often proclaimed, that Christ is the Head of the Church; but Paul here reveals to us a truth which is but seldom recognised, and at the present day almost forgotten. Christ is also the Head of society—not merely as an imaginative ideal, but as a matter of fact. Christ, the Son of man, is raised to the right hand of God; to Him is given all power in heaven and upon earth. The power and authority which is exercised here below by men is derived from Him; He is, in fact and in truth, King of kings and Lord of lords. If we liken society to a pyramid, the apex of it reaches to heaven; for Christ is that apex. As, for instance, in a monarchy the subordinate official is a servant of the king; as in an army the commonest soldier serves under the orders of the sovereign, and in so doing asserts his dignity and feels himself raised by that consciousness, just so is it here. The Christian to whom Providence has assigned a lowly position and one despised of men, knows that in his position he serves Christ, the supreme Ruler. And Christ is an omnipresent Ruler; His eyes are upon all His servants; their troubles and sufferings are all known to Him; He never forgets anything that has been done out of love to Him and confidence in Him; He is the most generous of kings in the rewards He showers upon His servants.

"Ye serve the Lord Christ." This consciousness raises His servant above all petty feelings. It makes him conscientious, so that he fulfils the duties of his position, even when no human being is overlooking him and no one would discover the secret transgression or dereliction of duty. He yields an upright obedience and seeks the good of his master. The consciousness of so doing makes him contented, and furnishes him with perseverance and patience, even when he is not appreciated by men and is ill-treated by those over him. It preserves him from slavishness and adulation. He has no reason to ingratiate himself with his earthly master, because he looks to a higher Ruler, of whose justice and goodness he is perfectly convinced.

Christ is the Head of all human society; He is the Lord and Judge of all. From this fact we can deduce what is the proper attitude of a master. Paul says: "Masters, give unto your servants that which is just and equal," "forbearing threatening: knowing that your Master also is in heaven; neither is there respect of persons with Him."

These truths are perhaps still recognised in the case of servants who form part of the family or of the household. In such cases, at least occasionally, there is still a consciousness of the fact that masters and servants are bound to one another by a moral tie; that reverence is due from those in subjection; justice, good-will, kindness, and cordial interest, from those in authority.

But all this ought also by rights to be the case between manufacturers and their hands. The master tradesman is not the only one who should care for his apprentices and shopmen, feeling a sense of responsibility for their moral as well as their physical well-being. The manufacturer, too, who works on a large scale, and employs a number of people, ought to have the same feeling towards his workpeople and their families. Riches, power, and influence are given to him by Christ. He should look upon himself as holding a commission from Christ, and employ all those gifts according to the will of Christ; for Christ, whom God hath set to be the Judge over all men, will call him too before His judgment-seat, requiring of him an account of how he has used the goods confided to his care.

However strange it may sound to the working class, it is a fact that they should honour the rich man who gives them employment, and serve him faithfully. They must not look upon him as an enemy, but as a father. "Thou shalt honour thy father and mother;" this commandment includes masters also. And why? Because all fathers should be masters, and all masters fathers. We must not wait for our superiors to act in a fatherly manner towards us before we show them honour. The duties of reverence and fidelity are of themselves binding, and must be fulfilled, because Christ the true Master is in the masters.

This life, in which Providence has made an unequal distribution of the goods of this world, is the school of preparation for the world which is to come. Here every one in his own place ought to show fidelity and obedience, practising those virtues by which he will be rendered capable of serving Christ in the future kingdom. At the judgment-seat of Christ there is no respect of persons. The soul of a poor man is, in the sight of God, of as much value as that of a rich man. He who has shown forth patience and charity here below in a humble position, will some day have it said to him, "Thou hast been faithful over a few things, I will make thee ruler over many things." When we look up to God as the Ruler of all things, and to the kingdom which is promised to us, then all feelings of impatience and envy die out.

The Christian verity teaches us to look upon the rich man in his true light. The poor man must recognise in such an one a being to whom God has entrusted much; he is not his master, that he should have a right to call him to account for the use he has made of the goods entrusted to his care. Another will do this; He who entrusted the goods to the rich man will also require an account of him. The rich may not despise the poor; the poor may not judge the rich. It is the less permissible for him to do so, because he, the poor man, cannot say that, if he were suddenly to come into possession of those goods, he would turn them to better account. To use wealth with temperance and wisdom, neither to hoard nor to squander it,—to maintain the Aristotelian mean between the two extremes,—is a great matter; and no one can say of himself that he would be able to do this without having actually been put to the proof and done it.

Contentment is a virtue and a duty which must be constantly preached; but we must not forget what great temptations in this respect the working classes are exposed to. It is a justifiable attempt on the part of the working men, at a time when all necessaries of life have risen in price, to strive for an increased value to be placed upon bodily labour, time, strength, and health; but any continued beneficial alteration in this respect is not to be expected, because with the increase of wages of the labourer, and partially in consequence of that very increase, the price of goods, whether manufactured or raw products, which the labourer requires also increases. Hence, by a natural law, in the course of time the old status is resumed, wherein unskilled labour, as it is termed, in which mere bodily strength is required, only receives just so much wage as will suffice for the procurement of absolute necessaries. Thus in reality that saying of Christ is fulfilled, "Ye have the poor always with you." Hence also arises the constant demand made upon those who are well-to-do to be benevolent.

One cause by which in our days contentment is rendered more difficult, is the result of a social development in which the individual has had no choice. Formerly every class had its corresponding mode of life, its code of honour, its ideas,—every one, whether citizen, farmer, or servant, felt that he was a member of a particular guild; he took a pride in his peculiar garb, and clung to ancient ways and customs. He did not strive for anything else; he was proud of being a man of mark in his class, and to bring honour upon his class, corporation, or guild. These distinctions are rapidly disappearing; hence, naturally enough, the lower classes do all they can to act the same as those above them. Just as the difference of apparel has disappeared, so that on a holiday a blacksmith may be mistaken for a baron, so, too, there has arisen amongst working men a wish to enjoy all the pleasures at the disposal of their superiors. The working man has been raised out of his proper position, which naturally brings with it a feeling of being ill at ease; and if he has not good and firm principles, it produces restless striving, envy, covetousness, and murmuring.

And yet there is here still a possibility of remedy, and even of cure. It was not in vain that Paul said to the needy for their comfort, "Godliness with contentment is great gain. Having food and raiment, let us be therewith content." Does the present generation still know that contentment, that peace of mind under want, that quiet homely joy in the most modest circumstances and pleasures, that was so often to be found amongst our pious ancestors?

Jean Paul tells us of his grandfather the old rector, Johann Richter, in Neustadt, on the Culm, how that he, being a man of faith and of prayer, was oppressed with the bitterest poverty even till his hairs were grey with age, and yet he was full of contentment and merriment. Hebel has left us in his poems a reminiscence of what peaceful joy, what childlike happiness, there was to be found even at the end of the last century in the cottages of the peasantry.

A spoilt child of rich parents will hardly look at the most costly toys; a genuine and modest child is pleased and overjoyed with the commonest playthings and the simplest pleasures. The rising generation is a spoilt, discontented, fretful, unbearable child.

The hidden source from which all our happiness comes is not yet closed, if we will only return to and partake of it. Man in his folly seeks for the cause of his discontent outside of himself. He has an idea that if he could only enjoy this or that pleasure he would be satisfied. He does not recognise the cause of all his troubles, which is within himself, in his love of pleasure and his own ambition. He does not see that these passions devour him like a raging fire. His pleasures do not serve so much to appease those passions as to incite them; and a man who has yielded to his passions when he has got what he wanted is always longing for something more. The heart of man is insatiable. This is the chief cause of all our misery. If this evil were removed, the external evils that we have put up with would be bearable. Christ offers us peace with God, that does satisfy the heart, and we are at peace with mankind. If this peace be established, we can enjoy the gifts of God even if they are given us in the smallest portions to partake of.

Dangerous blindness of our Socialists and societies of working men, who repudiate from their midst the principles of Christianity, and place themselves at the service of the misanthropic powers of unbelief! Such unhappy blind men, the opponents of Christian truth, are in a spiritual condition resembling hydrophobia, when the patient in his delirium avoids and repels the only element that could refresh him. Only amongst a Christian people and in a Christian State is help for the poorer classes possible. Where can any doctrine be found which is more apposite and terrible to the mind of the selfish rich man, or more comforting and balmy to the oppressed, than that parable of Christ which shows us the unmerciful spendthrift in the place of torment, and represents Lazarus as being consoled in the bosom of Abraham?

When ministers of religion properly understand their duty of awakening the consciences of those who have this world's goods by boldly proclaiming Christian truths, and thereby provoking noble feelings in them, it will not be without effect upon the community at large. Where Christian feelings are put into practice, where manufacturers and employers of labour, even if at present only in individual cases, are benevolent, and devote wise care to their workpeople, the latter are still found to be—thank God for it!—appreciative and thankful. Where they meet with Christian treatment, Christianity can still find a way into their hearts. It is not yet too late to avert the impending judgment, if the upper classes fulfil the duty of charity or brotherly love, and a legislature be introduced which shall be agreeable to the calling of a Christian Commonwealth.

CHAPTER XIV.

ON CRIMINAL LAW.

WHAT is the origin of the power of punishment vested in the State? What form should the exercise of that power assume in a Christian Commonwealth?

The existence of a power whose province it shall be to punish the evildoer dates from a period anterior to the existence of the State itself. The power of punishment has an origin existing before the State, and this was in the family. If we go back to the commencement of historic times, we find that the head of the family possessed the power of punishing all the members of his household. The family formed a comprehensive unit, and if it were attacked from without, the family had a right to defend itself and to retaliate. But things could not remain thus. The family was destined to grow into a tribe, the tribe to become a nation. A regular government was to be ordered, and the handling of justice and the protection of the common weal were to be placed in the hands of the authorities. As in the constitution of the family, so too in the constitution of a government, and its power of punishment, we ought to recognise a divine ordinance.

The transition from one condition to the other, it is true, only took place slowly, and the vestiges of the original power of punishment go deep into the historical times. The Mosaic law, and also that of ancient Rome, show us the traces of the transition. According to the Mosaic law, the parents of a disobedient son were to bring him before the elders of the town, and they were to pronounce the sentence of death upon him. The desire for bloody vengeance had to be got rid of. In the Mosaic law this does not occur all at once; it is there limited. The involuntary manslayer could fly to one of the cities of refuge; a regular trial was held upon him, and the avenger of blood dared not to lay hands upon him. His punishment existed in a species of exile or confinement in a fortified place. In the days of the Roman Republic the "judicium domesticum" still existed. The "patria potestas" over the life of the children survived longest amongst the Romans and Galatians.

In most of the ancient States great lawgivers arose as benefactors of mankind. Their pre-eminent wisdom was much looked up to. The citizens agreed to the proposed laws. The legislature was called into existence with the co-operation of the people and with solemn contracts, and solid axioms were set up as to what was to be considered a crime, and what the form of process was to be, what form and what extent the punishment was to take. That was the case with the laws of Lycurgus, Solon, and the twelve tables in Rome. Whilst an agreement was come to, the laws at once received a moral and religious consecration, and the exercise of the office of judge was built upon a religious basis. The law was administered with reference to the highest of their gods, Zeus, whose attribute was that he would not allow the evildoer to go unpunished. So also in the Mosaic law it is said "the judgment is God's;" and the judges, in that they gave their sentence as holding a divine commission, were called gods.

Out of these simple historical principles proceeds one very important consequence. As is the case with the State in a general way, so also more especially the power of punishment inherent in it has been at one time entirely deduced from a divine ordinance, at another, again, entirely from a social contract amongst men. These two aspects are not incompatible. The true conception lies in a combination of both. Both elements are mentioned in history: a primitive commission which passed from the family to the State, and an agreement by which the laws of the people were one by one established. The power of punishment, like any other privilege, is exercised by a commission from the community, and yet at the same time in virtue of a divine commission.

The Mosaic decalogue was the republication of an original divine law, which from the beginning was the basis of all human society. With the words, "Thou shalt honour thy father and thy mother, thou shalt do no murder, thou shalt not commit adultery, thou shalt not steal, thou shalt not bear false witness against thy neighbour," God took our families, our property, and our characters under His own protection. This is the protection which society requires. This protection He wields by means of the authorities; and for this purpose He has invested them with the power of inflicting punishment. Because this power proceeds from Him, it possesses an ethic character. It is based upon the commands of God; its duty is to put in force the justice and benevolence of God. It has to minister to the material and moral welfare of the people; for the one can only be maintained and advanced in combination with the other, and not separate from it.

Of such sort were the fundamental principles of justice in the antechristian States, irrespective of national peculiarities — recognisable notwithstanding all the darkness and error connected with a state of heathendom.

When, however, a nation accepted Christianity, what form was the right of punishment to assume amongst such a people? In such a case, one maxim which we have before discussed becomes of great importance. Christianity recognises all constitutional forms which it finds existing, as it also does actual laws or penal enactments. In such a case there never was any question of creating something new; on the contrary, the object was to bring national law, whether civil or criminal, into full force. The ministers of the Church have nothing to do with introducing or abolishing the power of punishment; they have no right to interfere in the matter.

Still, Christianity ought to make its influence felt even in this matter, and that in a threefold direction. First, it should uphold the commission, the power, the dignity of the government, and the sanctity of the judicial office; secondly, it should enunciate and elucidate the divine principles; and finally, it should subdue selfishness, hardness of heart, and cruelty. In that the servants of Christ proclaim the principles of the Christian moral law, in that they endeavour to fill high and low with a Christian spirit, their influence upon the penal code cannot remain in abeyance. When the true light shines forth, the dark remnants of heathenism disappear. Whereas ecclesiastics have no right to interfere in worldly matters, no laws to dictate, none to abolish, but are bound to leave intact the entire responsibility of the temporal power, still they too are bound not to remain silent spectators when, for instance, slavery or torture, the cruelty of sentences or the self-will of the judges, contravenes the mind of Christ. By instruction, warning, petition, and mediation, they will endeavour to procure that those vested with power, of their own accord and with the assistance of their legitimate advisers, shall gradually bring everything into harmony with the word of God.

Truly a great undertaking, and one which has as yet never been perfectly carried out! The carrying out of it would be very easy, if one could take the Mosaic law, and then and there proceed to apply it to a Christian people. But that is simply impossible; for that law, although given of God, was intended for the Israelites alone, and for no other people. As a matter of fact, it is quite unsuitable for application to a Christian nation; for in it the criminal law is interwoven with the ceremonial law, and this, if taken literally, has been utterly done away with for us. Besides which, it contains elements, such as the permission of polygamy and divorce, contrary to what Christ has declared. Finally, it presupposes at every step that intimate incorporation of Church and State which came to an end in Christ, and that in such a manner that the ordering of a Christian life and its success depend upon the capability of distinguishing between the spiritual and temporal spheres.

Still, we can learn much from the Mosaic law on this very subject of the right to punish. That law distinguishes itself from all heathen legislation by its combination of earnestness and mercy. The holiness of God, and disapproval of any intentional transgression of His commands, form one chief feature. The other consists in benevolence towards the lowly, protection of the helpless, and care for the poor. Are there not in the book of Deuteronomy a number of humane ordinances, which Johannis von Müller justly admired? In Egypt and Persia, in Sparta, Athens, and Rome, nothing was to be found comparable to it. In this general character of the Mosaic law, we see the glowing beams of that dawn which was to culminate in the full daylight of Christ.

For, looked at from an ethic point of view, what is the peculiar characteristic of the revelation of God in Christ Jesus? The holy earnestness against all evil is preserved, being asserted and developed to the utmost; paternal clemency and the unspeakable love of God appears in Christ, vivified and personified. Both are impressed upon the feelings of believers by the Spirit of Christ.

But the earnestness and the goodness of God must also be manifested to the children of men by means of the temporal powers. This ethic feature should be especially exemplified in the judicial office. If this be exercised in the proper manner, it at once becomes a finger pointing to the just action of the Divinity, and at the same time it assures the full enjoyment of those temporal benefits which Divine goodness has appointed for us poor mortals.

If we ask how far this ethic character is expressed by our criminal laws and the mode of their administration, the reply must be one that we are ashamed of; for in the whole history of the criminal law, since the introduction of Christianity into the Roman Empire, two contradictory elements appear to gain the upper hand alternately,—first of all heathen cruelty and hardness of heart, and then modern laxity and weakness. Both continue to the present time. To one of these Christian mercy must be opposed; to the other, Christian earnestness.

The one evil with which our penal code was too long chargeable was the severity which had been handed down from heathendom, and which was continued by the Roman law to the Middle Ages, or even to later times. It is true that the Roman civil law is, in its way, the most perfect that ever was framed. In it we find the most subtle exposition of all questions relating to *meum* and *tuum*, and science is obliged constantly to refer to these axioms; but, compared with it, the criminal law lagged far behind. The principles laid down in the ancient law were by no means amplified in a spirit of justice and equity, rather during the reign of the emperors they distinctly deteriorated. New and cruel modes of punishment were added to those in use in early times, such as condemnation to working in mines, castigation, increase of the terrors of the punishment of death, and exposure to death from wild beasts; besides which, the scope of the crime of high treason was largely increased. If the old distinction made in the treatment of freemen and slaves was evil, much worse was the distinction which now obtained between *honestiores* and *humiliores*.

Although Christianity has been accepted since the days of Constantine, there has been no improvement of the criminal law. The changes which have been made are, for the most part, only an increase in severity. Since the removal of the throne to Byzantium, the kingdom became more and more Orientalized, and the spirit of the ancient heathen East showed itself to be more powerful than the spirit of Christianity. The laws issued from Constantine to Justinian against heretics were evil; the regulations made for protecting morality and matrimony alone were a gain. The intercession of the Christian bishops occasionally intervened, with a view to tempering and alleviating too violent sentences.

The legal usages of the ancient Teutonic nations also lagged behind the requirements which Christianity imposes. They, too, contained cruel punishments; on other occasions, the compositions or money payments were contradictory to the idea of justice. Unfortunately, the introduction of any improvement from the Roman law was not to be looked for, as in the

Middle Ages it had been made an object of study under the form given it by Justinian, and had partially been put in force in the Roman Empire of the German nation; on the contrary, it rather increased cruelty and barbarism. Torture was introduced and fearfully practised. Whereas in Rome, the *quæstio per tormenta* was only originally permitted to be applied to slaves and strangers, but never to Roman citizens; amongst us Teutons, free men and women were subjected to it. This fearful evil came among us partly in consequence of the studies of the Jurists in Bologna, partly in consequence of the ecclesiastical proceedings of the Inquisition against heretics, and the trials for witchcraft which sprang from the latter.

The criminal punishments in the Middle Ages were so terrible, that the severe code of the Emperor Charles v., the details of which are now read with a shudder, was looked upon as a beneficent alleviation. The Reformation introduced some attempts to improve the criminal law, but in all principal points it remained as before. Our ancient German modes of procedure, by means of a regular charge, jury, oral and public trial, which have been maintained in England, but which in Germany were set aside by the Roman inquisitorial mode of procedure, were not restored at the time of the Reformation. The punishment of death for theft or infringement of the game laws still remained in force; the cruelties which took place at executions were not done away with; the rack, that insensate and unchristian means for the supposed extraction of the truth, was used at least as cruelly in Protestant countries as in Catholic ones. Occasional warnings were issued by the Pope against excess of cruelty. It is one of the most perplexing problems contained in history, why all ecclesiastics did not raise their voices in protest with greater effect. It is the greatest reproach which can be cast at the age of orthodoxy. Although individual Christian men, such as Meyfart and Von Spee, and after them Thomasius, protested and testified against these cruel abuses, they still continued to exist; and this relic of heathendom remained in force until the latter half of the eighteenth century; the abolition of it, which had been neglected by the acknowledged representatives of Christian principles, was brought about by another spiritual power.

This was that process of development which has already been spoken of before when treating of toleration; that which in the orthodox age had been shamefully neglected, was subsequently effected in the philosophic century. An alteration in the modes of criminal procedure, and of punishment, should have been insisted upon in the name of Christian humanity; but the introduction of this Christian principle was left for the opposers of Christian verity. These, the representatives of spurious French enlightenment, Voltaire and Rousseau, raised the standard of humanity apart from Christianity, and under this banner they applied for a reform of the criminal code. This was the manner in which they dealt with morality generally; whereas they treated Christianity with disdain, they boasted of their morality—for which, however, they were indebted to the former—as though they had themselves originated it. Men liked the fruit, and it was held up for admiration, whilst the axe was being laid to the root of the tree which bore it. Benevolent monarchs, such as Frederick II., Maria Theresa, Joseph II., Catherine II., adopted humane courses. The rack, ingenious modes of inflicting death, and the laws against heterodoxy were abolished. This is that great and permanent service which the age of enlightenment has rendered. Such are the advantages which accrued to the Christian world through a school of men who, having no Christian feelings or convictions, fought for a principle which is essentially Christian.

If the genuine source of all humanity be not recognised, that is to say, the word of Christ and His Spirit, then it becomes necessary to find another, a philosophic basis, for the duties of humanity. Hence it was sought to deduce the humane alterations of the penal code, which were acknowledged to be the business of the age, from that theory of a natural condition and of a social contract, which has been before treated of. But this theory excludes every supernatural element and any reference to God from the idea of a commonwealth. That is only to be a mutual insurance office for the protection of this world's goods. It has no longer any ethic source, and, as far as morality is concerned, has only to do with that because it is a very useful means of maintaining individual and public safety. But if the entire power of the State is based upon a social contract alone, the right of punishment must also rest upon the same. Its only object is the maintenance of general safety. It has nothing to do with setting forth the justice and goodness of God, nothing to do with the realization of an idea of eternal justice. The idea of retribution is eliminated from all punishment, and the only object in view is to render the criminal, because he is dangerous to society, innocuous,—to prevent the repetition of the offence by him, and to guard against the imitation of his crime by others. Then it is a consequent deduction that the injury inflicted upon the criminal shall be the least possible, concomitant with the public safety.

For, naturally, it must be presupposed that, in concluding the contract, every individual has only given up so much of his own rights and liberties as are absolutely necessary for the attainment of the objects of the Commonwealth.

The ancient teachers of a natural law, Grotius and Pufendorf, did not follow out to the full extent the consequences of their own principles, when they allowed the government to retain a power of life and death over the citizen. Beccaria was consistent when he denied generally the right of capital punishment, in his ecstatic work, *Dei delitti e delle pene* (1764). It could not have been an article in the original State contract, that the individual in the case of a serious trespass gave up his right to live. Granted that he wished to do so, he had no right to dispose of his own life; and why should he wish to do so, seeing that the object of the State can be obtained without this? Beccaria considers that compulsory labour has a more deterrent effect than capital punishment. It is true that Beccaria would have been quite consistent only if he had denied the right of the authorities to resort to any violent or death-dealing measures in putting down rebellion, or to carry on war at all. In both these cases the government deals with the lives of the citizens, and, what is more, with the lives of the innocent. What right it can have to do this will be difficult to determine from Beccaria's point of view.

The bias of the foregoing tendencies had a wholesome counterpoise, so long as earnest morality had not disappeared from public opinion; but a straight line which once departs from the right course always increases its divergence. Thus it would have been with this biased humanity, if a powerful counterpoise had not been applied at the right time. This was found in the philosophy of Kant.

It was an age when morality had been reduced to a theory of mere happiness. To Kant belongs the honour of having, in opposition to this, reasserted the idea of duty and its inflexible laws in all their true dignity. He performed the same service for the criminal law when he based, as he did in his *Metaphysical Elements of Jurisprudence* (1797), punishment upon the right of retaliation. This same active morality, which Kant revived and rendered capable of dispelling the mists of an impotent and sickly imitation, enabled him, in opposition to the vapidity of his contemporaries, to reject the doctrine of convenience, and to recognise in the judicial power of the State a reflex of eternal justice.

The corrective to ancient heathen cruelty ought to have come from the representatives of Christian traditions; but it came from the *quasi*-philosophers of the French school of infidelity. The corrective to pseudo-humanity, which became necessary, ought to have come from those who are appointed to declare the fulness of Christian truth; again, it was not offered by them, but by a great moral philosopher, who had embraced but few of the doctrines of Christianity, who was, however, imbued with many of the feelings of a true Christian.

Was the remedy applied by Kant effectual in its action? Unfortunately, we cannot say it was; on the contrary, up to the present day, the criminal law appears to be in a vacillating state. The doctrines of Kant, Feuerbach, and Hegel are partially at variance with themselves—partially, too, at variance with the doctrines of humanity, which, in the meantime, had made even greater progress.

With humanity, kindness, and forbearance alone, no family can be managed, much less a State. A wholesome severity is absolutely requisite, otherwise the most superficial objects of the State will not be attained. Feuerbach attempted to find a proper place for this severity, in his *Review of the Fundamental*

Principles and Maxims of the Penal Law (1799, 1800), which at the time acquired much influence; but he does not seek to attain his object in the manner sketched out by Kant. His principle is not retaliation, but intimidation, and the psychological effect produced by it. Punishment must be intimidating to the criminal and intimidating to others. It is true that, even if we retain the theory of a one-sided contract, this much may also be said; but, if we go no farther, we have still no ethical basis for punishment, and we are dangerously near proposing the most cruel punishments, as being the most effective means of intimidation.

In the theory of Feuerbach, too, the right of punishment is independent of ethics. It is certainly necessary to draw a line between the two. The administration of justice has only to do with the external demeanour of man, with such acts as can be taken cognisance of by man, and in so far as they affect the welfare of his fellow-men and the welfare of the community. The moral law, on the other hand, embraces the entire life of man; it refers also to that which is within, and works upon the corresponding feelings. But here it by no means follows that the two spheres of action are separate and divided; the distinction between them may not be looked upon as a separation. On the contrary, justice and morality have the same relation to each other that two concentric circles have; their superficial area is different, but they have a common centre. The divine will and the divine law is the basis of both. If the right of punishment is maintained without regard to this basis, it is then cut off from its source of vitality. The separation of justice from morality, in which Feuerbach and Fichte agree, contradicts our feelings of what is right, and appears to be one of those subtleties which can only be accounted for by the unpractical mental aberrations of our German speculative reasoners.

Feuerbach insists that, in the passing of a sentence, no regard should be had to the greater or lesser degree of moral obliquity of the action; not the immorality, but the illegality ought to be punished. "Civic punishments are not moral punishments; they are based upon the right of self-defence; their object is security and intimidation. It is not the breach of duty contained in, but the danger accruing from, the action, which renders amenable to civic punishment." If a criminal has been badly brought up, is ignorant, or of weak mind, these, according to Feuerbach, are no reasons for mitigating the punishment, but rather for increasing it. Such a criminal is in consequence more dangerous, and should receive a severer sentence. The deduction is logically correct; but it is, therefore, all the more a proof that some error must be contained in the axiom. If the right of punishment has no connection with the divine attributes and divine intentions, if it fulfils its object by means of terrorism, then the proper symbol to be displayed above the entrance to a court of justice would no longer be Themis with a balance, but rather a three-headed Cerberus.

Hegel, in his *Philosophy of Law*, which he lectured upon in the second decade of the present century, has very justly denounced this theory of punishment. He rejects the theory of a State contract; he admits the State to be a higher power placed over the individual; he designates the view, that crime is an evil to be got rid of, as superficial. He says: "It is a distinct question of right and wrong and of justice. By taking the other superficial view, the objective aspect of justice is set aside. The different motives of intimidation, improvement, etc. are quite in place; but they presuppose the justice of the punishment itself." Thus

Hegel inclines to the doctrines of Kant, and his philosophy, represented by Reinhold Köstlin amongst criminal jurists, was adapted to act as a wholesome antiseptic to the vapid doctrines of humanity which are in such favour now.

Meanwhile, however, these doctrines, in lieu of the antidote being applied, have been developed to an extreme degree, acquiring a preponderating influence upon public opinion and recent acts of the legislature.

An important advance in this direction took place as a result of the unwholesome development of the theory of monomania. Men are inclined to accept as an excuse for the criminal, that, although intelligent and accountable for his actions in other respects, still, with reference to the one point, he has been acting under an insane impulse. It is very true that evil passions, when a man gives way to them, acquire a power over him which is similar to insanity—a psychological process which is set forth in all its naked truth in Shakespeare's *Macbeth*. But just as true is the counter statement, that every step which a man takes on this road to ruin, by which he allows evil passions to assume such a mastery over him, is his own act, his own fault, for which he must be content to be held responsible. Heinroth, although he erred on the side of severity, was quite right in bringing this aspect of the truth into prominence.

Once arrived so far, there remained only one further step to be taken upon the path of error; and this has been taken by our most modern Materialists. A daring unbeliever has expressed it in the following language:—" With such nerves, such a bringing up, and such surroundings, the criminal could not act otherwise;" hence he was obliged to commit deeds of violence, arson, and murder. Whence did the State then derive its right to punish him? Those whom we call criminals are merely diseased, mad, or unfortunate persons. Therefore—and this is the necessary deduction—let us do away with houses of correction, and have instead asylums, hospitals, and houses of restraint; no more cells for rogues and murderers, but in lieu a PRYTANIUM!

The responsibility of man for his actions is an irreversible fact. Conscience is part of a man's being, and it is as criminal as it is futile to try and stifle it by sophistry or casuistry. Moral feeling and common sense teach us to treat a man who has committed a single evil action, not more mildly, but more severely, if it can be shown that his whole character is bad; for his character is the result of his own actions, and he is responsible for them.

Thus, then, the responsibility of man is a necessary and irreversible fundamental principle not only in the interests of morality, but also of the general welfare. This latter will not long remain unaffected, if we once reduce our administration of justice to a mere matter of police regulation, placing the punishment of a criminal on the same level with the safe keeping of a vessel containing virulent poison.

Punishment must be looked upon as retributive, and must assume the form of a just retaliation. This principle is in itself right, and must be maintained; still we do not overlook the objections that may be raised, the dangers with which it is surrounded, nor the limitations to which it must be subjected.

The first objection that will be raised is derived from the imperfection attaching to the administration of all human justice, even with the best laws and the best intentions of those who have to deal with them. This is really the case, and the experiences of the philanthropist must be very painful: the fact should make the dispensers of justice extremely careful. But still that is no reason for abolishing the principle itself, for throwing away the sword and scales of justice, for being content with the staff of the constable, and for using that as sparingly as is consistent with public safety. If perfection is not within our reach, still we must strive to carry it out in at least as approximate a manner as possible,—a principle which is of itself right, otherwise we might just as well abandon all attempts to realize any ideal in human affairs.

The next objection is, the impossibility of practically enforcing the *lex talionis* as Kant would have it. How is it possible, in cases of rape or arson, to retaliate upon the criminal in a similar manner? What barbarities would it not entail, if the Mosaic law of an eye for an eye, a tooth for a tooth, were to be enforced! But who obliges us to render retaliation so mechanical, or rather so indiscriminating? The science of ethics is something different to that of mathematics. There is no reason why every act of violence should be compensated for by a similar act; but the object in view is, that every infringement of the law should react upon the evildoer. The corner-stone of justice should be so firmly laid that any one who comes in contact with it, to upset it, should only injure himself. He who transgresses one of the laws, "Thou shalt not kill; thou shalt not steal," which have been ordered for the protection and welfare of the community, should find by experience that he has thereby injured himself, and that he is fighting against a power which is too strong for him. His misdeeds recoil upon himself, and he should be made to feel the greater or lesser heinousness of them by the degree of punishment which is inflicted upon him.

When we insist upon the doctrine of retaliation, we

are reproached with calling into play feelings of revenge and cruelty. This would be true if it were a question of private retaliation. The individual may not take revenge, and the community, too, is prohibited from being actuated by revenge. If we start with the notion of a one-sided contract, then, indeed, the mention of retaliation becomes very suspicious. From that point of view, morality calls for the punishment of criminals not as an act of retaliation, but in self-defence; and we are bound to use only so much violence as is necessary for such self-defence.

But it is very different if a higher Power reigns over us, and the human judge is to be regarded as an organ and exponent of His justice; then the sentence and its execution have nothing to do with human desires for revenge.

In a heathen State, retaliation may be accompanied by cruelty. In a Christian State, it is true that retaliation is terribly serious; but other considerations come into play to reduce its severity. Punishment is not intended to be injurious to the criminal, but, on the contrary, to bring him to reflection, and, in that he submits and confesses the justice of it, to save his better self.

If we maintain the principle of retaliation, it is not just to accuse us of inhuman intentions; for in that we do maintain that principle, we at the same time subject ourselves to retaliatory justice, and bind ourselves to accept whatever in that name may threaten us personally.

Our opponents would be entitled to reproach us with hardness of heart if we meant to say that retaliation should be the sole characteristic of punishment; but that is the peculiar feature of a Christian State, that room is found for mercy by the side of strictly just retaliation. That is the true Christian principle; the evil deed is punished, and yet at the same time the doer may and does find pity and assistance. Certainly, if there are still any penal establishments which are training colleges for crime,—if the released criminal does not find a helping hand stretched out to assist him in his return to a better mode of life,—both sentences and punishments have a taint of cruelty. The powers of the State, in whose name the sentence is pronounced, are bound to take care that there is no lack of spiritual care and comfort for the condemned. We must all of us get rid of that unchristian Phariseeism, which looks upon a man, who has once been found guilty of a crime, as shut out for ever from society. These are lofty subjects for the State to deal with, and any one who talks of retaliation must also bear in mind these duties. Who does not thankfully admit that at the present time many noble minds are working in this direction?

The power of punishing becomes dangerous when it is pushed too far, and it will be so whenever the idea of what the State is, is incorrectly taken up. Do not let us suppose that at present there is no danger of extending the domain of the State and its authorities too far. That occurs when, in modern fashion, all the actions of our lives are placed under civil surveillance, and all progress (a very indefinite and unsatisfactory term) is looked upon as under the control of the State. The temporal powers have just as little call as the ecclesiastical to do everything; and for that very reason it is necessary that the two spheres exist, and side by side, in order that there may be room for freedom.

If we may be allowed to regard the new criminal code of Germany of 1871 as a mirror in which we may see a reflection of the present position of penal science, there can be no doubt that in it a strong bias of humanity preponderates, just as in our modern educational establishments excessive gentleness and forbearance are too prominent, and the corrective of Christian earnestness is wanting.

Men are mistaken in supposing that seriousness of retaliation can be eliminated from our criminal code without injury to the safety of the public. If, in cases of serious crimes, the punishment bears no proportion to the offence, the popular feeling of justice and the national conscience becomes deadened; for we must not overlook the fact that, in the great majority of men, the distinction between good and evil, and serious moral decision, is much less maintained by what they were taught as children and still have preached to them, than by the equity with which they see the penal code administered at the hands of the temporal power. Once let it become the rule that crimes or public misdemeanours are either insufficiently or not at all punished, and the result will be that public opinion will come to look upon such things as no longer reprehensible. It is no question of the horrors of the cat-of-nine-tails or of military law, but of the effects produced by a proper administration of justice upon the popular conscience. That will be lulled to sleep if humanity becomes immoderately predominant; it is kept awake and active when in judicial transactions, as is the case in England, a solemn earnestness predominates, and in the publication of the sentence direct reference is made to the supreme Lawgiver and Judge, against whom the accused has sinned, and to whom he is advised to look for mercy. But enervation of the popular conscience necessarily reacts in a deteriorating manner upon the general welfare and the general security.

Let us here point out the various tendencies which a one-sided humanity assumes, and see whether the objects of the State—namely, justice and humanity—are really served by them individually.

1. In order to reduce the number of charges and proceedings, in order to prevent so many cases of crime coming to light, it has been determined with reference to a number of offences that they are not to be prosecuted by the State and punished at its instance, but that this is to be relegated to the injured individual. This is even the case in respect of rape, sec. 177, the next heinous crime to murder. Here the charge cannot be withdrawn; but in cases of serious bodily injury, the charge, once preferred, may be withdrawn at any time before passing sentence, sec. 232. Thereby powerful and influential criminals have always a chance of impunity, in that the injured parties may be bought off, or, owing to fear of ulterior consequences, will not come forward to prove anything. The door is set wide open for bribery and corruption; but if a poor man, or one without connections, has committed the crime, he may rest assured that he will be charged and convicted. Where do we here find any equality in the sight of the law? But even supposing that neither bribery nor intimidation takes place, still it is a serious matter for the injured party to prefer a criminal charge, as there is always an appearance of private revenge. No such invidious suspicion can attach to the State. When it prefers a charge, every one knows that it is only fulfilling a duty without any selfish object in view, and purely for the purpose of vindicating the law. The purity of the administration of justice, and the maintenance of the dignity of the law, seem to call for a revision of these professedly humane regulations respecting the initiation of charges.

2. The humane tendencies of the age have led to milder forms of sentence being awarded to attempts at murder and to manslaughter. At the same time,

the code contains severe punishments against cases of theft. If the code already contains a disproportion between the sentences applicable to these crimes, the well-known inclinations of our juries go still farther. They are very ready, in cases of murder and manslaughter, to recognise mitigating circumstances, but in cases of theft to allow the extreme of severity to come into play. In Swabia a short time ago, a man who killed his wife with a brick got one and a half years' imprisonment in the House of Correction. Had he been convicted of habitual theft he would probably have got ten years (sec. 244). It almost seems as though our jurors were influenced by heathen traditions, as though they had some faint notion of the ancient German compensations in cases of murder and manslaughter, and that in consequence these crimes did not strike them in their full enormity. If such really is the case, we have arrived at a point where ancient heathen traditions and modern ideas of humanity meet.

This evil has very wide bearings. First of all, the moral conscience of the nation is injured. Between crimes against the life and crimes against the property of our neighbour, there is not only a graduated, but a specific difference. The guilt of blood is of a different kind from that guilt which the thief has taken upon himself. This difference arises from the dignity of the person of man, whom God created after His own image.

The Mosaic law demanded the death of the premeditated murderer: the thief was to be punished with forty stripes and a four or five-fold restitution of the stolen property; if he was unable to pay, then the punishment of imprisonment in the form of slavery came into play, and this continued until the next ensuing Sabbath year. A similar standard should be employed by us in apportioning punishments for these two forms of crime. Any one who attacks the life of a man not only robs him of all his earthly goods, but he also wickedly interferes with the prerogative of God, who has reserved to Himself the disposition of life and death. He takes upon himself a load of guilt, which he can never entirely free himself from. A human life is something sacred, and that, too, in a totally different sense to that in which we say our neighbour's property ought to be sacred. Here we have something in itself sacred, the destruction of which calls for the severest punishment. If, in opposition to this, in our law and in our practice there be no difference, or only a difference of degree, made between attacks upon life and those upon property, or eventually men come to consider property more sacred than life, then the question may well arise, "Is this really maintaining the dignity of the person of man? Is this real humanity, or the contrary?"

Another very injurious consequence is, that the people feel a want of harmony in this matter between the human administration of the law and divine justice. Hence arises a dangerous conception regarding the authority of the government and of the law,— the right of punishment is no longer exercised as in the service of eternal justice, but as is most conducive to the interests of those who wield it; the divine commands are no longer reflected from its surface, but the avarice and selfishness of men. This is all fuel to the fire of the Socialists, who assert that all our social and civic ordinances are mere inventions, originating in the selfishness of men of property. He who promotes such ideas acts contrary to the common weal. That is undermined when property is deified, and crimes against the image of God are carelessly dealt with.

3. The punishment of death for the crime of infanticide has been done away with (sec. 217). Even in cases where it has been committed in a wicked and aggravated manner, capital punishment can no longer be inflicted.

This is an old and deep sore in the administration of our law that we here touch upon. In the days of terrible severity, the punishment of death was applicable; but even then the usual course was, that the seducer at the same time got off scot free; and yet in many cases he, by having brought an inexperienced and, until then, perhaps innocent female to this condition of desperation, is a participator in the murderous act—in fact he is a double murderer, both in the spiritual and bodily sense. Gretchen is beheaded, Dr. Faust goes his way unaspersed. This is how matters formerly stood; and it could not be allowed to remain so, the judicial anomaly was too startling. In this case the object should have been to make the seducer responsible as accomplice in the misdeed, and at least to award to him the punishment of loss of character. But it would seem that no such thing was thought of. The impunity of the heartless offender still continues. A false path was persevered in; and as men would not quit it, naturally it became necessary to assign the mildest possible form of punishment to the crime of child murder, reducing it to two years' imprisonment. Still the inevitable result is, that an impression gains ground that the legislature does not set so high a value upon the life of a child. Here we have humanity reverting into cruelty. We have already heard the voices of some godless men demanding that the procuration of abortion shall not be punished at all.

4. Out of our strivings after humanity which are not restrained by any stern morality, we find noxious

ideas have sprung up in modern legislature regarding matrimony, conjugal fidelity, and modesty generally. It is said to be humane to remove all obstacles to matrimony, even those which God Himself has decreed; to facilitate divorce, and even to afford the adulterous party an opportunity of remarriage. This same so-called humane spirit appears to have influenced some of the arrangements of our German penal code.

There is no prohibition of concubinage. No matter what offence open profligacy may give, the law affords no power of interference; neither the criminal law nor the police can intervene. In the Napoleonic Code there is a punishment laid down if a married man keeps a concubine in his own house; in accordance with it, the wife can require and obtain her removal. With us it is different. The wife in so pitiful a case will look in vain for any legal means of getting rid of the cause of offence, of asserting her own position as wife, her dignity as mother and helpmeet. Her only means of redress is an action for divorce.

Again, an action for the punishment of adultery is in no case possible, unless a divorce has been judicially obtained on that ground (sec. 172). The result is, that a man cannot bring an action against the seducer of his wife unless he has previously been divorced from her. Is not this similar to a denial of justice in one of the worst cases of injury? If the marriage be dissolved, an action for the subsequent punishment of the seducer can hardly have any object.

The trading in profligacy, which Origenes terms the pestilence of youth, which was successfully interdicted amongst the people of Israel, is alluded to in our penal code; but how? In the article on police misdemeanours. At the same time as the neglecting to destroy caterpillars, the carrying of a sword-stick, or driving a sledge within the limits of a town without bells is prohibited, we read: "A female who shall carry on a trade in unchastity, contrary to the police regulations, shall be punished with imprisonment." The thing itself is not punishable; it can only be punished when the local or district police regulations on the subject have been disregarded. Here we have one of the direst offences against the dignity of a man and a Christian placed in the same category as a number of indifferent and morally harmless actions. How can such a combination, and the entire course of procedure, act otherwise than demoralizingly upon the people? To them, that which is morally objectionable will also appear harmless; for at the same time the police have the power, in all cases in which it seems good to them, and under such conditions as they may predetermine, to grant permission.

It is deserving of recognition that our penal code does endeavour to restrain the most flagrant offences by the enactments against procuration (secs. 180, 181).

God grant that this may be seriously carried out; for a conscientious government, sec. 361 furnishes yet one point on which a position in accordance with duty may be taken up. It is made discretionary to enlarge the scope of the police regulations, which have been mentioned, to an unconditional prohibition; still it is deeply to be regretted that the true principle has not been maintained in our penal code, but has been insulted and denied.

Let us again resume: the weakening and abolition of the laws, by means of which in days gone by the sanctity of matrimony and purity of manners were protected, began more than a century ago. It was no fortuitous occurrence. It did not come about apart from the condition of the people. It was called into existence partially owing to a predominant degeneracy of morals. We may say such laws are the codification of a state of things already existing in the community. They are a terrible witness against our nation, which during its heathenish condition was remarkable for its conjugal fidelity and modesty of manners. But there is another aspect in which such laws must be regarded. They have their origin in an attempt to make the statutes accord with customs and manners prevailing at the time; and this is called humanity. But the fact is, this assumption contains a fearful untruth.

In ancient Rome, even during the commencement of the Imperial times, it was considered that wholesome and strict laws ought to be promulgated, as a dam to check the increasing corruption of morals. That very thing constitutes the majesty of the law and of the legislature, that they restrain the passions and vices of men, that they protect such good customs as still exist, and that they try to recover such as have been lost. So long as the laws are pure, there is still a hope that a powerful government may oppose the evil and co-operate to bring about better times. But in our days the opposite seems to be the principle which has been adopted, that the law must accommodate itself as much as possible to the wicked lusts of mankind. The offences which occur in daily life, and, it is very true, did also occur in former times, may pollute the stream of morality and of custom, but impure laws poison the very source. A beginning has been made in allowing the laws to diverge from the pattern which is eternally in force; where will the deterioration stop? What pledge have we that further concessions will not be made? Public opinion is changeable, moral feelings become more and more blunted under such laws as we now have. The calls for liberty of the flesh will be ever increasing, and is the law really to keep pace with the increasing corruption?

No; it ought to be a witness against the evil, and a protection and support to the good. The lawgivers are answerable for this. Even regarded from the shallow theory of a mere social contract, the duty of the government can and must be maintained, not only to care for the life and property of the subjects, but also for the respectability, morality, and purity of family life.

For whilst these good qualities disappear, all noble feelings die out, and a dark, lawless spirit, which is inimical to the welfare of the community, takes possession of the desecrated position. What, then, becomes of humanity? It was not true humanity or love for our brethren of the human race that introduced such laws, but a spirit of darkness inimical to the life of man, which, under the mask of humanity, sought in this manner to carry out its foul designs, which are the extirpation of all virtue and the ruin of the country.

In our criminal code the punishment of death is still retained,—that is to say, for cold-blooded, premeditated, and prearranged murder in general, and for attempted murder when directed against the life of the sovereign (secs. 80, 211).

These ordinances are at variance with the whole spirit of the code. The punishment of death in it appears an anomaly. It was at one time abolished, and we know how it came to be reinstated. The controversy on the subject is by no means concluded, and we may not shirk the question whether in a Christian Commonwealth capital punishment has any place at all?

It is here no question of capital punishment for other crimes, as it formerly existed, and which no one wishes to see revived, but with regard to the punishment of death in cases of murder or attempted murder.

Has the government the power, in extreme cases and for the most serious crimes, to award and to inflict capital punishment? If the reply be affirmative, is it advisable for it to exercise such power? And what if it declines to put such power in force? This would seem to be the manner in which the question must be treated.

1. Has the government any such power? The answer which we, as heralds of Christian doctrine, have to give is not optional. It is here no question of our own inclinations and wishes. We have the Holy Scriptures, and we must refer to them, being bound by their authority. On the authority of the Scripture we must say, "The government has such power."

When Christ stood before the judgment-seat of Pilate, who, as prefect of the Imperator Tiberius, had to decide upon the charge, which was a question of life and death, Pilate said to Christ, "Knowest thou not that I have power to crucify Thee, and have power to release Thee?" Christ did not dispute this power; on the contrary, He recognised it, and asserted in His answer that Pilate had not been charged with it by accident or by the will of man, but had received it from God. He said, "Thou couldest have no power at all against me, except it were given thee from above." The word ἐξουσια (translated in our text as *power*) which Christ used, for He spoke Greek with Pilate, does not denote illegal power, such as a robber possesses over those who have fallen into his hands, but a legitimate power. Pilate understood the reference to God; he felt his conscience touched, and reflected upon his responsibility. "From thenceforth Pilate sought to release Him." If Christ had considered the power of the government in dispensing life and death to be an assumption, or a human invention, or anything of itself improper and objectionable, He would have expressed Himself very differently. With these words of Christ, the teaching of St. Paul in his Epistle to the Romans perfectly agrees: "The powers that be are ordained of God. . . . He is the minister of God to thee for good. But if thou do that which is evil, be afraid; for he beareth not the sword in vain: for he is the minister of God, a revenger to execute wrath upon him that doeth evil." He speaks here primarily of the Roman power, and the sword which it bore was the symbol of the *jus vitæ et necis.* He beareth not the sword in vain. What can this mean, other than that the power can in extreme cases make use of it against the evildoer? When Paul was arraigned upon a capital charge, and defended himself before the Roman prefect Festus, he said, "If I be an offender, or have committed anything worthy of death, I refuse not to die" (Acts xxv. 11).

In all these cases it is heathen authorities to whom this power is ascribed, so that there is an original commission, applicable to all nations and continuing for all time, which is the source of such power; and we shall probably not err when we state that both Christ and Paul in their assertions referred to that divine ordinance which existed even in the days of Noah: "At the hand of every man's brother will I require the life of man. Whoso sheddeth man's blood, by man shall his blood be shed: for in the image of God made He man" (Gen. ix. 5, 6).

Man dare not take the life of man, for he certainly cannot give it to him. This is a pure truism; and if it were only man dealing with man, the objections to and inadmissibility of any capital punishment would be evident. It is only when a higher form of justice reigns over us, and when it makes use of men upon earth as its ambassadors and instruments, that we can entertain any idea of the disposition of life and death being in the hands of men.

That which is said in Scripture regarding blood-guiltiness finds its confirmation in the consciences of men. Cain wanders restlessly and a fugitive, finding no peace. Macbeth cannot sleep any more. So it is too at the present day, and it will be thus so long as there are men upon earth. The consciousness of having committed a murder, the recollection of the dead, constantly pursues the guilty man. It is no superstition induced by education, it is the divine voice which calls to him, "Where is thy brother Abel? What hast thou done? The voice of thy brother's blood cries unto me from the ground." Granted that the criminal is able in the bustle of the world, or by exciting or engrossing pursuits and pleasures, to deaden the sound of this voice for a time, still in the sleepless hours of the night, or in dreams, it will make itself heard, all the louder, in accusation against him. The numbers who, not being punished by men for blood-guiltiness, have gone mad or committed suicide are sufficient proof of this. If a murderer is moved to confession, and really repents of his crime, he feels himself impelled not to ask for his life to be spared; his own conscience confirms the justice of capital punishment. It does sometimes occur that such a criminal not only welcomes death as an atonement and a relief from his misery, but actually begs that capital punishment may be inflicted. Capital punishment may be abolished, but who will abolish the Eumenides who pursue Orestes?

We may not require of the authorities to expunge capital punishment from the code. If it be only retained for the most rare cases, still it remains as a wholesome warning, as the awful background of the entire legislature, a witness to the connection existing between human and divine justice.

2. But now we approach a very different question. How about the exercise of this fearful power? Is it advisable? Ought not a Christian government rather to desist from using it, and in all cases to allow a mitigation or alteration of sentence to take effect? Here we touch a point upon which the opponents of capital punishment have much to say that is true and worthy of being laid to heart. The danger of judicial murder taking place is seldom completely excluded, especially now that a jury have it in their power to find a verdict of guilty upon circumstantial evidence, and that personal confession is no longer absolutely necessary, as was formerly the case in Bavaria, according to the *Codex Maximilianeus*. It is better that nine guilty men escape death, than that one innocent man should suffer it.

The scenes which occur upon the scaffold, and the undoubtedly barbarizing effect which public executions produce upon the spectators, undoubtedly have much weight. In such cases there arise in men of coarse feelings something of that fiendish pleasure with which the heathen Romans used to look on at the gladiatorial combats. That brutality which feeds upon the sight of Spanish bull-fights finds here congenial aliment. Public executions do not diminish the number of criminals; even the horrors with which executions were accompanied in former centuries do not appear to have deterred, but rather to have awakened a pleasure in cruelty, and thus indirectly to have increased crime. If an execution must take place at all, the carrying of it out in the court of the prison, in the presence of selected witnesses, is the lesser evil.

It is a fearful thing that amongst a Christian people crimes worthy of death and executions should occur at all. Richard Rothe was quite right in saying that the day on which an execution takes place should be passed as a day of mourning, humiliation, and repentance by the whole nation.

If capital punishment is retained in the code, sufficient care must be taken that the necessary supplementary paragraphs are also there. In many cases, to push the literal reading of the law to extremities becomes the greatest possible injustice. If this should occur in a case where life and death are at stake, care must be taken that an antidote be available. In order to find such a remedy, our modern lawgivers have allowed extenuating circumstances an extensive scope, and the consideration of them is remitted to the jury.

Trial by jury, oral examinations, and publicity of trial are all great benefits. The German people had a very ancient right to them; but they were long withheld, and at last given back in the year 1848. He who knows from experience what the former course of procedure was, will know how to value these blessings. As in an organized State the people have a right to participate in the legislature, so, too, it is only right that they should have a voice in the decision affecting the life and liberty of a citizen. According to the ancient German principle, every one has a right to trial by his peers. This is effected by the institution of trial by jury.

Jurors have to deliver a verdict upon the facts. Still it by no means follows that they, more than others, are also capable of deciding as to extenuating circumstances. Here we have some of the most difficult questions, as to free agency and soundness of mind, calling for consideration. If the decision upon these points is handed over to the jury, then we have those mitigated verdicts which have been mentioned above, and which are utterly at variance with justice. The legal advisers of rulers, who have a wider range of vision than jurymen, would probably be more capable than the latter are of weighing attendant circumstances, and appraising the degree of mental responsibility. Hence the English mode of procedure appears to be the most commendable; agreeably to it the jury have nothing to do with extenuating circumstances, and are not permitted to allow them to exert any influence upon the verdict. But if any such have come to light during the trial, the jury have the power, in delivering their verdict, to recommend the guilty person to the clemency of the sovereign.

The proper complement of the stringency of the law consists in the power of mercy vested in the throne. If a contradiction arises between the letter of the law and feelings of moral justice, between the human and heavenly command, the difficulty finds here its proper solution, in a gracious resolution of the sovereign. He, by mitigating or remitting the sentence, exercises his highest and most glorious attribute. He acts in such a case as the representative of the highest Lawgiver, and his action becomes thereby the reflection of divine action, in which justice and mercy are combined.

3. If a government should deem it right not to exercise the power of life and death, or to renounce it, what is then to be said? Answer: Ecclesiastics are not entitled to interfere.

The Empress Elizabeth of Russia never signed a death warrant, but always commuted the sentence into banishment to Siberia. If our rulers choose to do the same, it is not fitting that any objection should be raised. They have the right, if they have so much confidence in their people, to try what effect so much clemency will produce upon the community. If, as is the case of the latest Swiss federal constitution, capital punishment be erased from the statute-book, it would be unworthy of the servants of Christ to protest against this. Christian bishops, in ancient times, assumed a different attitude.

Ambrosius, Augustine, and other great teachers of the Church, did, it is true, recognise the power of the authorities to threaten the criminal with death; but when it came to be put into effect, they exercised in many cases their right of intercession in favour of the condemned man, and saved his life.

CHAPTER XV.

WAR AND INTERNATIONAL LAW.

How is war compatible with a Christian Commonwealth? Does it not form the most complete antithesis to the feelings with which every Christian should be filled, and to that condition of material and moral progress which is the object of the State, and more especially of the Christian Commonwealth?

There is only one ground upon which war can be justified; it is the same, and can be no other than that upon which the right of punishment rests. The government is called upon, and it is its duty, to protect those who do right from injury and violence, and to inflict penal justice upon evildoers. For this purpose is the sword, of which Paul speaks in his Epistle to the Romans, given into its hands. It is nowhere written that any other sword has been given to it. Authority does not carry two swords. The sword of justice is the only one confided to it by God. If it desires to carry a second,—apart from the exercise of justice to carry a sword for the execution of selfish objects or for satisfying revenge,—this becomes a usurpation which it cannot base upon any divine permission, and for which it cannot produce any divine commission, being opposed to the divine commands. A Christian ruler will only put his power into force for the purpose of executing justice, and will enter upon warlike action for no other purpose.

The government owes to its subjects protection of

their rights. That is the reason why it employs the sword against the murderer and rebel, the internal enemies of society; and for the same reason, too, it is bound to draw it against the external enemies of the State. Every nation has a right as such to exist, and the government is bound to defend the country against foreign attack. Where no State exists, the duty of defence against predatory attack devolves upon the individual. In cases of necessity, where no governmental assistance can be invoked, the individual in defending himself and his property acts in the name of the government, and the act of self-defence is subsequently, when the government is made acquainted with it, recognised by it as justifiable. In an organized State, this duty devolves exclusively upon the government. Private war must disappear. Connivance at duelling by a Christian State is a denial of Christian principles, and at the same time a contravention of the authority of the law, to say nothing of the absurdities, barbarisms, prejudices, and anomalies with which duelling is connected in the form it at present assumes.

When Christ said, in His Sermon on the Mount, "Resist not evil," He enjoined that brotherly feeling by which all His disciples ought to be bound together. He in that sentence no more withdrew the commission of the authorities to resist evil and to punish it, which He on other occasions solemnly recognised, than He did away with the paternal right of chastisement. No father has a right to lay his power down, and to look passively on at all sorts of evil in his family; just as little is the government called upon to lay down the sword of justice.

The making of war in the service of justice is recognised as being possible, and is admitted in Holy Scripture. If it were otherwise, and every war were declared to be iniquitous, it would on no pretence be permissible to exercise the profession of arms; but such an occupation is expressly permitted in the New Testament.

When the soldiers came to John the Baptist and asked, "What shall we do?" they were not told, "Take your discharge, and give up the profession of arms," but, "Do violence to no man, neither accuse any falsely, and be content with your wages." When Christ showed His pleasure in the centurion of Capernaum, and when Peter ordered the Roman centurion Cornelius and those who were with him to be baptized, no word was said about their renouncing military service; in accordance with which, the ancient Christian Church, taken as a whole, considered it permissible to accept military service even under heathen commanders.

War is the most fearful scourge of heaven, not only because it spreads untold evils over both the nations who are at war, but more especially because it almost inevitably gives occasion for the letting loose of devilish passions in many individuals. For this very reason, on every occasion when war is declared or carried on, there rests upon the authorities an enormous responsibility, such as in no other case supervenes. For the same reason, too, Christianity and humanity enjoin us to obviate as much as possible, by international contracts and conventions, the cruelties and deeds of horror which follow in the footsteps of war. The task is difficult, but one that must be undertaken. The Convention of Geneva, which has already done so much good, and the Congress at Brussels, belong to the most comforting occurrences of our present century.

Suffering humanity longs for peace. The Christian Church sends up a prayer to heaven: "Give peace in our days;" "Take away ambition and lust of conquest from the hearts both of rulers and of people!" Is it possible to consider ambition or lust of conquest as noble qualities? When they come into play and influence the actions of the State, the Christian calling both of the authorities and of the nation is denied; and when they penetrate amongst the people, the morality of public opinion is ruined; for such passions are completely antagonistic to Christian principles. National hatred cannot co-exist with Christianity or with humanity; it, like every other species of hatred between man and man, is a sin.

Xenophon tells us that Cyrus learned in his youth to hate a lie; for, in the ideas of Zoroaster, that was the object of education. The Persians taught their boys to use the bow and to tell the truth. When Cyrus had become a young man, and was instructed by his grandfather in the art of war, he heard with surprise of quite a different doctrine,—how to deceive and by stratagem to defeat an enemy. Upon inquiry, he was told that this was only allowable towards an enemy and in time of war; that, as regards friends and countrymen, the duty of truthfulness existed in full force.

The surprise of Cyrus ought to exist amongst us, and in a higher degree, seeing that we are Christians; for in the present day deceit and cunning are employed in war. We require much clearness of perception and conscientious discernment, in order to prevent a degeneration taking place in our moral ideas.

The art of self-defence consists of feints and surprises, by which the opponent is taken unawares and overcome; they are part of the art, we expect their employment. In this respect, the art of fighting is similar to that of chess. In war, feigned attacks and retreats are made in order to deceive the enemy as to the real intentions of the campaign. This occurs when war has been declared. The declaration of war contains an intimation that such means will be employed. Thus both sides understand, men are prepared for them; and if such take place, the opponent raises no objections—they constitute no betrayal of confidence.

Here we have the distinction. Confidence may not be abused, it may never be employed to the disadvantage of the enemy; the noble-mindedness of the opponent may not be deceived—as, for instance, by a fraudulent hoisting of the hospital flag. Fidelity in the maintenance of contracts, a punctual observation of an agreed armistice, punctilious respect for the bearers of a flag of truce—these are duties which admit of no exception, no evasion. The proper military feeling of honour looks upon any breach of them as disreputable and detestable. It becomes, therefore, a question of deciding what the situation is; what are the cases in which confidence has been expressly declared at an end, and those in which it is affirmed and expected.

If peace be concluded, both parties are bound to consider it as a real peace, and, as becomes Christian people, to look upon it as a basis upon which mutual confidence is restored. The continuance of arts of deception during a condition of peace is detestable; but that is unfortunately the mournful part of our present position. There is neither open war nor yet peace between the States of the continent of Europe; or rather, it is war under the hypocritical mask of peace. None of the Powers has confidence in the others; evil deeds and bitter experiences have been prominent; noble and Christian principles have disappeared. None of the powers expects to find such in the others. Fierce passions in the people and leading men amongst them are the predominant motives of action. This latent condition of war, quite unworthy of the Christian appellation, antagonistic to humanity and political virtue, is the severe chronic malady under the burden of which the nations groan. The effects of the evil display themselves in a twofold manner. The present position of affairs destroys the characters of statesmen; hence diplomacy has become the art of lying, and lies have become political science. From the same evil arise the monstrous armaments, the endless increment of standing armies, and in connection therewith the increase of poverty and moral depravity.

It is the first duty of our statesmen to recover from this position, by a recognition of Christian principles, by calling noble feelings into play, and by paving the way for a union of nations, founded upon truth and justice, by establishing an international law.

Notwithstanding all the endeavours of science, from Hugo Grotius until now, we are very far from the introduction and holding sacred of an international law. It is impossible to bring that about in practice, or even in theory, except Christian principles are recognised as furnishing the pattern which is to be followed.

In heathen antiquity, a stranger was looked upon as an enemy; the nations, sharply sundered, and held together by no common moral bond, fought with inhuman cruelty. History and the monuments of the East are full of such records. Even in the doctrines of Plato and Aristotle, that brutality is not overcome. Any thought of an equal and common dignity of man, and of any duty incumbent upon all to love as brethren, was very foreign to their ideas. To possess slaves, and to enslave the conquered, was looked upon as quite allowable. It is true that the Roman laws of war contained noble feelings of honour and humanity: "To spare the conquered and to humble the proud. . . . A magnanimous lion is satisfied with having prostrated the bodies; the fight is at an end when the enemy lies at one's mercy." These are genuine Roman sayings; and yet the prominent characteristics of that iron empire were, lust of conquest, severity, and deceit towards the nations that still opposed them.

In Christ there first dawned upon the world a light, in which a just and humane attitude of the nations to one another appeared to be a desirable and attainable object of pursuit. Paul was obliged to come and announce this great fact to the philosophers at Athens: " God, that made the world and all things therein, seeing that He is Lord of heaven and earth, . . . hath made of one blood all nations of men for to dwell on all the face of the earth, and hath determined the times before appointed, and the bounds of their habitation; that they should seek the Lord, if haply they might feel after Him, and find Him, though He be not far from every one of us : . . . as certain also of your own poets have said, For we are also His offspring" (Acts xvii. 22–27). The unity of God, the common Father, and the unity of the whole race of men, was proclaimed; and upon these truths is based the duty of brotherly love, justice, good-will, and fidelity — as from every individual towards every individual, so also on the part of every nation to every nation, and from State to State. It is nowhere stated that this duty is only incumbent upon us in our relations with Christian men and Christian nations, that a Christian nation ought to wait until the neighbouring nations become Christian before they can enter into brotherly relations with them. The object was then set forth, and the way to attain it revealed; but although the Roman Empire, as such, recognised the Christian religion, the entire task was a long way from being accomplished. The ancient heathen notion of a universal rule still worked on,—that notion of repelling, and the lust of conquering, those nations which had not submitted to the Empire. In the Middle Ages the way was paved for a better state of things. Princes and people did entertain the idea of one Christian family of nations. In the Pope, that common guardian of our barbarian forefathers, as Johann von Müller calls him, there appeared to exist an authority fitted for intercession and establishing peace amongst the whole of Western Christianity. But that grand idea was marred by a want of toleration towards those who differed in faith. In the Crusades there manifested itself a reprehensible mixture of Christian watchwords and apparently Christian spirit, with bloodthirstiness and want of integrity towards infidels. And how was it possible that any mutual attitude based upon integrity could exist amongst Christian nations, so long as the wicked maxim was maintained, "that it was not necessary to keep faith with a heretic"? By the persecutions of the Moors in Spain, and of the Jews in the whole of the West, the Christian international law was denied. The federation of Christian States ought to hold out their hand to such nations as are not Christians, and, without requiring any acceptance of creeds or baptism, invite them to recognise and practise those humane and just principles which we owe to the doctrines of Christ. The Mohammedans, Jews, and heathen ought to have been able to recognise the truth of the Christian religion from the actions of Christian nations; instead of which, the European conquerors in America, by their conduct towards the heathen, have incurred an immeasurable debt of guilt.

Still, for such nations as were within the pale of Christianity, great blessings flowed from their recognition of the fact that they all formed one family, enclosed in a sacred bond. These good things have fallen into decay since selfishness and self-idolizing of rulers, lust of conquest and intrigue, became predominant in the time of Louis XIV. In the eighteenth century the moral bonds between State and State were almost entirely destroyed. The Revolutions, the approach of which Leibnitz foretold when he saw all nobility of political principle passing away, and the Napoleonic empire, filled with the spirit of ancient Rome, were not adapted to draw those bonds closer. Then came the wholesome reaction which took place at the fall of Napoleon. With the return to a lively Christian faith, there arose a general feeling that the age of lust of conquest and hatred of nations had come to an end, and that from that time forth a compact based upon justice and charity should arise amongst Christian rulers and European nations. The intelligent philosopher, Franz von Baader, composed his memoirs "On the necessity produced by the French Revolution for a fresh and intimate connection of religion with politics," which served as the cause, or at least as the inducement, for Alexander I. of Russia and Frederick William III. of Prussia, in connection with Emperor Francis I. of Austria, to set up the Holy Alliance. This was the most important attempt ever made to bring into actual practice a code of international law worthy of the Christian name, and to put an end to that disgraceful and injurious condition of hostile and suspicious suspense. The fundamental principles were: The solemn recognition of the fact that Christ is the Head not only of the religious, but also of the civic community; that temporal rulers derive their dignity and authority from Him, and that, consequently, they are in duty bound to exercise their powers according to the mind of Christ, with justice and mercy; and that there exists a brotherly bond of union amongst Christian nations, which ought to be recognised and held sacred.

It would be very wrong to refuse to admit the benefits which Europe owes to the Holy Alliance. Therein lay salutary progress, compared with the state of international law during the Middle Ages, and compared with the religious wars of the sixteenth and seventeenth centuries. In this alliance the three great divisions of the Church were recognised as being, what they really are, members of one Christian body,—three mighty branches borne by the same stem, not three separate bodies which have nothing to do with each other, and devoid of mutual duties. The Greek Catholic Czar of Russia, the Roman Catholic Emperor of Austria, and the Protestant King of Prussia, made a compact on the common ground of Christianity. To the idea which was thereby expressed, we owe the quiet and happy period during which the three confessions on the whole lived together in peace and mutual respect,—a position which, unfortunately, owing to later events, has been put an end to. Europe owed to the Holy Alliance a peace which endured for forty years,—Germany, indeed, enjoyed it for fifty years,—disturbed only by partial disturbances. Meanwhile, the principles which had been agreed to as the basis upon which the compact was made, were not faithfully adhered to by the governments themselves, not properly appreciated by the people, and in the course of decades lost footing everywhere. This very lamentable result may be traced to a fundamental error made in originating the alliance. The principle of international law which was set up was correct, but the true principle of statute law was wanting. This was only formulated in a very incomplete manner, and in the background there remained one truly pernicious prejudice, which biased all three governments. At that time only two political parties were recognised, the party of Reform and that of Conservatism; and as, in the French Revolution, the Reformers had been guilty of crimes, all reform was looked upon as dangerous and to be rejected. The Conservatives were always looked upon as being right, the others wrong. The fact was completely ignored, that both principles, that of authority as well as that of liberty, were equally necessary to the life of the State and equally justifiable. Both can be overdone, and both the extremes which arise therefrom are objectionable. Prepossessed by that shortsightedness, and guided by a superstitious dread of revolution, the governments introduced the system of protection under which the people suffered, and were excited to want of confidence and exasperation. Of the rights of the people, of the privileges of parliaments, and of guarantees for freedom, no mention was made in the proceedings of the Holy Alliance; and in that the governments opposed all those things, the evil, which Napoleon in his displeasure on the island of St. Helena had prognosticated, became a realized fact, namely, *C'est une alliance des rois contre les peuples.* Hence the revolutions of 1820, 1821, 1830, and 1848. The whole system became so rotten, wanting in vital truth and power, that its dissolution was inevitable. A new Napoleonic empire arose in 1851, which declared the treaties of 1815 to be void; and the last remnant of the system of States set up in connection with the Holy Alliance, the German Confederacy, was broken up in 1866.

Since then the temple of Janus has been thrown open afresh, and its open condition is permanent. The system of international law nations proclaimed in 1815 has disappeared; a new, better, or even partially satisfactory one has not taken its place.

An attempt is being made to prepare the way for setting up a code of international law by means of science. The present intellectual tendency endeavours to establish this new law apart from Christian principles. It is this "modern international law of civilised States" which Bluntschli has attempted to formulate in the shape of a statute-book, a code of 862 paragraphs. However excellent the material in its individual sections may be, the groundwork is utterly insufficient: humanity not based upon Christian doctrine. It was the great mistake made by rationalistic Protestant theologians, that they presumed to proclaim moral doctrines without the doctrines of faith: morals without religion. It is a similar mistake for jurists to wish to isolate international law from Christian faith. The feeling of right and wrong, moral tact, disregard of all low-minded and unworthy means, fidelity to treaties, and mutual confidence, are elements indispensable to an international law. Whatever of such feelings existed in ancient times, sprang from the primitive religion and its traditions; when they fell to pieces, those feelings were lost too. The Christian religion has confirmed, regenerated, and refined them for us. If it be undermined, those noble principles are also in danger of dying out. They are not dry goods, which can be laid by and taken out for use at pleasure, they are living impulses which cannot be cut off from their source; and that source is Christ, who by His doctrines, His institutions, and His spirit, produces and maintains such ideas and feelings. If Christ be hidden from the nations, and His spirit banished, no philosophy, no legal doctrines, can resuscitate the expiring political virtues, reverence for the law and brotherly love; the fruit, once separated from the tree, perishes. If in our days morality and rectitude do exist without religion, it is only in exceptional cases, which may simply be explained by the fact that the spirit of Christianity, under the influence of which we have all grown up, even when its origin is disavowed, continues to act for a time. When the sun has actually sunk below the horizon, daylight continues for half an hour. Who is so bold as to deduce from that fact the assertion that no sun at all is necessary, and that we could have light just as well without it? The religious reaction of 1813 and 1814 was a gleam of sunshine in the present century; the conclusion of the Holy Alliance also was a ray of light, which unfortunately soon passed away. We ought to look back to that epoch and take a fresh start from there; the nations ought to call upon their rulers to return to the principles then proclaimed, not of statute, but of international law, and to act accordingly.

The wants of the age point to the fact that congresses of the European Powers—not of the rulers alone, but combined with representatives of the people—might be the means of averting threatening wars. One glorious example has shown that even great powers, without injury to their dignity or influence, can determine a proximate *casus belli* by arbitration, wherein England and America brought the question of the Alabama claims to a happy issue. Such commencements afford, at least, a glimmer of hope.

The extreme party, which has formed the so-called "League of Liberty and of Peace," talk about a mighty, peaceful, Union of Republics. This must remain a mere visionary dream, if for no other reason than that amongst the people the state of mind requisite for a permanent condition of peace is at any rate not present in a greater degree than amongst the governments. The monarchical form of the European States is not the obstacle standing in the way of setting up an international law which should bring peace; it is the decay and absence of Christian principles.

CHAPTER XVI.

THE DUTIES OF SUBJECTS.

GENTLENESS and justice on the part of those placed in authority, obedience and fidelity on the part of subjects, and self-sacrifice on the part of every one for the sake of the common weal and the country, are pre-Christian commands, which were well known to ancient heathendom. The moral greatness of antiquity consisted in its political virtue. There were just kings, such as Zaleucus; and some who sacrificed themselves for the sake of their people, as Codrus. From Germanic antiquity tradition has handed down to us, like a glorious inheritance, the fidelity of the liegeman who would not even in death desert his leader in battle.

When a prince and people take up Christianity, no new relation is created thereby, no new duties are imposed; but the old connection is indeed permeated by a new spirit, a new light is cast upon existing duties, and a new measure of divine support is accorded to rulers and to people, in order to enable them to fulfil those duties: the bond between them is drawn closer. The Christian subject is shown that obedience, reverence, and fidelity are not only civil, but also religious duties; it is the will of God that they be religiously fulfilled. Every duty, whether of rule or of obedience, should be performed in the fear of the almighty and omniscient One, to whom we are responsible for all our actions. Rulers have to thank the Christian religion for the fact that their subjects are bound to them by the strongest tie that there is, namely, that of conscience. From this arises the conscientiousness of the Christian in paying taxes, in the exercise of official duties, and in the management of goods confided to his care. The ancient Christians were remarkable for the punctuality with which they paid taxes—not from any fear of men, lest they should be found out and punished for want of honesty, but for conscience' sake; because the Government is the handmaid of God, and should exercise a commission from Him for the protection of society, being therefore justified in demanding from all subjects the means requisite thereto. Paul has taught us this (Rom. xiii. 5-7). One of the original, immutable duties incumbent upon a Christian nation, and upon every Christian, is the duty of offering intercession for the authorities; and it is immaterial whether they are Christian or not, and whether their rule be mild or oppressive. But the intercession is not an empty form nor a flattering piece of adulation; it is based upon a consciousness that God directs the hearts of kings, and that a just and benevolent government is among the most precious of earthly gifts that God can bestow. His own wants compel the Christian to offer up the intercession; because it is only under the protection of a just and humane government that it becomes possible for a Christian community to fulfil its task, lead a godly and honourable life, and bring the truth to the knowledge of all men. By an upright participation in the prayer for kings and all authorities, we are at once protected from temptation and error; every one must feel that scoffing, reviling, and insubordination are not compatible with such intercessions. It is morally impossible that the two antitheses can co-exist in one and the same mind.

To the Christian, a mystery has been revealed which

is hidden from the profane intellect. The latter, swayed by false ideas of the origin and nature of society, looks upon the king as chief constable—or, as a modern Greek has sarcastically expressed it, as chief butler, whose duty it is to see that every one is served. We, on the other hand, see whence the dignity of the ruler comes; we know that all authority is derived from Christ, the Lord of lords and King of kings; it is His invisible support that maintains the existing authorities in their places. With the existence of so many bad passions, subversive principles, and wild revolutionary ideas in society, as it now is, the fact of there being any order, authority, and power with which the government still rules the people, the protection which is afforded to kings, is a continuous miracle performed by the divine might. Thus the Christian sees something of the honour and majesty which are in Christ transferred to the head of the State; and in however small a degree, yet partially also to all who have part in the commission, and are placed in subordinate offices or other places of honour. This is the basis of the Christian's reverence for the government, as Peter has impressed upon us: "Submit yourselves to every ordinance of man for the Lord's sake; whether it be unto the king" (this was the title in Greek of the imperator), "as supreme" (who is over all, and only under God); "or unto governors, as unto them that are sent by Him for the punishment of evildoers, and for the praise of them that do well. . . . As free, and not using your liberty for a cloak of maliciousness, but as the servants of God. . . . Fear God. Honour the king" (1 Pet. ii. 13–17).

This respect for authority is far from being a base conception, a slavish homage, or flattery; because it is based upon the fear of God and not of men, it contains the most powerful corrective to the errors of servility.

We honour in the ruler not the mortal, sinful, and often faulty individual, but Him who has bestowed this office and authority; we may not derogate from his dignity because of any blemish that may attach to his private life, but also just as little may we extol such blemishes or consider them to be right and proper. Luther says, " A wicked government must be obeyed, but not praised." Every one is bound to know the ten commandments; and if the government requires anything of us which is contrary to the moral law, we must, as Peter reminds us, never forget that we are servants of God, and in such cases, with all due respect, decline to obey.

This was held to be the case even by the strictest Tories in England under Charles I. and James II. In such cases passive resistance is the duty of the Christian. This is not rebellion; we accept the consequences, and to suffer is to obey. Thus did the Christians act in olden days: if they were called upon to sacrifice to the gods, to swear by the familiar spirit of the emperor, or to burn incense before the image of the emperor, they declined to do so, suffering the punishment and glorifying God by their martyrdom.

But questions of a different sort are stirring men's minds at present. What is to be done when a government bearing the title of Christian exceeds its competence, and uses its power to attack the rights of the people?

What is the duty of a Christian when a revolution is drawing nigh? How ought he to behave during the revolution and after it?

There are lawful means for opposing the abuse of power; of these the Christian ought to make use, so far as is compatible with his particular position in society, —as, for instance, as official, clergyman, or military man. If it be a question of defending existing rights and ancient laws, he too must resist encroachments;

and where his calling obliges him to speak, he must come forth with boldness of speech as an example to others. How far the lawful means may extend, and where they cease, cannot be determined by any general Christian principles; it becomes a question of positive right and wrong, and should be decided by jurists, not by theologians. As early as 1287, in Aragon, the nobility obtained the recognition of their right to resist the encroachments of the royal power by force of arms. Whether, in extreme cases, the representatives of the people may refuse to pay taxes, can neither be affirmed nor denied upon general ethic grounds, but depends upon the constitution and laws of the particular State.

Still we must not overlook the fact that the Christian, when he feels it to be his duty, as representative of the people, as author, or in any other capacity, to oppose the action of the government, is animated by a very different spirit to that which generally inspires the individuals composing the opposition with us. He fulfils such a duty, not for the sake of bringing about a violent convulsion, but in order to prevent it. He raises his voice in opposition, not to bring himself into notice, to bring the government into difficulties, or to gain the applause of the masses, but only for the sake of fulfilling his duty towards the community and the government itself in a satisfactory manner.

He is careful to avoid the mistake of supposing that he is wiser and better than those who actually are in possession of power; he does not fondly imagine that if he were offered a seat in the cabinet all would be well. He is conscious and mindful of the enormous responsibility resting upon those who rule; and that consciousness urges him to sympathize with those who are in such a position, and to be temperate in any expressions which he may employ in objecting to their mode of action.

That which is most objectionable in the manner in which, at the present day, men generally take up the part of opposition, is the self-sufficiency and the ignoring of the common fault, the insolent spirit of complaint, which only seeks for the causes of the evils from which we suffer in those set over us. "Ye people, do not quarrel with your princes and their councils. Do not seek in them alone for faults and crimes which are common to the whole mass of the people. The government is only an artificial focus in front of the reflector formed by the community. If every individual for his own part, and the community in general, would refrain from all evil, the worst government would soon be radically improved. Whenever such complaints arise, it generally occurs that the fault comes quite as much from below as above, and an earnest desire to get rid of it should come unanimously from both parties." These are words of Goerres in the *Rhenish Mercury*, 9th April 1815. They contain the same truth which Origenes long ago uttered: "God punishes the sins of a nation by giving them a wicked ruler." In the existence of a tyrannical government, we must not imagine that we have an unintelligent and aimless caprice of fortune, but a wise intervention of divine Providence.

If all lawful means are exhausted and yet no benefit produced, still the Christian patriot has one more hope, —that the Almighty, who has reserved to Himself the judgment of princes, and has forbidden us to take matters into our own hands by rebellion, will hearken to the prayers of the oppressed that He will, at such time and in such manner as may seem best to Him, assist them. He does not require any transgression of His commands on our part to enable Him to intervene and to save; on the contrary, if we exalt ourselves and clamber up into the judge's seat, which belongs to the Lord and not to us, we spoil a good cause and destroy our claim to divine assistance. The worldly proverb runs: "Heaven helps those who help themselves" (*Aide-toi et le ciel t'aidera*). In such a case, where it is a question of revolutionary action, the contrary is more correct: "Heaven does not help those who help themselves." More than one nation has had to learn this by bitter experience. No good comes of it. A revolution caused by unlawful means does not produce any satisfactory results. In the whole course of legitimate action, we are called upon to use our intelligence and all our powers; but we may never put our hands to illegal means. The Holy Scriptures, and in accordance with them the conscience of a Christian also, condemn the principle of doing evil that good may come. That principle is, and always will be, objectionable, whether in private life, in national affairs, or in political matters.

"Revolutions are like death," says Goerres, "of whom only cowards are afraid, but with whom only fools dare to play. These catastrophes in history are of such terrible import, and productive of such serious consequences, that only madmen or desperadoes desire to bring them about."

They do not arise by accident. When, in the year 1848, the popular movement raised its head like the raging waves of the sea, King Ernest Augustus of Hanover was advised to order out the artillery. Whereupon he truly said: "When an entire nation becomes uneasy and revolts, there must be some mighty and just causes for it." He determined upon nominating Stueve, the leader of the opposition, to a seat in the Cabinet, and he had no cause to repent of his resolve.

Where an overthrow has taken place, like the fall of the Bourbons in France, Naples, and Spain, it is, as a rule, not difficult to detect the objective justice of it. We see therein the hand of the Guider of the world, the supreme Judge, of whom it has been said: "Wisdom and might are His: and He changeth the times and the seasons: He removeth kings, and setteth up kings" (Dan. ii. 20, 21). But with all this, the violent and rebellious are not thereby acquitted of guilt. Both sayings are true, "Their deeds are displeasing to the Lord," and, "They are instruments in His hands, by which, without their knowledge and understanding, a divine intention is carried out." For the action of Providence in the history of the world is on this wise: "God punishes the godless by means of the godless. He employs the bands of the wicked as His scourge; and when that has done its service, He throws it into the fire." The Christian is called upon to assume a very different attitude. Those who fear God cannot allow themselves to be made the instruments of revolution. Just at such times it is most necessary for them to uphold the law, and to insist with the greatest determination upon the maintenance of divine ordinances and commands. [The Grecian war of independence (1821–1827) was of a very different kind to the revolutions which we have been speaking of above, and must be dealt with in a special manner. The author has attempted to do this in his work, *The Fortunes of Greece from the Commencement of the War of Liberty*, Frankfort-on-the-Maine, 1863.]

With reference to these questions, errors have from time to time crept into Christian doctrines. On the part of the Pope, the erroneous doctrine has been sedulously proclaimed, that the highest spiritual authority has the power to release a nation from its oath of allegiance to an excommunicated and heretical ruler. Pius v. in 1569 acted thus towards Queen Elizabeth of England, and thereby produced untold misfortunes; amongst others, the decapitation of Mary, Queen of Scots.

Certainly a prince, as member of the Christian community, is placed under pastoral care and oversight; and when he transgresses the commandments of God, the minister should refuse to him, as well as to any other person in such a case, the administration of the sacraments. Ambrosius was quite right in refusing to allow the Emperor Theodosius to enter the sanctuary, on account of his blood-guiltiness. But the regal authority may not be impugned. The king, as king, is only subject to God; we may not refuse to obey, to intercede for, or to be faithful to him. The decision of the question whether Elizabeth was the lawful queen of England belonged to the Parliament in London, and not to the Bishop of Rome.

Similar is the question of assassinating a tyrant. The Spanish Jesuit Mariana took upon himself, in his book *De rege et regis institutione*, which, strange to say, is dedicated to King Philip III., to justify the assassination of Henry III. of France by the Dominican monk Clement. He maintains that against a tyrant,—that is to say, against one who has seized upon the throne by violence, who acts contrary to the laws and suppresses the true religion,—such means are allowable. Ehud acted thus, in the Book of Judges, when he smote Eglon, the king of the Moabites, with a dagger, thereby freeing the people of Israel (Judges iii. 12-30). According to ancient ideas, it was a praiseworthy act in any one to free his country from a tyrant at the risk of his own life; in Rome, the first and second Brutus did so, and in Athens, Harmodius and Aristogiton. Melancthon was also of the same opinion; the most eloquent exposition of it, however, is to be found in Schiller's *Tell*. Still it is a dogma which can never find acceptance in the ethics of Christianity. The tyrant of Mariana, when once he is in possession of regal power, must be regarded as ruler. The legal representatives and heads of the nation may refuse to obey him or to recognise him, and may declare war against him; but the individual subject is not empowered to resist him, much less to proceed against him with treachery and assassination. Mariana's error proceeds from a confusion of heathen and Christian morality; it is the same admixture of the two elements which is observable in art and poetry, in Michael Angelo's pictures and Tasso's *Jerusalem Delivered*. Heathen mythology should not be mixed up with Christianity; even from an æsthetic point of view this cannot be justified, much less in a moral aspect. In the days when the Christian Church kept itself pure from any admixture of heathenism, men had other conceptions. During the great persecutions, no Christian was ever guilty of an attempt upon the life of a Nero, Decius, or Diocletian, in order to free the Church from her sufferings.

Strange to say, the same confusion came from quite another direction, in the case of Oliver Cromwell and his party. He was impressed with the idea that a divine commission had been laid upon him (which he thought to be able to show by the results—that is, the victories gained in the civil wars), empowering him to carry out the revolution to the end, and to condemn the king to death. Thus extremes met. On the one hand, it was the Pope who assumed to himself the right of judging rulers, which Christ had never given to His servants; on the other, it was the Calvinistic Puritans who had the hardihood to cite their king, in the name of the community of believers, to appear before the judgment-seat of his subjects. In later times, Merle, in *Le Protecteur*, has dared to justify the execution of Charles I.; and, further still, to compare Oliver Cromwell, as a perfect Christian character, with Paul and Luther. So that we see it is possible to be a famous historical writer upon the subject of the Reformation, and yet be utterly ignorant of wholesome doctrine and devoid of divine light.

When Christians come into the unfortunate position that the legitimate ruler of their country is violently overthrown and a usurper becomes possessed of power, how are they to act? Certainly Christians, and especially ministers, should be heedful of tendering their allegiance to the new government in too great haste. It was a grievous fact, when, on 24th February 1848, Louis Philippe, the benefactor of the clergy, was driven away by the Revolution, that on the following day, in the Cathedral of Notre Dame, the response should be sung, *Domine salvam fac rempublicam.*

Conscientious men, in such a case, tender no new oath until they shall have received permission so to do from the ruler to whom their former oaths bound them, and they prefer to submit to some amount of persecution rather than be guilty of fickleness. Such occurrences are so rare, so intricate, and so varied in their attendant circumstances, that it is impossible to regulate beforehand what course should be pursued in all cases by laying down a set of casuistic rules. Much must be left to the discernment and conscience of the individual.

When a new power has established itself and taken root, the Christian community may not refuse to offer intercession in services of public worship for this new authority; for it is only the existing authority, and not the one that is overthrown, which can afford that protection required by society, upon which order, peace, justice, and the flourishing of all Christian virtues depend. For all these benefits we are dependent upon the existing government; hence we pray for wisdom and assistance for it from above. When the ecclesiastics present this intercession at the head of their congregations, the duty of reverence and obedience is thereby recognised; but no opinion is expressed as to the origin of this new power, nor of the principles upon which its institution was based. There is scarcely a State in which the present form of government has not been, at least in part, the result of revolution and usurpation. We are at all times ready to honour the existing power in the State; but we reserve to ourselves the right neither to commend nor to approve of any revolution or usurpation, whether proceeding from above or below.

With the constant change which is going on in human affairs, new relations of duty and of rights spring up. Even if the origin of any particular government be marked with an unclean spot, still between it and the people a moral bond of union may in course of time grow up and be confirmed. It is similar also in other affairs of life. If an ordination has taken place in defiance of any ecclesiastical law, it is on that account irregular, but not invalid. If a marriage has been celebrated in the face of some existing *impedimentum prohibens*, for instance, without the requisite paternal consent, there arises a moral objection, but no invalidity of the marriage. Here the principle holds good, *Non faciendum, sed factum valet.* If a government which was illegitimate in its origin has actually assumed a position, it intertwines itself at least so much with the people that no one can be held criminally responsible for adhering to it. The contrary mode of procedure would be unjust and cruel, as is now being exemplified in the civil war in Spain. It is a beautiful and humane principle of the English law, that no one who has taken up arms for a *de facto* government can on that account be dealt with for the crime of high treason.

The heralds of Christian morality do well in affording room for the free exercise of conscience in every individual, as to what political party he may choose to belong to; and yet Christian doctrine does not favour the ULTRAS of either party. The effect of Christianity is to temper extreme views; hence we may expect to find it attacked and blamed by both parties. And we do find that a purely scriptural form of creed is stigmatized by one party as superstitious, by the other as heretical. It does not fare better with Christianity than with her Lord and Master, who was crucified between two thieves; so we need not wonder if the position of a Christian in the time of political storms and revolutions, as here described, should be reprobated by the one party as servile, and by the other as revolutionary.

CHAPTER XVII.

THE DUTIES OF RULERS.

The ruler is a servant of God, and he is placed in that position for the good of the nation. This is the sum of Christian doctrine. Not only is an idea expressed in these words; they are the embodiment of a reality, a great fact, which remains unchangeable and unchanged in all times, and notwithstanding all the changes in the opinions of men. This fact may have become obscure to the consciences of men, and it may be denied a thousand times over, but still there it is and remains unaffected. The duty of any Christian ruler is to recognise this fact, to maintain his real position, notwithstanding the inclinations of his own heart—notwithstanding, if it must be so, the opposition of the whole world.

Three wholesome moral impulses will arise from this actual bond of relationship, so long as it is vivid and present to the mind of the ruler.

He will feel himself responsible to God for all he does and permits as ruler; for regal power is not a private possession, given to be employed according to a man's own pleasure, it is a loan committed to his hands by the King of kings, who is Himself the source of all power and might. He is bound to exercise it according to the mind and commands of the Giver, who is the real owner. The ruler is the incumbent of an office, and he will have to give an account of his stewardship to the supreme Judge.

"God is no respecter of persons." "We must all appear before the judgment-seat of Christ." These, and similar passages in Scripture, should be guiding stars for the manner of government of a Christian ruler. They will fill him with a holy fear, they will prevent his assuming too much to himself, they will protect him against his own passions, and they will at all times incline him to prudence and conscientiousness.

This same truth is the Archimedean point, situated outside of this world, upon which a ruler can lean for support to overcome the world. In the execution of his onerous duties, the consciousness of his mission from above will endue him with firmness and calm confidence. The fear of men is a power which will fetter every one who has no point of support other than this world affords. Great as is the duty of a free man not to tremble before the threatening countenance of a tyrant, still greater is the duty of the ruler calmly and imperturbably to resist the "depraved ardour of an excited mob." The Christian ruler finds strength in his confidence in the Almighty, from whom he has received a commission to protect and foster what is right.

The Christian ruler will constantly derive fresh strength from the same source, to confirm his love to his people and to make him ready to sacrifice himself for their good; for he is the servant of God, and he is placed in the position which he occupies for the good of his people. To secure this, the greatest benefit Providence has granted to mortal man, is the ruler's calling; for this purpose, and for it alone, has such extraordinary power been bestowed upon him. It has not been committed to him in order that he may employ it to satisfy his own selfish will, not that he may exalt himself above his brethren and look proudly down upon them, not that he may consult his own pleasure and gratify his insatiable lusts, but that he may be the greatest benefactor of his people.

Between him and his people there exists a sacred bond, and according to the divine intention it should be a bond of love. A Christian ruler will not wait to see whether he is beloved of his people, before commencing to fulfil his duties of love towards them; he will follow the example of that mightiest of sovereigns, Christ, who first loved us, and gave Himself for His people, before they recognised His love for them. It is the way of this world, that with the best intentions we must look for ingratitude and a want of recognition. The ruler, too, is not spared learning this bitter truth by experience; on the contrary, he has a greater amount of it to experience than others. But even that will not make him misanthropical; he will not visit upon all what some, and it may be many, have neglected in their duty towards him. Love, by which he is inspired, is a flame which many waters cannot extinguish; he will not lose courage or hope, he will not become bitterly minded or conceive a mean idea of mankind. In reliance upon the divine love, and impressed with the task which it has given him to do, he will always be ready to devote himself to his calling, endeavouring to elevate his people and to render them happy. The whole time and bodily powers of a ruler should be devoted to caring for his people. An enlightened ruler will be industrious, like Frederick the Great, and will consider day and night how he may benefit his people, like Maximilian II. of Bavaria. If a bishop were to refrain from devoting himself to the good of the flock confided to his care, if he misused his position to seek his own good and to advance that, the verdict of all right-minded people upon him would be a very severe one. Would not a ruler deserve the same, who should forget that he is called upon to live entirely for his office and for his people? For rulers are also bishops and shepherds of their people: Homer, for instance, terms Agamemnon a shepherd of the people, and Holy Scripture uses the same symbolical language in speaking of kings.

These are no new truths; they are contained in an ancient, much used, often objected to, but deep-meaning and eternally true formula, *Dei gratiâ*. From time immemorial, the rulers of Christian States have termed themselves princes by the grace of God,—or, as the Greek expression runs, ἐλέει Θεοῦ, by the mercy of God. A curious misapprehension has attached to these words. Many—one may almost say public opinion—in the present day look upon them as designating absolute monarchical power. They have become a bogie, behind which people imagine they can detect a system of oppression and of enmity to the people peeping forth. Such a mistaken conception can only be accounted for as resulting from a long and grave misuse of power by those in authority; the reference to divine grace became a desecration of the divine name in the mouths of unworthy bearers of the office, and only thus was it possible that so much cavil and objection should arise. The actual meaning of the words is not responsible for that. Properly understood, the inscription *Dei gratiâ* around the effigy of our rulers upon coins is rather a pledge for a just and humane form of government; for in that a ruler proclaims that he is what he is by the grace of God, he admits that he has not to thank himself or his own merits for his power or his illustrious position. He admits that he is not worthy of the crown which he wears; it has been lent to him, in consequence of an undeserved confidence which the Ruler of all things has been pleased to repose in him. He will have to account for that which has been committed to him by the grace of God; he may not use it according to his own wishes.

Further, if the ruler is appointed by the grace of God, he must regard himself as a gift, made of divine clemency to the people; as an instrument by which the Almighty will carry out His benevolent intentions, administer justice, afford protection, and maintain the welfare and peace of the nation. In all this there is certainly no justification for the ruler to exalt himself above the law, to tear down all limits to his power, and to infringe the rights of his people; for the same superhuman power, to whose goodness he owes his royal dignity, is also the Protector of justice and of the law.

Now, whether the highest position in the State has come to its possessor by birth and inheritance or by the election of the people, in both cases its derivation from the mercy of God is still a fact. Regarded in a true light, republican magistrates, judges, commanders, and presidents are all what they are by the grace of God. Even they, however limited their duties, however short their term of office may be, are, like kings, the servants of God, placed in the position which they occupy for the good of the people.

Instead of demanding that the phrase *Dei gratiâ* should be erased from the title and from off the coins of our rulers, people ought rather to insist upon its retention, in the hope and desire that it may also be inscribed upon the hearts of rulers, in order that their nobleness of mind and the character of their actions may correspond to the admission and the vows which are expressed in those two words.

The majesty of a princely calling will be a spur to a Christian ruler for working indefatigably to render himself competent for the same. There are callings in life for which one can thoroughly prepare oneself by a course of study, in a certain amount of time; here it is otherwise. The requirements of a position of rule are manifold and almost immeasurable, and frequently only a very short time is given for preparation before taking up the highest office. On that account, a ruler should always learn to extend the horizon of his mind, and to labour indefatigably at his own improvement. He will be careful to avoid the foolish notion that aptitude for his calling was conveyed by the accident of his birth. He will be far from supposing that he is an oracle, or that inspiration from above gives him a correct insight into everything without any trouble or painstaking on his part. He certainly may hope for the assistance of divine wisdom, and he ought in prayer to seek for divine guidance and protection; but, at the same time, he will not leave a stone unturned, by diligent exertion and by employing the means which Providence has placed at his disposal for that purpose, to qualify himself for the duties entrusted to him.

There is one very ancient book which contains the wisdom of twenty centuries, and is in all parts specially written for the use of rulers. Should a Christian ruler allow the Holy Scriptures to lie on his shelves unused? That book is full of information regarding the duties of rulers, the dangers and temptations of their position, the divine punishments and rewards which a king must look for according to his actions. Amongst the books of the Apocrypha, there is one which seems to come next to the Scriptures in value, and may aptly be termed the mirror of princes, namely, the "Wisdom of Solomon addressed to Tyrants," commonly called the Book of Wisdom. Christian ethics are, above all other sciences, worthy of and require careful study by a ruler for the proper understanding of his duties.

Princes must endeavour to acquire their knowledge of religious duties from the unadulterated ancient traditions of the Church.

If there be amongst those who are teachers in the Christian Church, men who with the unreservedness of the ancient prophets, with the courage of John the Baptist and Paul, reprove kings when they depart from the ways of God; who are firm, like the ancient bishops; who tell their rulers the truth, like Luther and some of the Lutheran court preachers of the sixteenth and seventeenth centuries,—a Christian ruler will do well to keep such men about him, and to listen to their exhortations.

The truths of our faith, the commandments of God, and the principles of Christianity have to be learned by us, and by our rulers as well, from the Scriptures, from tradition, and from the lips of the servants of Christ; the highest as well as the lowest are all obliged to apply to these sources of information. But that is no reason for supposing that a ruler would do well to select ecclesiastics as his counsellors in state matters. It does not correspond with the divine order or intention that cardinals, bishops, or theologians should officiate as Cabinet ministers or assist in ruling in temporal matters. In the deciding of political questions, in all matters connected with the government, a ruler should hearken to his temporal advisers. Skilful jurists and practised men of business, in whom he may expect to find firm moral principles, are those whom he should select for his confidants and instruments.

"When the age was more pious, the ruler still had friends; ecclesiastics and nobles held positions about his person, as familiar acquaintances. If he contemplated any ill-considered act towards his people, a friend, in form of a knight, would step forward and say, 'Honour forbids it,' or a minister of the Church would say, 'God disapproves of it.' As long as the age continued pious, the ruler honoured his old friends; when things took an evil turn, he got rid of them, as being troublesome legacies left by a morose father. Then the ruler was left alone; but loneliness produces ennui, and ennui arrogance. Hence it comes that, from time immemorial, the nations have pondered how again to furnish their rulers with companions from amongst the people who shall know the truth and speak it, in lieu of those boon companions whom chance may throw in their prince's way."

Exhortations such as this, taken from the *Rhenish Mercury*, will find a response in the mind of an intelligent ruler; he will look about him to discover the most excellent men for every branch of the State economy,—for war, finance, trade, and agriculture, for law and education. The political views of individual men will have less weight with him than their capabilities; he will strive to attain to that rare art which Napoleon I. possessed in a high degree, that of finding the right man to fill the right place. He will hunt up the old and experienced, and not trust himself blindly in the hands of new-born talent. He will give heed to the counsels of his ministers, following the parliamentary discussions with attention; he will encourage the utmost freedom of speech in the council chamber. He will require from the officials that they are considerate and prudent in their remarks upon the government to outsiders, but unreserved to their superiors. He will welcome the freedom of the press, and make use of it; he will not depend implicitly upon his informants, but read for himself, in order to become acquainted with the wishes and difficulties of the various parties.

Happy is the ruler who, like Frederick the Great and John of Saxony, has served in every office of the

State, from the lowest upwards, and has thus learned to know every branch of government, whether political or legal.

Because our lives only embrace a span of time, it is very necessary to glean information from the experiences of earlier centuries; and for whom could the study of history be more attractive and useful than for a prince?

Treasures of experience are to be found in the writings of the great historians of antiquity; splendid examples, noble principles, in Livy, Plutarch, and in the incomparable Tacitus, who gained the deepest insight into the hearts of princes, who has recorded for us the errors into which they so easily fall, and the degeneracy of which they are capable. He who will matriculate in the higher branches of statesmanship must study the constitution of England and her history. The two great epochs of modern days—the English and French Revolutions—are full of inexhaustible mines of instruction for rulers. The writings of statesmen like Lord Bacon and Sir Edmund Burke contain the most precious materials for nourishing the mind of a prince.

Yet let us pause here, in order not to go too deeply into a subject foreign to our own; for we are not dealing with statesmanship, but with ethics. We will therefore endeavour to show how, from the centre of Christian truth, rays of beneficent light fall upon various points in the extensive circle comprising the calling of a ruler. As in every other sphere of human action, princes too are exposed to be tempted by arrogance and weakness. We will speak first of these two different sorts of temptations, and then touch upon certain of the positive duties of princes, bearing in our mind always the peculiar dangers and requirements of the present day.

None of the evil passions of the human heart are so deeply rooted, so obstinate, and so tenacious of life, as self-exaltation and pride. The temptation to yield to these is stronger in the case of a ruler than in others. The pernicious results of this passion, too, assume great dimensions in his case. A Christian ruler will watch more carefully over himself, and beware of arrogance, for the very reason that he is not accountable to any earthly superior for his mode of government; he will keep his eye the more steadily fixed upon his invisible Judge. Whilst maintaining his dignity and authority as regards other men, he will always preserve the humble position of a subject towards God. The splendours which surround him, the honours which are accorded him, must not render his heart foolish; for all these are not tendered to him individually, or to his personal qualities, but to his office. If he is addressed in terms of fulsome praise, he will reply in the words of Charles v.: "Your language and the praises you ascribe to us remind us how we should conduct ourselves."

There can be no aspiration more dangerous than that a prince should long for absolute power. Uncontrolled despotic power, if placed in the hands of any individual, is the cause of ruin to himself and to others. In a slaveholder, all noble feelings, if he ever possessed such, are destroyed by his position. He looks down upon his fellow men; he cannot bear contradiction; he silences the language of truth; he hates and suspects all independence of character; he becomes entangled in an insane conceit of his own greatness; and, once arrived at that stage, nothing can any longer restrain him from criminal acts. Cambyses had an excellent father; but he inherited from him an evil legacy, that of despotic power. Nero possessed brilliant talents, and for the first five years he governed well. Both, under the baneful influence of their positions, fell into that condition bordering on insanity, when they would no longer submit to any restraint imposed upon their criminal lusts.

The arrogant despot not only ruins himself, but also all about him,—his subjects and his kingdom; he finds most characters weak, but he completes their ruin. Tiberius, when he entered upon his government, found a Senate inclined to gratify his despotic lusts: *O paratos ad servitium homines*, were his words as he left the council room. After a reign of twenty-three years, he left the Senate a mass of irremediable corruption.

A Christian prince will carefully instruct himself as to the limits imposed upon his power by the legislature; he will take the coronation or constitutional oath in deep and holy seriousness. A very ancient intellectual error, and a wicked self-deception of the human heart, combine to confound sovereignty with arbitrary power. The arrogant ruler sucks in such nonsense like a sweet-tasting poison, persuading himself that his despotic lusts are consecrated and justified from above; he ensconces himself behind the mistaken idea, that absolute regal power is an original gift from God, of which he cannot divest himself. This erroneous doctrine works disintegratingly upon the morality of the ruler and the existence of his kingdom; a notion arises that the prince or leading statesman has a special divine mission to establish absolute power, that he is at the same time empowered to get rid of every obstacle at any price. Such a statesman or ruler becomes so dazzled with the idea, that, to attain this end, he fancies himself no longer bound by the moral law; but it is blasphemy to invoke the name of God as an authority for infringing the commandments of God.

From this point of view, the despot imagines himself always at liberty to retract promises or to cancel privileges which he has conceded to the people. Thus he destroys confidence, and undermines the foundations of his throne. Occasionally we see in a menagerie, at feeding time, how the keeper will hold up before a wild beast in a cage a piece of meat on an iron fork, and take it away again, repeating this until the animal is furious with rage. Unfortunately we have seen governments which, having forsaken the paths of true wisdom, have, in incomprehensible infatuation, acted thus towards their people.

An inquiring young prince of our day asked a learned man, whom he honoured with his confidence and friendship, "Whether kings, who are placed in such an unusual position, are equally with other people bound to obey the moral law?" He received the expressive reply: "King Philip of Macedonia handed over his son Alexander to Aristotle to be instructed in mathematics, with a request that the philosopher should not oblige the young prince to go through all the usual drudgery and labour in learning the science. Aristotle replied: 'O king, there is no royal road to learning mathematics.'" As in mathematics, so too in morals.

That which the soft voice of the deceptive heart whispers to princes, "That God will not be so particular with them, and that from them the usual virtues of private life cannot be demanded," was distinctly enunciated by the courtiers of Louis xiv. in their wicked saying: "Le sang des rois ne souille pas." The difference is merely one of degree. If a royal youth is once allowed to depart from the path of virtue, no one can say for certain where the degeneracy will end.

Princes, not a whit less than other men, are answerable for the purity of their private lives, and perhaps are rather more so, on two accounts. First of all, the actions and habits of a prince do not remain hidden, however much he may desire it or imagine that it is so. Every private individual is more capable of concealing his sins than a prince. But, in addition, we must remember the extensive influence which the example of a prince exercises. So to say, the entire authority with which he is clothed enters the service of evil,—it becomes a certificate of character for sin. All who have similar wicked inclinations feel justified and permitted to do likewise.

"Quite right," some will say; "the same laws of morality, justice, and honour are applicable to the private lives of princes as of other people. But here a line must be drawn. There is a totally different sphere, which may not be confused with the former—that of higher political economy, regarding which the limited intelligence of the subject may not form an opinion. In matters of royal and State action, a timid regard for the moral law must not be insisted upon."

This pretension is by no means new; it is as old as the falling away from Christian principles. This, as is well known, was first put into shape at the time of the so-called *renaissance* in Italy. Modern Epicurism was then developed; then it was that godless despots and politicians simultaneously rejected and abjured all moral principles. As usual, it was first put in practice, and then theoretically justified. This theory was asserted by Nicolo Machiavelli, the Florentine Secretary of State, in his *Principe*, written at the time of Leo X. and dedicated to the Medician Lorenzo. He was the first who dared to assert that a prince might avail himself of morally reprehensible means for the compassing of his ends; that he was not bound to be guided by the moral law, but by State reasons. In other countries of Christendom, better principles still prevailed. The Spanish general of the Jesuits, Pedro de Ribadaneira, in the year 1595, dedicated to King Philip II. a refutation of Machiavelli and all similarly-minded politicians; but in the evil times of Louis XIV. those wicked principles spread from the court at Versailles almost all over Europe, and brought about the ruin of political virtue. Better ideas have since gained ground, and some brilliant examples exist; but the times in which we live are much afflicted with the same disease. The wicked tradition takes root, the course of the world exercises its power, and high-principled characters become fewer and fewer. Men say that there is no such thing as political morality, and we must give up such ideas. If a question arises regarding the greatness of our country, even those means are permissible which in private life would be reprobated. The strongest expression which we remember of this false doctrine is to be found in an Italian newspaper, which said, "Italy would enter into a compact with the devil himself to attain her unity."

The whole of this distinction, together with the proposition that the higher branches of political economy are exempted from the application of the moral law, is a denial of and a challenge to the Almighty. In the chamber of the heart, in the family circle, and in private intercourse, Christian religion is still allowed a place; but in State affairs it must be got rid of. That is to say, they wish to debase the living God to a minor house deity; in the large State edifice there shall be no more room found for Him, and in the most important concerns of human life He shall no longer have a voice. He shall no longer have a right to interfere when nations, statesmen, and princes depart from the paths of virtue, truth, and justice!

It is the apostasy of our days which speaks in such language. We might expect that at least one party would strenuously oppose this. "The priest's lips should keep knowledge, and they should seek the law at his mouth; for he is the messenger of the Lord of hosts." Such is the manner in which Holy Scripture speaks of the duties of ecclesiastics and theologians. They should, by their fearless testimony, support morality to the last.

When, in the French court, morals were destroyed, and the pernicious example spread to the courts of other countries, the Jesuits sinned in that they weakened and subtilized the strictness of the moral law, in order to bring it into accord with the then state of social ideas, and to preserve their own position and influence as confidants and confessors in noble houses. Do the theologians of our day stand up manfully for the divine commands? When flatterers, those dangerous enemies of Christian royalty, absolve rulers from their obedience to the divine laws, do the theologians oppose this, as their profession and dignity require them to do?

We will not take upon ourselves to reproach the whole class, but one single shocking example must not be passed over here in silence. An evangelical theologian, Professor von der Goltz, professor and doctor of theology in Basle, in an academical speech (printed in Gotha 1872, pp. 12, 13) says that he maintains the aphorism, "that in politics much is good which in private life is bad, and that means which would otherwise be objectionable are sanctified by the end." "I hold it to be superfluous," he continues, "to enter upon a refutation of those applications which the Jesuits have made of the principle, The end sanctifies the means. But the principle is in itself not so false as is generally supposed; it is only the Jesuitical application of it to hypocritical ends, and to absolutely reprehensible means." "In the service of the State, the standard by which actions must be judged, as to their goodness or otherwise, is different from that in use in private life; and the moral task of regulating the life of a community sanctifies many means, the employment of which in personal interests would be reprehensible."

Thus speaks a false theology. Is no Pascal to be found to hurl his winged lightnings against it, and wither up our modern sophists? Is there no philosopher now alive, like Kant, who can throw a ray of light into this dark chaos of mistaken ideas and unconsidered language?

A Christian prince will keep this misleading doctrine far from him, even though it be garbed in ecclesiastic attire. In the flattering and toadying ideas which it contains, he will see nothing but a series of insults to his royal as well as his Christian dignity. He will consider it absolutely necessary to the preservation of his royal honour, that he turn his back upon such preachers. The temptations which the spirit of this world brings in its train, and those which arise from the heart of man himself, are trying enough for every mortal; but especially for those set in high places, there is no need that they be made more deadly still by a theology which conforms itself to the world.

The reflections which are most adapted to protect a Christian prince from such errors are these. In the execution of our duty, dangers, embarrassments, and apprehensions do doubtless come before each of us. In order to bring about the realization of an object which is in itself allowable, the crooked way of base and immoral modes of action occasionally appears to be the safest. Still He who gave the moral law foresaw this; none of these difficulties were hidden from His omniscience; He made us subject to the moral law; and in that He permits us to be surrounded with obstacles, He makes trial of our obedience, promising such as stand firm under the temptation, and hearken more to His divine voice than to the suggestions of the deceitful, wicked, and desperately foolish (although it is supposed to be so wise) heart of man, a reward which defies computation." In such feelings of duty and confidence in God, the Christian ruler finds strength to deny himself the assistance of any unsanctioned means.

Moreover, he will remember that Christ has said: "Whoso shall break one of the least of these commandments, and shall teach men so, he shall be called the least in the kingdom of heaven." This is the standard by which he will judge such teachers.

In accordance with this harmonizes that well-considered lesson which has been imparted to us by those great representatives of philosophic morality, Kant and Fichte, who say: "All moral laws are imperative; he who disturbs one of them damages the whole code; they must be obeyed without regard to the pleasantness or unpleasantness of the result."

Napoleon once, when upon the island of St. Helena, raised the question as to whether a ruler should be guided in his action by his conscience or by the applause of the world. The conclusion he came to was characteristic of his sinister mind: it was by the applause of men. He considered that a ruler who followed the dictates of his conscience might be a good and noble regent, but not a great man. Not a great man! Certainly not one of those whose path streams with blood and tears; not one of those who are looked upon as scourges of mankind.

When a powerful ruler is wanting in knowledge of himself, when he omits to watch over his own actions, when he departs from the consciousness of his responsibility to God, those passions will obtain the mastery over him that bring the greatest misfortunes upon nations, in that they cause wars which could be avoided without any dereliction of duty. Ambition, once inflamed, becomes a powerful demon, which darkens our moral judgment and deadens all feelings of humanity; it hurries the ruler along on a mad course, as though the patient, obedient, industrious people were only created for the purpose of shedding their blood to increase the glory of his crown. The ruler who, without being obliged by his duty, brings war upon his people, is responsible in the eyes of the eternal Judge for all the blood that is shed, all the scenes of misery and all the acts of cruelty which even the best of officers cannot completely prevent during a war. When the Emperor Ferdinand II. lay on his deathbed, his prayer wrung from the terrors of his soul was, "Cleanse me from the sins of others, O God." It is not improbable that those fearful deeds which the imperial armies had committed in the years 1618-35 passed then before his mind.

So much for the temptations of arrogance; but there are also temptations of weakness.

It is weakness which leads a ruler to suppose he is bound to ratify everything that the majority of his Parliament determine. In almost all our constitutional States, without exception, the royal prerogative still exists; the Crown still has the right of veto, and not merely a suspension veto, but a peremptory one. The sovereign is legally justified in refusing his sanction to any proposed measure, which is opposed to his conscience. It is, of course, more pleasant to swim with the stream, to give way to the spirit of the age, to agree through thick and thin with the mass of the people and their demands; but it is a denial of, and repulsive to, the royal dignity and duty.

It is a sign of weakness in a ruler when he supposes

that he is bound to subscribe to all that his ministers propose to him, without regard to his own judgment. Certainly they are responsible, and the arrangement is not a bad one which renders some minister of State responsible to Parliament, and, on appeal, to the Court of Chancery also, for every decision of the king. By such means the conscience of the royal advisers is kept alive; their business is to assist in bearing the burdens of State, but not to relieve the ruler entirely of them, to render him a mere puppet, a writing machine, a nonentity. By no means; he still has the power of personally deciding, and with it the responsibility of exercising that power. Adequately to fill the position and calling of ruler, not only is the spirit of wisdom necessary, but also that of fortitude. Where it is wanting, even good qualities may be injurious to a ruler. He must guard against weak councils; he must take up his position in confidence in God, and be ready to assume the responsibility for his decisions.

Queen Elizabeth of England, at the end of her long reign, was able to say that she had never formed an opinion as to the guilt of an accused person upon the first reports which reached her. This is a sign of a strong mind and a character accustomed to self-government. It is weak to allow oneself to be guided by a first impression, to be filled with aversion and prejudice, instead of hearing both sides of the question and calmly considering all the circumstances of the case. Suspicion, fear, antipathies, and narrow-minded obstinacy are the concomitants of weakness of character.

Such errors assume their worst form when rulers do not listen to the advice of their legitimate and responsible advisers and counsellors, but allow themselves to be influenced by the suggestions and back-stairs influence of favourites. It is only a weak-minded prince who lends his ear to backbiters; a man of character and of a good conscience holds them at a distance.

The burden of the crown is great, the cares multitudinous, the peace but rare; the position of the ruler is lonely, his experiences bitter. A ruler cannot but fear lest those about him should be self-interested, and on that account disguise the real thoughts of their hearts. Selfishness, hypocrisy, and subserviency meet him at almost every turn. Where can he find the consolation of friendship? where disinterested good-will or confidential candour? The deprivation of these must be some of the heaviest trials a ruler who has a heart is obliged to submit to. One substitute he can obtain, and that is when he can take a noble helpmeet to share his life. In her society he can refresh his jaded mind; here he has no coldness, no disguise, to be afraid of. A ruler, more than any other man, requires to be happily married in order to enjoy his human existence. If he is so fortunate, let him know how to appreciate his happiness.

But he must also endeavour to understand the true position of his consort. She has been given to him as helpmeet, in order to help him to bear the burden of life, but not of office. She may be endowed with the rarest qualities of mind, and yet she has no business to mix herself up with the government, or to rule the king. Even a surgeon, an ecclesiastic, or a judge, if he is a wise man, will not drag his wife into the weighty cares of his calling. These he is not called upon to share with his wife, and she must not assume to herself any influence in that sphere. Similarly with the profession of king. The influence of a queen upon affairs of State belonging to her consort may be more noble than any other unjustifiable influence, but it is not on that account justifiable; it does not excite confidence, it is not wholesome, it is not a sign of strength of mind and insight on the part of the ruler.

Yet a word or two on the chief positive duties of royalty. The administration of law and of justice is the chief debt a ruler owes to his people. He can only fulfil this duty by the employment of good instruments; hence he will exercise the greatest prudence in the selection of men to fill high positions, especially of his judges, and he will courageously proceed against such as are unfaithful and unjust. The independence of the judicial bench will be sacred to him; it is true that they dispense justice in his name, but not under his influence.

King John of France said: "If allegiance and good faith were lost upon earth, they ought still to be found in the hearts and in the mouths of kings." To keep faith is the best, the wisest policy, and the one enjoined both by reason and Christianity.

Prudence in deliberation, maturity of resolution, and, when once a decision is arrived at, firmness in determination; to be slow to excite hopes, but, when once a thing is promised, to accord it uncompromisingly,—these are characteristics which make a government strong, and ensure the joyful obedience of the people. What can be more incentive to dangerous attacks upon the throne and the government than promises made in fear and haste, out of weakness or false cunning, afterwards repented of, and, with a change of circumstances, withdrawn?

Admitted that a ruler, badly advised, had conceded more than was necessary, more than prudence permitted, of the prerogatives of the crown, he will certainly avoid the dangerous resolution of retracting such a concession. He will see that the confidence which is produced in a nation by the inviolability of his promised word is worth more, and is a more valuable pledge for the stability of his throne, than any extension of royal privileges which may have been too much circumscribed.

In a healthy form of government, the course of the legislature, when it is a matter of promulgating new laws, should be circumspect, dignified, and majestic. The hurried mode of legislation which at present takes place in some of the Continental States, makes the contrary impression. A cautious monarch will counteract this as much as possible; for it conduces, more than men imagine, to a weakening of authority and mutual confidence.

The kings of England promise in their coronation oath to preserve the Christian Church in peace. Even without that oath, the duty is incumbent on every Christian ruler. Peace for the Christian Church from the violence and insults of her enemies; peace between her and the Powers of the world by reciprocation and explanation; peace within the Church by obliging the different parties to respect each other, and by the powers of the State being careful in theological quarrels not to take the part of either side, thereby only embittering the strife,—these are objects and aims worthy of a Christian ruler.

Jung Stilling in the commencement of this century said: "Those rulers who can look on in silence whilst their subjects deprive Christ of His divine sonship and royal majesty, will some day have to learn by experience how that Christ will look on in silence whilst they are being robbed by their people of their own sacred dignity." When we quote this remarkable saying, we by no means wish to advocate any compulsion of conscience, by which only hypocrites can be created and nothing durable or wholesome can be built up. From any such misapprehension, all that we have before said about freedom of conscience fully exonerates us; but the conservation of the sacred things belonging to a Christian people is a very different matter to compulsion of conscience or obligation to perform religious ceremonies. We still have laws which forbid blasphemy or rude attacks upon the foundations of morality, such as matrimony, modesty, and property, against actual scoffing at morality and decency. Unhappily, the courage and resolution requisite to put them in force are wanting. In this respect Germany is at present worse off than France; still we may assume that those whose duty it is to interfere, only require to be set in motion by their superiors to make them carry out their duties at once.

Where the laws do not suffice, the example furnished by those in high places is capable of producing extraordinary results. The ruler is, as a result of his position, not only the source of all authority, but also of all honour; he is bound to appear in all his conduct as the "first gentleman," a nobleman *sans peur et sans reproche*. The tone of society is taken from him; his ideas and his actions establish the rules of taste in the upper circles, and much farther downwards in the social scale. Queen Victoria has succeeded, by the firmness and integrity of her will, in achieving a remarkable feat. She has abolished duelling amongst the officers of her army and navy; she will not permit the officers of her own forces to engage in deadly combat with each other. What in Germany is looked upon as impossible, has been carried out in consequence of the feeling which emanated from the English court.

If a ruler and his family furnish a brilliant example of pure morality and conjugal fidelity, if he personally looks upon vice as dishonourable and despicable, if he banishes it from all court ceremonials, and lays the weight of his displeasure upon it, it may be expected that far and wide in his kingdom a proper moral feeling will increase, that virtue will acquire respect and value, and that vice will be obliged to hide itself from the light of day, creeping back to those noisome caverns whence it came.

A ruler may not lay aside his dignity; his appearance in public should correspond thereto, and should command reverence and respect. But it is only a weak or misanthropical mind that would consider the retirement and unapproachableness of an Oriental despot as necessary to the maintenance of majesty. In the light of truth, the ruler knows himself to be not only ruler, but also father of his people; hence he will provide that, at suitable times, even the lowest of his subjects can obtain access to him. If he has true nobility of mind, he will run no danger thereby of provoking contempt or impertinent boldness. A Christian ruler does not despise the poor and uneducated; he is only mindful of the fact that he belongs to all his subjects, and that a sacred bond connects him with the poorest and most insignificant member of his people. He has a right to require love and confidence from them. Let him try to awaken these feelings in them, by allowing them from time to time access to his person.

The interests of the well-to-do classes are more than sufficiently represented in our great bodies of State, the First and Second Chambers. The proprietor class can help themselves; but the day-labourer and artisan are differently placed: they must depend upon the sympathy of the Crown. It may be hoped of a Christian ruler, that, as the protector of those who cannot protect themselves, he will initiate large measures, which, without interfering with property, shall prevent usury, diminish the sufferings of the working classes and their families, and advance the material as well as the moral welfare of the needy.

King Alfred the Great on his deathbed said to his son: "Endeavour to be a lord and father of your people. Be the father of the orphan and friend of the widow. Assist the poor, protect the weak, and with your whole might convert what is wrong into what is right. And, my son, govern thyself according to the law. Then the Lord will love you, and your reward shall be with God."

THE END.

www.ingramcontent.com/pod-product-compliance
Lightning Source LLC
Chambersburg PA
CBHW032110230426
43672CB00009B/1696